JAMES INVERNE TALKS TO

THE IMPRESARIOS

Photographs by John Timbers

Oberon Books
London

First published in 2000 by Oberon Books Ltd.
(incorporating Absolute Classics)
521 Caledonian Road, London N7 9RH
Tel: 020 7607 3637 / Fax: 020 7607 3629
E-mail: oberon.books@btinternet.com

Copyright © James Inverne 2000
Copyright photographs © John Timbers 2000

British Library Cataloguing-in-Publication-Data
A catalogue record for this book is available fromthe British Library.

ISBN: 1 84002 135 7

Cover design and book design and layout: Jon Morgan

All photographs: John Timbers

Printed in Great Britain by Alden Press Ltd, Oxford.

1 3 5 7 9 10 8 6 4 2

DEDICATED TO THE MEMORY
OF MY FRIEND AND MENTOR,
SIR DAVID ENGLISH

CONTENTS

Acknowledgements

It was a big job, and could not have been completed without the help of several people, to whom I owe thanks. Family first; Sue, Jill, Jodie and Daniel for moral support, my father Richard particularly for his patient proof-reading and expert advice.

My publisher, James Hogan, who has now trusted me with a big project twice, and editors Humphrey Gudgeon and Torben Betts. Sarah Wherry for being a wonderful sounding-board, and everyone else at Oberon Books.

Anna Arthur for her commitment on the publicity front.

Bob Lynton at *Performance* for indulging my prolonged absences and for being a friend as well as a boss.

For their helpful comments, Ina Miller, Roger Wingate, Sir Charles Mackerras and Chris Woodward.

Veronica Wadley, also Paul Rossiter and the librarians of the *Daily Mail* for granting me access to that invaluable archive. The Theatre Museum for their tireless assistance in aiding me with my research.

John Timbers, for being a vital co-conspirator in this arduous but wonderful project, and of course for his exquisite photographs.

Finally, the impresarios themselves – and those who work in their offices – all of whom gave unstintingly of their time and co-operation, and were good enough to believe in this book.

FOREWORD

Ever since Philip Henslowe went out looking for angels to back Shakespeare's earliest plays at the Rose, they've been with us – the impresarios. The word means 'undertakers of exploits' and, carrying the address books of your dreams, they preside over the theatrical souk with the taste of the Medicis and the speculative instincts of Bill Gates.

Once, actors put themselves on and so became managers; amateurs owned theatres and could indulge their own whims; then actors became directors but were overtaken in turn by full-time directors who then ran buildings and harassed the government. But, with a few notable exceptions, producers don't double as anything else – they do one job that comprehends all the others. And like old-fashioned movie moguls, they suffer from a familiar thumbnail sketch – the cigar-smoke, the trigger-happy temperament, the ruthless bark – that does them scant justice.

Binkie Beaumont, it is said, used to have a little door in the floor of his office through which he would observe both the auditorium below and the stage, simultaneously counting the house and keeping a ruthless eye on the standard of performance, particularly at a matinee – his authority on both subjects was beyond question. My own tenure in my first West End show over 30 years ago was secured by Michael Codron at a moment in rehearsals when a panicky director wanted to fire me: called in to pass judgement, he quietly instructed me to get an immediate haircut and always to wear a suit to rehearsals, adding a well-timed word of encouragement to help the medicine go down. The director, confronted by this physical image of the finished character rather earlier in rehearsals than usual, immediately calmed down.

Another interviewee in this book is Bill Kenwright. Now, if being with Michael Codron is like being gently held in a grey velvet glove, working for Bill is like being dipped in a heady blend of sensuous oils – rock 'n' roll, football and the gambling table. On one show of which he was inordinately proud, but which looked for a time as if it would lose him a packet, he told me that he would sit in his office with the previous night's figures and weep, come to the matinee and feel as if Everton had won the Cup, and then go back to his office and weep again.

What these stories and their subjects share is, of course, the unexpected. A good producer will, like Hotspur in *Henry IV*, cavil on the ninth part of a contractual hair, but then spoil you with an extravagant Christmas present. The impresarios can be surprisingly loyal, suddenly reckless, more insightful than the people they hire to be insightful, far from cynical, and inclined to back the most unlikely hunches. For that reason, these talented people have changed the face of the theatre this last half-century. Whether your tipple is tragical-comical-historical-pastoral, the brand new play or the classic revival, the reconsidered musical, the brilliant ensemble or the dazzle of the imported star, scene individable or poem unlimited, these are your only women and men. For the price of a ticket, they will renew your interest in what we do. We sometimes can't live with them, but we certainly can't live without them, and the lunches can be fantastic.

Michael Pennington
London, 2000

THE IMPRESARIOS

Magical and mysterious, the word "impresario" has its own lustre, a suggestion of hidden marvels, the treasures of the stage to be unfolded from within its cloak. But over the years we have become less certain about its precise meaning. According to the *Oxford English Dictionary*, an impresario is "one who organises public entertainments".

The by-the-book definition is as follows. Impresario is an Italian term which migrated to England in the mid-eighteenth century. It refers to the person who hires a show or an act that is already in existence, hires a performing space and presents them there. He or she (mostly he so far, with notable exceptions, such as Lilian Baylis, Ninette de Valois in the past, and those interviewed for this book) is often his or her own promoter, overseeing all of the publicity. A producer has an even wider scope, creating his own show from the ground up – finding and paying for the play, the director, the cast, the theatre, the publicity, the marketing and anything else that crops up.

However, the role of the impresario / producer has over the years widened, and in the theatre, producers are also often impresarios. Duncan C Weldon, who has strong views on the subject, is one of today's leading producers. However, as he points out, "on very rare occasions I may transfer a Royal Shakespeare Company or National Theatre production to the West End, which is the impresario's role." And sometimes in these cases, the impresario may have some influence over the production in the first place, particularly if the initial deal involved a West End transfer. This happened with Sir Cameron Mackintosh and *Les Miserables*. It was always a Cameron Mackintosh production in every sense, yet his deal with the director Trevor Nunn (then artistic director of the RSC) stipulated that it fly under the RSC banner. So the musical began its life at the Barbican Centre before transferring to the Palace. And Sir Cameron was impresario and producer at once.

The distinguished producer Robert Fox has made something of a speciality of bringing hit plays from Broadway across to London, which makes him an impresario. However, he then takes creative control of the London productions, often alters the casting and anything else that he sees fit, which makes him a producer.

In theatre, therefore, the distinction is often uncertain. In the lyric arts somewhat less so, although in opera just to confuse matters the director is called the producer. But even the purest of impresarios – Harvey Goldsmith, say, or Victor Hochhauser – sometimes stray into the realms of the producer. They are all in the same business, and they are of the same breed.

"Producers," says Michael White, "must be dictators. Because their shows must reflect their personal taste." This, perhaps, is why the producers and impresarios who work in the commercial sector are such strong, fascinating characters. Many are eccentrics – whether one thinks of the occasionally explosive Harvey Goldsmith throwing over a lunch table at a business colleague, Michael White enviably still "young", still partying at clubs most nights in his sixties, or Bill Kenwright precariously balancing dual careers as theatre producer and owner of Everton Football Club. Characters such as these are not so readily found in the subsidised sector, where leadership is a democratic process, usually done by committee, and where the stakes are much lower – there is always the comfort blanket of the subsidy, and the artistic director of the RSC, say, never faces having to sell his house if a production fails. Autocracy – fuelled by the vital need for success – is much more interesting; and that is why this book focuses solely on the commercial sector.

Today's producers come from a long, rich line of larger-than-life characters. Although space limits me to writing about those who are still working, it is fascinating, without even delving into the pre-war years, to glance briefly back at their immediate predecessors, who dominated the middle of the twentieth century. Bestriding the West End, clinging on to his power with an iron grip for more than 40 years was Hugh Beaumont, known to the theatrical world as Binkie. Through his company H M Tennent, Beaumont dictated more than any other single figure the shape of the commercial West End.

Just as famous, perhaps more so in retrospect, was the man who set the archetypal image of the impresario. Besuited, sitting behind the desk, chequebook in hand, enormous cigar in mouth. It has become a caricature, but Lew Grade lived it. A colourful figure who started his career as a world champion Charleston dancer, Grade was one-third of a famous trio of brothers, all of whom became producers. Leslie Grade until his untimely death worked with Lew, and Bernard Delfont (he had changed his name for his own dance act), became the enormously successful force behind the Royal Variety Show and much else. Both Lew Grade and Delfont received peerages and, to the last, they were close yet competitive.

The Grades weren't the only sibling-act in town. Emile Littler and his elder brother Prince dominated the pantomime scene, although Prince left the impresario's role behind to become one of London's most important theatre owners. Val Parnell, the formidable supremo of the London Palladium, established that theatre as one of the world's most prestigious variety houses. The variety show, a form that has all but disappeared, was the impresario's playground and nobody bettered Parnell. Under his ever-watchful eye, hundreds of the world's top stars from Bob Hope to Judy Garland played the Palladium's famous stage. He demanded absolute respect for his beloved theatre, and once fired the Rolling Stones on the spot for making a mess of their dressing room. Indeed Lew Grade attributed his habitual cigar-smoking to the need for a comfort blanket in dealing with intimidating people like Parnell.

After Parnell, another major figure at the Palladium was Robert Nesbitt, who always clasped an ubiquitous glass of champagne and was known as "The Prince of Darkness" because his shows employed a new invention, the lighting board, and he used to sit in the gloom to light his shows himself. When variety died, the Palladium was home to the glitzy musicals of Harold Fielding – who brought us the likes of *Singin' in the Rain* and *Barnum*.

Musicals were also a speciality of Jack Hylton, the successful bandleader who became an impresario at the age of nearly 50. Though he produced a wide range, from concerts with the London Philharmonic to *The Crazy Gang*, his reputation was sealed with a string of American hit shows – *Kiss Me Kate, Call Me Madam, Ring Out the Bells, Paint Your Wagon, Pal Joey* and *Kismet*.

Until quite recently, the musicals field was occupied (though not solely) by the stylish Robert Stigwood, who counts among his successes *Hair, Jesus Christ Superstar* and *Evita*, as well as the films of *Grease* and *Saturday Night Fever*. He also presented pop acts such as the Bee Gees, Cream and the 15-year-old Stevie Wonder. He as much as anyone illustrates the instability of this business – a millionaire at 28, Stigwood had a couple of failures and was bankrupt at 31. He manufactured a triumphant comeback, became one of the richest men in Britain and then abruptly scaled down all his operations and went to live in the peaceful surroundings of the Isle of Wight.

Binkie Beaumont aside, the world of theatre had other important dictators: Sir Peter Daubeny, formerly an actor, turned to producing after losing an arm in World War II. His World Theatre seasons at the Aldwych became legendary; the gentlemanly Sir Donald Albery whose family constitutes a theatrical dynasty – his grandmother was Lady Wyndham, after whom Wyndham's Theatre was named, his son Ian Albery is now a significant theatre proprietor. Meanwhile, far away from the suits and cigars and more likely to be found wearing a cap over her cropped hair, Joan Littlewood held sway with her socialist Theatre Workshop in London's East End. Trying to create a theatre for the working classes, Littlewood's successes included *Oh What A Lovely War*, Shelagh Delaney's *A Taste of Honey* and the glorious Cockney musical *Fings Ain't Wot They Used T'Be* by Frank Norman and Lionel Bart.

There were also the actor-producers, a species no longer to be found in abundance. A valiant and much-admired exception to this was Kenneth Branagh's Renaissance Company in the 80s. For five seasons Branagh brought Shakespeare and other playwrights to the commercial West End. Part of his ambition was to involve the actor in all parts of the creative process. This resulted in some fine productions – notably *Much Ado About Nothing* directed by Judi Dench and *Hamlet* directed by Derek Jacobi. Eventually Branagh moved the company – and the Bard – to the worlds of film and radio. Decades before, Sir Donald Wolfit had regally toured the provinces, his companies meticulously tailored to showcase his own talents. Laurence Olivier, of course, fashioned the Chichester Festival Theatre and then launched his dream – the National Theatre of Great Britain. On a smaller, but no less inspiring scale, the actor Bernard Miles fulfilled his own ambition; in 1950 he turned an old school hall next to his house into the Mermaid Theatre. The venue's biggest success was always an annual production of *Treasure Island* in which Miles would always play Long John Silver.

As a teenager, I was privileged to encounter one of the great, and largely unsung, British actor-managers; Geoffrey Kendal, father of Felicity, who took Shakespeare to far-flung corners of India. When I met him, his windswept shock of white hair and grizzled beard made him look like a latter-day Prospero, mystical and fierce. One can imagine the effect he had in places where the locals had never even seen *The Tempest*.

There is less commercial activity in opera, ballet and classical music, but certain blazing achievers of yesteryear stand out. Sir John Christie built an opera house in his garden, creating the Glyndebourne Festival. His son and successor George, who has distinguished himself no less than his father with his daring rebuilding of that theatre, features in this book. Still as active as ever as the century turns, the last of his generation of impresarios, and he is also dealt with more fully later – Victor Hochhauser, aided and abetted by his wife Lilian. Earlier in the 20th century Lilian Baylis' reign at the Old Vic was the stuff of legend, alongside Ninette de Valois, the founder of the Vic-Wells Ballet, now the Royal Ballet. De Valois had danced for Serge Diaghilev, who brought classical ballet from St Petersburg to the rest of Europe.

These then were the British showmen of a bygone age, the people behind the circus, who themselves were often as fascinating as any stage act. So it is with their successors, although a different style now prevails.

Most of today's impresarios may be less formal than Binkie Beaumont and his contemporaries, but they grip the reins of power no less tightly. And in Cameron Mackintosh has arisen a figure who has pushed the financial might of the theatre producer far beyond anything previously achieved. The Society of London Theatre's Wyndham Report in 1998 noted that Mackintosh's production of *The Phantom of the Opera* had taken £1730 million around the world, almost twice the takings of the highest-grossing film, *Titanic*.

Despite this level of success, almost all of the current generation complain that the costs of putting on a show have risen beyond all measure in the last 40 years. And if Duncan Weldon espouses the most drastic view, that this is the last era in which it is financially practical to be a commercial producer, he is by no means alone in his concerns.

Yet there *are* young producers already beginning to forge their empires, and they are less pessimistic. The final chapter deals with a few of the new breed and the perils that they encounter on the way up.

It is undoubtedly difficult to get started in the business, more so perhaps than ever before, but as David Pugh – the young producer of the hit play *Art* – discovered, with an international roll-out and the possibility of film royalties, the potential rewards are greater than they have ever been.

Failure along the way, however, is inevitable. Richard Jordan, one of today's youngest producers (and a protégé of Michael Codron) tells me with a grin, "Michael

Codron once said, 'If you're a producer you can't have a heart, because it gets broken many times'. And you don't understand that until you do it."

Yet the producers in this book do have heart. One surely must to enter such a precarious, strange profession. Certainly it takes something to overcome the obstacles to be faced along the way, from exploding theatres to disappearing actors to police raids and reviews which can kill a show stone dead.

Still they have prevailed, and each has brought particular interests to bear and carved out a well-defined area of expertise – their trademark – Cameron Mackintosh and musicals, Michael Codron and new writing, Duncan C Weldon's penchant for headline stars, Thelma Holt and international theatre, Harvey Goldsmith and Raymond Gubbay and their operas and concerts for the masses, Michael White and the avant-garde. They are all rightly proud of their fiefdoms, and – though they all know each other and some are even friends (and the opposite, in one or two cases) – they guard them well.

There are special cases. The actor-manager has been all but replaced by other creative figures. There is the composer – Andrew Lloyd Webber, who finally moved away from Cameron Mackintosh to become his own producer. Even if he only produces his own shows, given the scale of his operations that still makes him a major player. And his influence is set to increase since at the time of writing he has just bought the Stoll Moss group of theatres, making him more than ever one of the most powerful theatrical figures in the world.

There is the director-producer. *The* director, Sir Peter Hall, who has shaped the theatre scene of Britain as much as anyone, and left the subsidised sector for a glorious commercial adventure: the Peter Hall Company, a repertory company in the West End, whose range stretched from Shakespeare to Tennessee Williams to David Rabe. Like Lear on the heath, he faced an epic struggle, an old-fashioned idealist facing out the financial winds of a society that more and more prefers the long-running "sure thing".

There is the choreographer-producer. Matthew Bourne's successful production of *Swan Lake*, with men dancing the swans, was an international hit that established him and his company Adventures In Motion Pictures as a significant – and ultra-fashionable – force.

Finally the unsung loner-innovator: Alan Sievewright – in love with opera – who has been doing his own thing for years, rediscovering neglected works, beavering away as producer-presenter-broadcaster and now about to emerge as a cultural force on the internet.

There are more, and some I have not been able to include in this book. Space regrettably obliged me to pass over Paul Elliott, today's pantomime king, and the very active Peter Wilson, while Robert Fox – a stylish producer who chooses his productions with meticulous care – was unavailable for interview. I have also concentrated on the classical art forms, so rock impresarios are out with the exception of Harvey Goldsmith, who is included by virtue of his work in opera and classical music. As will be obvious by now, this book focuses on British producers, though Broadway of course has its great characters.

The individuals you will meet over the following pages are extraordinary. Each of them goes to work ready to tackle whatever unique situation their strange and glorious profession might choose to throw at them. Often against daunting odds, they have survived, and continue to stamp their personal tastes on our cultural lives. In this selection of interviews I have tried to convey the experience of meeting such vivid personalities – how they impose shape on a chaotic business, what drives them on. And always I have sought to recognise the particular part of their soul which they impart to their productions. For the commercial theatre pulses with the heartbeats of its single-parents; the impresarios.

Each one of them has a story to tell: variously exciting, heart-warming, provocative, glamorous, optimistic, pessimistic, nerve-wracking, hard-nosed and humane.

James Inverne,
London 2000

PETER HALL

"You're here to audition, right? Follow me." It is a startling proposal. When I arrived at London's Old Vic Theatre I had simply announced that I had an appointment with Sir Peter Hall. It seems, however, that my appointment has coincided with Sir Peter's auditions to re-cast his successful run of

Peter Shaffer's play *Amadeus*. The original cast are off to Broadway, and London replacements are required.

Now it just so happens that I know the lead role of Salieri, or at least parts of it, thanks to a university production for which I learnt

PETER HALL
*poses mischievously in Salieri's wheelchair after
rehearsing Amadeus on stage at The Old Vic theatre*

all the lines but which never actually materialised. Could this be the chance to redeem all that wasted work?

An audition for Sir Peter Hall is tempting indeed, for he is a man who has made many careers, and not just those of actors; many playwrights, other directors and opera singers have also felt the munificent Hall touch. That he is one of the most important figures in the post-war British theatre is beyond doubt. The Peter Hall story is the story of the Royal Shakespeare Company, the National Theatre and much more besides.

He was Suffolk-born, from Bury St Edmunds, where his impoverished parents sacrificed much to give their son a good education. Despite earning only £3 a week, Hall's father managed to send him both to a private kindergarten and piano lessons. That his son eventually graduated from Cambridge University with a relatively modest 2:2 degree was due not to any lack of scholarly ability, but rather the fact that he directed no less than five drama productions in his crucial final year.

Hall was already addicted to working in the theatre, and this set the pattern for his life to date. He is, famously, a workaholic. By 1954, he had been appointed director of the Oxford Playhouse. In 1955, at the age of 24, he was made director of the Arts Theatre in London. This is where he first won serious critical attention for his brave championship of new, often experimental plays. The most famous of these was Samuel Beckett's *Waiting For Godot*, which he gave its British and English language premiere when much larger companies (and several famous actors) would not dare to touch it. The production won the advocacy of Harold Hobson, the influential drama critic of *The Sunday Times*, and Hall's career was made.

His next great challenge came in 1960, when he took over the Shakespeare Memorial Theatre in Stratford-upon-Avon. Despite powerful opposition and at great financial risk, Hall turned the seasonal festival into a major repertory theatre company with a London home (the Aldwych Theatre) to complement the base in Stratford. He persuaded Peggy Ashcroft to lead the company, and as Hall admiringly says, "where she led, the profession followed". He brought in brilliant young actors – including Judi Dench, Peter O'Toole, David Warner, Ian Holm and Dorothy Tutin – and created a resident ensemble. He revolutionised the speaking of Shakespeare, concentrating on a "house style" of clarity through the natural rhythms of the verse – a practice which reached its early zenith in *The Wars of the Roses* cycle of Shakespeare's history plays which were directed by Hall and John Barton. He continued to seek out the best new plays, including Harold Pinter's *The Homecoming* and the British premiere of Jean Anouilh's *Becket*. And he changed the name (declaring that the Shakespeare Memorial Theatre sounded like a gravestone) to the Royal Shakespeare Company. Finally he won for the company government funding, and the RSC in its current form was born.

After leaving Stratford in 1968, Hall inherited the National Theatre of Great Britain from Sir Laurence Olivier in 1973. If Olivier had created the company, it was Hall who had to mastermind the move into the new building on London's South Bank. This was beset by problems, not least the crippling trade union strikes in the late 1970s. He prevailed, and remained with the NT for 15 years. During that time, there was controversy (in 1986 *The Sunday Times* instituted a vigorous campaign condemning Hall's occasional transfer of successful productions to the West End, when he would collect a percentage of the box office – a necessary perk which Hall defended as standard practice) and there were also triumphs. Hall's own productions of *The Oresteia*, in which the actors wore Greek masks, and Shakespeare's *Antony and Cleopatra* starring Anthony Hopkins and Judi Dench, were hailed as landmark successes. When Hall finally handed over the reins to Richard Eyre, his successor inherited a healthy, vibrant company.

Not many directors are equally inspired in both theatre and opera. Hall is, and between 1984 and 1990 he brought his managerial skills to the Glyndebourne Festival Opera, where he served as its artistic director. Despite magnificent productions of Verdi's *La Traviata*, Bizet's *Carmen* (starring Hall's second wife, the mezzo-soprano Maria Ewing) and Mozart's *Don Giovanni* (a

production which, when it toured, brought to public attention the shining talents of the young baritone Thomas Allen), Hall's tenure ended prematurely. A new production of *The Magic Flute*, by the American Peter Sellars, had cut all the dialogue. Nobody told Hall. Outraged at the sacrilege and furious that nobody had informed him of such a drastic decision, he resigned.

So he embarked with a will on his latest grand idea, a great adventure in the commercial theatre. The Peter Hall Company had been established in 1988, as a joint venture with Duncan Weldon's Triumph Productions. It had the best of all possible starts, when Vanessa Redgrave caused a sensation in Hall's production of Tennesse Williams's *Orpheus Descending*. The show transferred to Broadway. A year later, the company repeated the success with Dustin Hoffman in *The Merchant of Venice*. So when Hall cut his ties with Glyndebourne in 1990 the stage was set for him to work towards his dream – a repertory company in the West End of a calibre to rival the RSC and the National. And it is about this, and his work in commercial theatre leading up to this, that I have come to talk. So my audition will have to wait.

I am shown up to a practically bare rehearsal room, and left there. I prepare my notes, and sit at the only table. Ten minutes pass in silence, before I hear the rickety old lift (it is an ancient apparatus where you actually have to turn a lever to ring for the carriage) begin its steady, whirring odyssey through the floors of the theatre. It clunks to a halt, the iron grille slides open, and Sir Peter Hall appears in the doorway.

Broad, bulky, with an immensely commanding presence, he is one of the more striking figures in the theatre world and much has been written about his appearance (Jack Tinker, the *Daily Mail*'s late theatre critic, described him as an "Oriental mandarin", the playwright John Osborne was less subtle and simply dubbed him "Fu Manchu".) On this occasion he seems equally exotic, wearing a black fedora and a poncho-like cape. A Mexican bandit-leader perhaps? His shoulders droop a little since, as he readily admits, he is tired from rehearsing and auditioning all day. As he sits, he seems to revive and his steely eyes gleam as he prepares to talk about his favourite subject. Theatre.

There was very little subsidised theatre in Britain when Hall was a teenager in the 1940s. I asked him to detail his early theatrical influences. He takes a deep breath and begins by reeling off a string of names:-

"As a very young man, Peggy Ashcroft, John Gielgud, Ralph Richardson and Laurence Olivier. Gielgud and Ashcroft at the Haymarket in the war years, Richardson and Olivier at what was then the New Theatre (now the Albery) in St Martin's Lane. I saw everything they did. Tyrone Guthrie was a huge influence as a director. Then the young Peter Brook. I saw

his *Love's Labours Lost* at Stratford in 1947 or 48, when I was still a schoolboy. Peter wasn't much more than a schoolboy himself, he was about 21.

"They all affected my perception of what theatre could do. But generally the main influence was the…" – here his eyes sparkle to match the adjective, which he takes care over choosing – "*glittering* West End of the impresario Binkie Beaumont and his company H M Tennent Ltd. Practically all the good work was done by them." He checks himself – practically all the *work* was done by them – except the Old Vic company at the New Theatre. My memory of that West End was of one very stylish unit. It was not in pockets, like it is now."

Binkie Beaumont, perhaps the most powerful of all commercial producers, is a figure who fascinates Hall. It is tempting to speculate that he saw in the older man a role model. A man who, as Hall has since done, controlled almost every aspect of his business.

"Binkie dominated it all. In the early years he even dominated Stratford. He was a governor of the Shakespeare Memorial Theatre, and the style of the place under Anthony Quayle was all modelled on Binkie's West End. Michael Redgrave, Peggy Ashcroft, Robert Helpmann and the rest were all Tennent's stars, and the designers were all Tennent's people. I even worked for Tennent as a young man and I learnt a great deal from Binkie, who I think is the cleverest impresario I have ever met.

Even when I later defied him in taking the RSC into London, we remained friends."

I ask whether then, given its commercial nature, Beaumont's West End was centred around a star-led culture. This leads Hall to a subject which has long-troubled him: "We have always had a star-led theatre and always will have. Much depends on how you make the stars. We do not have theatre stars any more. Now the stars come from film or television. If they are any good for the theatre they *become* theatre stars, if not they go back to their screen. But it is very hard to think of anybody at the moment who has actually been made famous by the theatre."

Rising to the challenge, I submit a few names: Rufus Sewell, Rachel Weisz… I am interrupted before I get very far. "True, they started on the stage but they are made famous by television and film."

This rankles, there must be someone. Anthony Sher, for instance is an undoubted superstar of the stage, he fills houses on the strength of his name. Hall becomes animated. "Yes, to us he is a superstar, but lots of people haven't got a clue who he is. That proves my point!"

When Hall was called up for national service in the mid-1940s, he was fortunate enough to receive his training at a base near Stratford, allowing him plenty of opportunities for theatregoing. Interestingly, however, he actually served in Germany in 1948, by which time the country had been devastated by the war. The contrast, I suggest, must have been immense. He nods in agreement.

"It was a rough time. Germany was very rough. And yet, among the ruins, it still had its repertory theatres and its repertory opera. I managed to see most of the operatic repertory during my year in Germany, in Hamburg and Hanover. That had an impact on me, the fact that German society, even when they had insufficient to eat, nevertheless was still concerned about their culture, about their art."

That philosophy of preserving the arts was, he insists, far more firmly embedded than in Britain at that time, which only began to nurture its arts establishment after the war ended: "The theatre and dance and music in Britain drew energy from the war. The Arts Council was born out of that period and the idea of state subsidy did not start until after the war. Since then, the golden age – and we *have* had a golden age for the arts in Britain – has been largely subsidy-led."

When Hall took over at Stratford, though, it was not subsidised. And his insistence on bringing the company to London was extremely risky and brought him into conflict with his much-admired Binkie Beaumont.

"Binkie took me out to lunch at the time, and said, 'I'm not having you coming in to the West End and ruining it. Because once you do repertory theatre in the West End the actors will no longer want to play eight times a week, and the dramatists will no longer want to give me their plays when they could have them nurtured by the repertory system. I am not putting up with it.' He told me that he would resign from the Stratford board if I went ahead. He kept his word, but he did it very decorously and very quietly, there was no great public row, and we remained close.

"In a certain sense he was quite right. But the time had come for a change anyway. Because by the middle of the 50s, the Royal Court was there and it had changed the whole nature of what we thought drama was. The tone had altered irrevocably. After that, the RSC arrived in the West End by 1960, and the National Theatre opened in 63. This was a time of enormous change."

Was it possible at such an early stage, I wondered, for Hall to foresee that London theatrical life would become so led by these huge companies?

"I didn't see that, but I did see that with the coming of the National and the increased development of subsidy, English theatre was growing up. There was suddenly a chance for it to become, in a proper sense, serious. If you look today at the list of what is on in the West End, as far as plays are concerned 80 per cent of it has emerged from subsidised houses. And Andrew Lloyd Webber and Cameron Mackintosh have said that they would not have been able to do what they have done in the musical field without the talent that came out of those houses."

"I have got nothing against the commercial sector. I work in it, I grew up in it, I owe a lot to it. But it *couldn't work now*. Plays do not make money, unless we are talking about the mega-musicals that run for years and years. Theatre is specialist, hand-made and very uneconomic. And if we didn't have a subsidised sector at this moment, the West End would be exactly the same as Broadway, with most of the theatres dark, the landlords eager for redevelopment."

That RSC move to London could have financially destroyed the company. It was an immensely stressful time for Hall. But he won through, he was vindicated. Yet so many other times in his life, not least very recently with the trials of the Peter Hall Company, he has had to face similar financial barriers in the face of formidable opposition. I suspect that he must get tired of fighting the same battles, and say so. But he pounces on the tail-end of the sentence, with obstinate resolve.

"*No*. Then I will die." After a moment's pause, he bends slightly. "I do get tired of seeing the same stupid mistakes being made by a different generation of stupid people. But that is one of the perils of growing old. I mean, as we talk now it hurts me more than I can tell you to see the Arts Council diminishing all the little theatres up and down the country because they actually want to close them." His eyes half close, as though in pain at the illness of a favourite child. There is no artifice here, he feels these wounds to the theatre as if they were his own. "They think that these small houses don't play to big enough audiences, and are expensive to run. So they decide just to concentrate on the big boys. This is a rational business decision. But it is *death* for the future of the theatre, for the training of actors, for the development of playwrights and most of all for theatre audiences."

I add that the Arts Council seems to think that they can rely on a staple diet of big shows in the West End, with musicals and guest appearances by film stars.

"Ah, but where do you find these film stars?" he continues. "At tiny theatres like the Almeida or the Donmar Warehouse, for very short runs. Then if they work, you transfer them – for very short runs – at very high prices and you make a killing. But then the film stars go and the theatres are left empty. The theatre ecology has gone. It is not there any more."

There seems to be a great sadness in Hall as he talks of the beleaguered British theatre. It seems to override any sense of pride in what it is still managing to achieve now (productions from the West End currently all but dominate Broadway). It may simply be fatigue from the rehearsal, but I wonder if this most battle-hardened of campaigners is not beginning to find that the war is taking its toll.

I turn to the Peter Hall Company, and he brightens as he explains its *raison d'être*, which turns out to be rather simple.

"When I left the National Theatre I wanted to enjoy something of the same conditions in the commercial theatre." He chortles at his own audacity. "I wanted to direct the plays of my choosing, I didn't want to be a hired hand, I wanted to use actors with whom I had forged working relationships over many years and I wanted continuity in my work. I thought, and I think I proved, that I had an audience. Not a huge one, but 50 or 60 thousand people who were prepared to see what I had to say, if I did it well. And I have done about 30 productions with the company." He pauses and reflects, before adding proudly, "Rather a lot."

He went to Duncan Weldon, who backed the company. The initial plan was to present all of the company's productions over three years at the Theatre Royal, Haymarket. In the event only the first production, *Orpheus Descending* played there. For a long time subsequently, Hall was frustrated in his attempts to secure a single theatre for a long-term tenancy. He and Weldon went their separate ways in 1991.

Next, Hall joined forces with the millionaire author and businessman Jeffrey Archer, who allowed him use of his Playhouse Theatre. There followed a season which included Molière's *Tartuffe*, Tennessee Williams's *The Rose Tattoo*, *Twelfth Night* and Ibsen's *Hedda Gabler* (directed by Deborah Warner). The starry casts included Felicity Kendal, Paul Eddington, Julie Walters, John Sessions, Eric Porter and Fiona Shaw. Six months into the season, Hall was informed that Archer was selling the theatre.

Bill Kenwright stepped into the breach and forged with Hall a partnership that lasted for seven years. This culminated in 1996 when Hall announced that the Peter Hall Company was now a permanent ensemble, and a very distinguished one at that, which included leading actors such as Michael Pennington, Peter Bowles, Denis Quilley, Anna Carteret and Alan Howard. They played at the Old Vic, and then at the Piccadilly Theatre.

If Hall had for a long time missed the continuity of a single venue, he had attracted a loyal group of actors. Pennington, for instance, had stayed close to the company since its inception. This gave Hall the company identity he sought. He denies, however, that there was any grand artistic policy from the start.

"I have never worked like that. I work on the people and on what seems communicable at a given time. For instance, I have recently produced quite a number of translations by Ranjit Bolt and I think that through these Ranjit has opened up French drama to the English audiences in a perfectly immediate way. I have done two Ibsens, I have done Shakespeare obviously. There has been quite a variety. Yet there is a pattern that emerges from working with the same designer, John Gunter, and the same lighting people and sound crew. And, of course, the actors whom I love, from Judi Dench down. And there were some exciting new discoveries like Victoria Hamilton and that wonderful actor who played Hamlet for me, Stephen Dillane."

I point out that he is in a most unusual position, being a major producer as well as a great director. This, it seems is a source of pleasure to him.

"Well," he rejoins, "I have produced about 800 shows." The great bushy eyebrows raise in amused amazement at the figure, and he issues forth a snorting chuckle.

Someone in such a powerful position must have to some degree an urge to affect the theatre culture. Hall considers. "If you have spent 25 years running the National Theatre and the RSC, you presumably have some expertise in running a theatre. And what irritates me about a lot of producers is that they are directors *manqué* or writers *manqué*, or even actors *manqué*, and they have never actually considered the fact that their primary duty is to be efficient managers. The management level among producers – particularly film producers – is appalling in my experience."

Hall himself has dabbled in film and television, without yet making any breakthrough to match his stage successes. It is the only currently lucrative area, in his opinion: "A lot of films don't make money, those that do, *make money.*' He is reluctant to detail his own financial successes, but he is no stranger to hit shows of the kind to delight a bank manager's balance sheet. Besides, as we talk it becomes clear that it is the work that he loves, and given any excuse he will talk for long minutes about favourite authors and their plays. I try to pin him down about financial benefits to the company of *Orpheus Descending*.

"It went to Broadway. That was a good start, thanks to Vanessa Redgrave and Tennessee Williams. I knew Tennessee very well. Miss him, miss him." There is real sorrow in his voice, even after all these years. "When I was 24," he continues, happy to be discussing one of his idols, "he gave me the rights of his plays in London to direct. That was a pretty fabulous gift, for which I will always be grateful. It was all because he came to see *Waiting For Godot*, which was really the turning point in my life. And, incidentally, that was an enormously successful play that the commercial theatre wouldn't do – it's interesting."

When *Orpheus* transferred to Broadway, there was an infamous incident involving air-conditioning, which gained Hall some notoriety in New York:"The Nederlanders, who owned the theatre, had not maintained the air-conditioning. If it was on, you could not hear the actors, and if it was off, everyone was sweating. So I went up on stage and got the audience to take a vote on it. They decided to sweat." I had read that Hall was booed off the stage. "Not at all, I was cheered and clapped. Fifteen people left angrily and it made the front page of the *New York Times*. I was the hero of the hour."

Are Broadway audiences notably different to a West End audience?

"I have worked a lot on Broadway over the years, and I was rather startled when I went to Los Angeles to be introduced at a dinner as 'nine times Tony nominee'. I was dreadfully embarrassed!" He laughs at the ridiculousness of the accolade.

"Up to a few years ago the Manhattan audience for the first 10 or 12 weeks of a play was the best in the world. They were absolutely sharp as a razor, a real cracker – phew!" His exclamation mingles fear and respect. "All the Pinter plays that I have done on Broadway from *The Homecoming* in 1966 on have had wonderful responses from the audience in those early weeks. Once you have run through the Manhattan audience, you reach the coach-trade and things slow up a little bit.

"Unfortunately, though, I don't think that audience goes to the theatre any more. The reason is that there isn't much straight theatre in New York now, there isn't much to interest the public. There are usually one or two British imports which become hot and fashionable, and there are long, long, long, long, long, *long*-running musicals. So the Manhattan audience goes out to dinner. They haven't got a Royal Shakespeare Company or a National Theatre. They haven't got a Royal Court. They haven't even got an Almeida – because Off-Broadway, however good it is, is not working at that level. So their theatre is very impoverished by our standards. The danger is that London is moving the same way."

Hall cast an American star in his next production, when Dustin Hoffman played Shylock in *The Merchant of Venice*. I had heard that Hoffman had originally wanted to play Hamlet. Hall nods. "Yes, he did. He rang me up and said, 'It's Dustin Hoffman. Can we have a drink?' I knew him slightly but I had never worked with him. So I met him, we had a drink and he declared, 'I want to play Shakespeare and I've decided to come to you.' I replied 'Thank you very much, what do you want to do?' and he said *Hamlet* and I immediately said, 'You're mad.'

"He was a bit taken aback and asked me what I meant. So I told him, 'You're far too old and – what is more worrying – if anyone who has never done Shakespeare thinks that they can start with Hamlet then they are riding for a fall.'" Hall grins. "So he liked all that!" I wonder if anyone had ever been so frank with Dustin Hoffman. Hall continues, "He thanked me for being honest and asked me what he should play. I replied, 'You should do one of those parts that steal the show but don't carry the play. There are three wonderful parts that Shakespeare wrote: Malvolio in *Twelfth Night*, Angelo in *Measure For Measure* and Shylock. They are all quite small, only about four or five scenes, they completely steal the limelight and everybody else does all the work.' He decided to do Shylock and I thought he was brilliant. By the time we got to Broadway he was the best Shylock I ever hope to see – absolutely fantastic."

The production marked two hits out of two for the Peter Hall Company. Two critical successes, two box office winners, two Broadway transfers. American stars tend not by nature (or by training) to be great Shakespeareans, but one might have expected Hoffman, who is Jewish, to have felt a natural affinity towards Shylock. I ask how important Hall feels it is to have a Jewish actor in the role.

Race and Shakespeare

"One of the good things about today's theatre culture is that we take race seriously. You don't have the humiliating and embarrassing spectacle of English classical actors putting endless amounts of putty on their nose and going 'Oy oy oy'. Even Alec Guinness's performance as Fagin in David Lean's film of *Oliver Twist* I find a bit embarrassing now. In our day and age, you have to either be Jewish or part-Jewish, or have something very Jewish about you. And I think that is wonderful. We are honouring race."

The corollary of that, I suggest, is that Hall would never again direct *Othello* with a white actor. He agrees, "No, I don't think I would." This is intriguing. I put it to him that so far, for various reasons mainly to do with training, there are not yet as many black actors with the technical skill and ease with the verse to carry off a major Shakespearean role like Othello. This does not alter his viewpoint.

"You are right, there aren't. But they are coming. There is a new generation of black actors who are really going to surprise us in the next ten or twenty years. We should, I believe, wait for them to arrive. I just can't take the idea of somebody blacking up. Yes, you can always argue that actually Othello is a moor and moors are not black. Yet the fact remains that Shakespeare's imagery is all about being black." He warms to his theme, and expands it: "Shakespeare wrote two great plays which are anti-racist: *The Merchant of Venice* and *Othello*. And he wrote them in a racist society, a *rabidly* racist society. That is extraordinary. We have to honour him now by casting those parts accurately."

Hall is enjoying the discussion now – we are on his territory, discussing the meaning of Shakespeare's plays, the texts, the cultural implications. This is what he has devoted his life to exploring. I am particularly glad that he feels that *Merchant* is not an anti-Semitic play, which is a charge often levelled at it. I tell him so and, with an 'Oh!' of disgust at the idea that anybody might think that it is, passionately defends his corner: "Not at all. The reverse! I mean, look at that speech he puts into the mouth of Shylock, 'Hath not a Jew eyes…'It is the most extraordinary plea for tolerance."

I am interested to know how then he defends Shylock's speech where he talks about Antonio to the audience, saying 'I hate him for he is a Christian.'. His answer is to the point: "Yes well, I would hate somebody who was a Christian if he had done to me what that man has done to Shylock. Shylock loses his daughter and is driven mad by these bigoted Christians. And I think the *most* important thing to remember is that Shakespeare's play was written as a response to Christopher Marlowe's big hit, *The Jew of Malta*. The Jew

of Malta, the title-character, is an out-and-out villain. The response to *The Jew of Malta* is *The Merchant of Venice*. Who *is* the merchant of Venice? Not Shylock. Antonio."

Hall encouraged Hoffman to play the part almost as a comedian, a man who uses laughter to try and win social acceptance. "How else," he remarks gravely, "do you survive in the ghetto?"

Dustin Hoffman, though, is a method actor, as are several big names with whom Hall has worked (another Oscar winner, Jessica Lange, among them). How, I ask, do they manage to fit into the very different British style of acting?

"They fit because they want to fit. Dustin wanted to learn how to speak Shakespeare, and he applied himself rigorously. Memorably one morning he strode into rehearsal and he took me aside and said, 'I understand now, it's clicked! You're quite right. You can't improvise this shit.'" Hall throws back his head and rocks with easy laughter. "Well, you *can't* improvise this shit, he's right. Improvisations help you get there, but they can't help you actually say the shit."

Success with Oscar

After *Merchant*, Hall had to wait a couple of seasons for another comparable success. It came in 1992, from the most unlikely source. A rarely performed play by Oscar Wilde, *An Ideal Husband*. It is a work which he has long championed: "It's a play that I have always wanted to do; it's always been on my list. The thing that I loved about it was that I was always convinced that there is a hidden play within it. There is, if you like, a covered play that Wilde wanted to write about a bisexual courtship and a bisexual marriage, that is obviously to some extent autobiographical, and he could never write that in those days. For years I have been convinced of the existence of that hidden play and I have never seen anybody reveal it on the stage. I did. And it ran for six years. It ran in Australia, it ran on Broadway. I never thought it would do any of *that*. I thought it might be a nice four months."

Indeed, so successful was the production (of which Nicholas de Jongh, critic for the London *Evening Standard*, remarked "I never dreamed a time would come when a play by Oscar Wilde would overcome me with emotion as well as laughter") that its listing appeared in the "long-runners" section of *The Times*, alongside such such unmovable extravaganzas as *Miss Saigon* and *The Woman in Black*. In the past, Hall himself has criticised shows that run past their sell-by date. I question how he can possibly maintain the sense of spontaneity.

"Oh, you can't. It is very difficult for the actors. I became more uncomfortable the longer the show ran. It's tremendously hard – all the constant replacements you inevitably have to make become, however hard you fight against it, slightly mechanical. Because you're not starting from scratch and saying, 'What is the problem that we've got to solve here?' since half the cast are probably already in it *now*. So you're merely slotting in one or two people. It's very tough, all that. For aesthetic reasons I prefer repertory, because in repertory productions get better." He corrects himself. "*Good* productions get better, bad productions collapse."

Is that why he chose the system for the Peter Hall Company? He weighs his answer carefully. "Ye-es, partly. It's better for audiences, it's better for plays, it allows you to nurse plays. When I put David Hare's *Plenty* on at the National it got a very bad press. If we had been in the West End it would have closed, unquestionably. I liked it, and I scheduled it on Fridays and Saturdays for three months. And it became a hit because the public liked it. Then it became a film. Now, all these years later, it is being given a starry revival with Cate Blanchett at the Almeida. That success would not have existed, I promise you, without the repertory system."

Beckett and Pinter

Hall, ever the champion of new writing (aside from Beckett, Pinter and Anouilh, he has directed the premieres of plays by Tennessee Williams, Edward Albee, Peter Shaffer, John Mortimer, John Whiting, Alan Ayckbourn, David Edgar, Simon Gray and Pam Gems) set up a "New Plays" season which ran alongside the classics. It was part and parcel of the Peter Hall Company, but the new works were directed by Dominic Dromgoole. For Hall, new writing is an essential artistic policy for any company.

"New plays tell us about now, they tell us about ourselves; how we are living and how we are screwing up. They express our current sensibility, and unless actors and theatre people are alive to that they have no right to be doing Shakespeare. They have got no chance of making Shakespeare live if they can't listen to their own writers."

The "New Plays" season, as Hall admits "didn't unearth any great jewels". But, not wishing to admit even partial defeat, immediately balances his admission with a comment about his past record in this area: "I suppose I'm so old that I remember when Samuel Beckett had not been heard of, when Harold Pinter was simply an unknown playwright who sent me a play. I had the chance to direct their great early work, which was lucky." I note, not for the first time, a sense of nostalgia, perhaps a longing for his youthful energy.

After several critically successful seasons during which the Peter Hall Company hopped from theatre to theatre, its director returned to the most famous of his early discoveries: *Waiting For Godot*. The production, which starred Ben Kingsley and Alan Howard, coincided with Hall's appointment as artistic director of his favourite theatre, the Old Vic. Why, I enquired, did he feel the need to revisit this particular play? He does not hesitate.

"Oh, it's like *The Marriage of Figaro* or *Hamlet* or *Twelfth Night*. A masterpiece. I am sure that what I did this time round bore absolutely no relationship to my original production in 1955. I don't actually

remember what I did in 1955. But I think I was better able to do the play now than I was then because I now know what Beckett was." He pauses to allow the implied genius of the man to sink in. "When I did it first one was trying to find a new country, a new language. It was very strange and extremely exciting."

The production was an unqualified success, extending its run and eventually continuing through a change of cast. It had seemed to me that Hall had pointed the marvellous vein of black humour in the play, that the play is full of positives and negatives, all of which cancel each other out and that he reflected this in the physical direction of Alan Howard and Ben Kingsley as Vladimir and Estragon (the two tramps who are forever waiting for the mysterious Godot). The very last image accentuated this, as Howard looked up and Kingsley gazed into his lap. Hall is pleased that I remember the detail, and elaborates: "Absolutely. Absolutely. They're totally contradictory and totally ambiguous, but at the same time they are like two lovers, two siblings, a man and a wife, two friends. They are everybody and everything. They always miss each other." He laughs with delight at the brilliance of the concept. "That's the comedy of it."

Shakespeare's verse
The composition of the Peter Hall Company is interesting. I suggest that Hall has employed a mixture of actors from the grand tradition of what one might

call "operatic" verse speakers, like Alan Howard and Michael Pennington – those who pay great attention to the music of the verse, in a way the stylistic descendents of Sir John Gielgud – and more consciously "modern" interpreters. Yet with the RSC, even more so at the National – when he antagonised more than one actor (Robert Eddison walked out of his production of *Cymbeline*) by reportedly insisting on "end-stopping"; (pausing at the physical end of every line on the page) – he had always insisted on a strictly uniform approach. He disagrees.

"They all speak verse in exactly the same way. Alan has a tendency to sing, but that is not to do with the verse. He is a very musical actor.

"My technique hasn't changed at all. I don't end-stop, I do not believe in it. What I do believe in is marking the end of the line, which is not stopping. It's phrasing, a bit like lifting the pedal on the piano in order to define a phrase when you are playing. The primary person who taught me verse speaking was Dame Edith Evans, who herself was taught by the revolutionary Shakespearean director at the end of the last century, William Poel. She played Cressida for him when she was 17.

"Poel was in many respects an eighteenth-century man. He believed that you should speak Shakespeare's text fluently, wittily and 'trippingly on the tongue' as Hamlet says. Edith taught me exactly the same, as

did George Rylands – the Cambridge don who tutored myself, John Barton, Richard Eyre and Trevor Nunn in the Marlowe Society [the famous Cambridge drama society to which they all belonged].

"I haven't changed at all. All that has happened is that I have become less inclined to persuade actors to do it who don't want to, or who think that there is some imposition being made upon them. If you don't want to do it, don't. That's my view now.

"The quarrel with Robert Eddison was not to do with his verse speaking – there are a lot of myths in this business, as you know. It was to do with the fact that he was very ill, very old and couldn't learn the lines. Really a very unhappy old bear. It was awful because I loved him. He was a good verse speaker on his day. He came out of the Marlowe Society too, so he should have been."

Looking for a good home – the Peter Hall Company

By and large, the itinerant Peter Hall Company has been a success – certainly critically, and it has formed a challenging counterpoint to the National Theatre and the Royal Shakespeare Company. It is perhaps worthy of comment that Hall's first great project, the formation of the RSC, was a struggle to make a commercial theatre operation subsidised – and here he was, all these years later, using techniques learned in the great subsidised institutions to create a commercial rival to them.

Nicholas De Jongh, again writing in the London *Evening Standard*, caught the general feeling when he wrote in 1997 that, "Under Sir Peter Hall's vigorous leadership the Old Vic demonstrated the allure of the old idea of an ensemble of admired actors working together in a repertoire of classic and modern plays. There were hitches and misses. But all along [the company] engaged us."

Alas, even Sir Peter Hall could not forever withstand the commercial pressures of running a major repertory company in the commercial West End. In 1997, the first of two crises broke. The Canadian owners of the Old Vic, Ed and David Mirvish, put the great old theatre up for sale. This was, says Hall, "A total surprise, for all of us – we had all, including the Mirvishes, planned to continue with the work we were doing at that theatre." Neither does he really know why: "I shouldn't think we will ever get at the real truth. What I believe to be true is that they had decided that the time had come for them to get out of England. They were winding up all their business affairs here, ready to go back to Canada. And that is what they did."

At the time, Hall was quoted as suggesting that they might have brought him in to add a touch of glamour to the theatre, in order to push up the value before they sold. In retrospect, he is more moderate: "I don't know whether that is true. They were perfectly happy for me to move in; certainly we were talking about five years initially. It

was a blow. However, they were very generous and kind to me. Apart from that one instance, for which they had their reasons, they always dealt openly with me. I think they *had* to sell it, or they had some deep psychological need to wind up their English interests. I just don't know."

Hall pushed on, and his company moved to the Piccadilly. Roger Wingate, the chairman of Associated Capital Theatres, which then owned the venue, remembers the 1998 season as, "A disaster, artistically and at the box office. Hall was trying to do too much to fill the theatre's quota. He was not giving as much of himself as a director to each production as he usually would. And the company knew it – morale was very low."

Matters were redeemed somewhat when Dame Judi Dench joined the company, playing a prostitute with a heart of gold in Eduardo De Filippo's *Filumena*. Audiences flocked to the play, the critics loved it and it seemed as though the company might after all survive the Old Vic catastrophe; (indeed the Old Vic – which had at one stage been under threat of being turned into a lap-dancing club – had in the interim been saved, and Hall was planning a production of Peter Shaffer's *Amadeus*.

Until, that is, crisis number two, when Hall fell out with his long-time backer Bill Kenwright. And although *Amadeus* went ahead and has since made the time-honoured trip across the Atlantic, Hall went with it, and he plans to stay. To compound his other troubles, he had applied for an

Arts Council grant to continue the Peter Hall Company and was refused. One might speculate how much the refusal had to do with the years of outspoken criticism that Hall has heaped upon the Arts Council's collective head. If they thought to crush him, it seems they are mistaken and would have been better advised to give him his grant.

Less than a month before our meeting, Hall announced the formation of a "Shadow Arts Council", designed to monitor the government body's every move and loudly protest when necessary. It was, he protests, "not his idea", but he has been elected the chairman, and has the support of much of the arts industry. He has already scheduled a lunch with the chairman of the Arts Council, Gerry Robinson. And what will he say? *"Get it right!"*

America calls

Later, Hall left for Los Angeles, where he set up a company of native American actors, including a few well-known names like Kelly McGillis and David Dukes, to perform Shakespeare. They have since staged *A Midsummer Night's Dream* and *Measure For Measure*. The company is sponsored and non-profit-making. Is the aim, I ask, to set up a permanent Shakespeare company in LA? Hall frowns, and sounds uncharacteristically hesitant: "Ye-es…I'm going where the work is." But might the venture grow into something like an American Shakespeare Company? Again, he is non-committal. "It might do."

Would he like it to? "Ye-es, not a very enthusiastic yes. There's an awful lot of work to do with American actors, to establish a tradition of speaking Shakespeare. I don't know whether I can do that. I'll try."

For the best part of the year 2000, Hall has been mounting John Barton's epic ten play cycle, *Tantalus* – a joint production by the RSC and the Denver Center for Performing Arts, assisted by his son, Edward Hall. The production cost over six million dollars and is set to tour the world after the Denver opening. Sir Peter is already well into his *Tantalus* diaries for publication in 2001 (Oberon) which charts the ups and downs of one of the largest theatrical ventures of our time; the Trojan wars told afresh, which took John Barton over 15 years to write. In any other European country the money would have been found to mount the production at home; and what is six million dollars compared to the colossal sums which many believe have been wasted on the Dome?

Despite the lack of support in his own country, Sir Peter's heart remains on these shores, as he freely admits: "I would love to go on with the Peter Hall Company here. But as we speak, I have no home in the West End. I have no backer and no prospect of working in the commercial sector. Nor, really, even in the subsidised sector on any long-term basis. I mean, I could always go and do a play at the RSC or the National; but not with any continuity."

Why, I ask, is he not content to travel around Britain and Europe as a "hired gun"?

"I don't like being a freelancer, it doesn't please me. If you are freelance, you are as good or bad as the last piece of work that you have done. And if you have a flop, say, in Brussels, you can't go back there again." He chuckles morosely. "I have a big family – six children – and I enjoy seeing them and want to be near them. I like life in London and there are about 400 actors who I love to work with, plus about 20 dramatists. So of course I long for continuity here, and the benefits that it brings."

I venture a more cheerful topic, and ask him to describe what he feels are the distinguishing features of a Peter Hall production.

"I have absolutely no idea. If I said to you what are the distinguishing features of your handwriting…" I interject with an instant reply – spidery. He considers this and decides that it is quite amusing. "Spidery? All right. Well, I won't say *that* about my productions! I hope that they are clear, I hope that they are not self-indulgent. I hope they use the time economically, I hope that they tell the audience something worth listening to. I hope they are not decorative."

A recurring theme in Hall's choice of plays with his company is social responsibility. This interests him and he concedes the possibility, though he is not conscious of it. It is, however, an area which he feels theatre must address:- "Good theatre is essential for a healthy democracy. I believe that it is far more than entertainment, though it should be entertaining of course. It must also teach us."

He looks ahead. It is difficult to believe that this man, who has been such a mainstay of the theatre scene in England, so instrumental in shaping it, will be absent from these shores for long. What does he think is the future of theatre here, I ask, and what would he realistically like to see happen? His reply is a credo, an evangelical statement of principle. And it is fully consistent with all that he continues to achieve.

"I would like to see theatre put back in the centre of the agenda. And that does mean, in this country and in America, government support. Because it won't ever become commercial again; theatre is handmade, something special for you tonight and therefore increasingly expensive. You can't ever play in a space that holds more than about 1000 people, because you cannot have bigger actors. The game of imaginative make-believe between actors and audience is very special, it is different every night. And it is very precious."

"Things are dumbing down, and they are starting at the school level. The mentality has got to change. I would like to see society recognise that theatre is above all essential for children. Why do children *play*? It is the same word. To learn how to live. And we go to plays to learn how to live."

BILL KENW

The Highest of Highs and the Lowest of Lows:
living on adrenalin

RIGHT

Those who have become regular West End theatregoers in the last 15 years will have grown up on the productions of most of the impresarios in this book, and not to have seen a Kenwright show is a statistical improbability. Bill Kenwright has something for everyone. His range is decidedly catholic and comes close to guaranteeing what everyone in virtually every age group wants – a good night out. And he has done it as much with top class straight theatre and prestige productions as with widely popular musicals. An ebullient man hailing from Merseyside, he has proved again that

BILL KENWRIGHT *in his office on the Harrow Road*

the distinction we make between so-called commercial theatre and culture is false. Standard "safe" works, Molière for example, that one might find on any school syllabus have drawn the crowds as much as Beckett's *Waiting for Godot*, once a baffling play to many, pioneered in the English version by Peter Hall years before. The 1997 Kenwright revival, again directed by Hall, came out of Kenwright's involvement with the Peter Hall Company which, sadly, was to end two years later when the two men fell out.

Bursting into the big time with a revival of *West Side Story* in the 70s, Kenwright has since treated audiences to a long succession of musicals, straight plays, old and new, and classics including Shakespeare. In one year alone (1993) his productions ranged from the disturbing insights of Harold Pinter to the majestic Greek classics. Diana Rigg starred in Euripides' *Medea* and took it to Broadway, there were revivals of Rattigan's *The Deep Blue Sea* and *Separate Tables*, a new play by Peter Shaffer, *The Gift of the Gorgon*, and Goldsmith's *She Stoops to Conquer*. And in every year of the last decade of the century he has produced an equally glittering repertory, much of it through his association with the Peter Hall Company. After all, what is "commercial"? Diana Rigg made *Medea* commercial. The spectacular production which began at the much-loved Almeida Theatre in Islington equalled anything you might see at the National or the RSC. But what of the man?

Bill Kenwright likes to strike the pose of the hard-working, lucky and somewhat accident-prone entrepreneur. More than that there is about him something of the celluloid hero, at least that is the prevailing impression he gives in the stories he tells. He loves films like *Shane* and *Rocky* – stories of lone men who overcome insurmountable odds – and his career has followed a similar path. Yet as with most crusaders, there is a sadness behind all the bravado. Are they chasing the horizon, to escape the melancholy which dogs their heels?

A working class lad from Liverpool, Kenwright burst out of his home town with those other heroes of the day John, Paul, Ringo and George, and seized his share of the limelight. First, there was Bill Kenwright the actor who found early television fame playing Gordon Clegg in *Coronation Street*. Then came Bill Kenwright the pop singer, not quite as successful. There are other Bill Kenwrights – the film producer, the lifelong fan and owner of Everton Football Club, the theatre owner. Yet it is as an impresario of the theatre that he has become master of his trade. He has produced over 500 plays and musicals and become a staple, not only of the West End, but of regional theatres the length and breadth of Britain.

All of these Kenwrights co-exist in the one man, but, as far as his professional life goes, he is the most loyal of lovers. This means that his various enthusiasms pull him in different directions and, unable to resist, he summons up more energy, more adrenalin on which to run. Interviewing him, one is irresistibly drawn into his exhilarating world of wonders. And – although he has often been criticised for the variable quality of his productions – he displays the same passion for *Elvis; The Musical* as for *Medea* with Diana Rigg. The paradox is, of course, that he rarely pauses for breath for long enough to fully enjoy what he creates.

By the standards of most of his colleagues, his office is remarkable, ostentatious behind the deceptively plain, unmarked door on Shaftesbury Avenue – what a location for an impresario, in the heart of Theatreland! Then up two flights of stairs, another white door, and then there is no doubt that you are in the archetypal impresario's office.

Spaced around the walls at regular intervals are grandly framed theatre posters of Kenwright productions. There is a proper reception desk, at which sits Leigh, Kenwright's PA. To the left of her there is a large fishtank, through which – bizarrely – can be seen a portion of Kenwright's office, magnified and distorted through the water; is it for people to see in, or for the man himself to observe his visitor and decide whether or not he will grant an audience? On the right, a pair of closed king-size doors await the decision.

I arrive early, and pass the time by squinting through the fishtank. He is there all right, holding a meeting in the enormous and opulent room, sitting on a sofa beyond a cream grand piano. Leigh knocks and pokes her head round the door to announce my arrival. A fragment of the conversation drifts out, Kenwright jovially entertaining with an anecdote: "…and he gave me the worst fucking review I've ever had!" The door closes. He will be with me in a second.

After a while the men file out and Kenwright himself appears at the door, all smiles, to show me in. I warm to him instantly. He is dressed in black trousers and a billowing open-necked white shirt which lends him a rather cavalier, almost renaissance air. Quite a thickset man, he is quite handsome (throughout his life, the tabloids have linked him with a string of beauties, and his current, long-standing partner is the actress Jenny Seagrove), with a face that is growing soft topped by an attention-grabbing mane of white hair.

When he begins to talk, I recognise his defining feature. His voice. It is not just the Liverpool accent. There is an edge there – nothing unpleasant, extremely friendly – but every word is charged with an energy that could ignite without warning and send him racing on a new mission. It never lets you doubt for a moment that the instincts which propelled him out of Liverpool have not yet dulled, or that he might make a formidable enemy. Not that he is anxious to be rid of his home town. He cites it, in a long impassioned homage, as his single greatest inspiration.

Liverpool

"I am terribly proud to be a Scouser. It's like a different world, Liverpool. We feel we're different. It's a port, it's got a unique accent, we think it's our own little United Kingdom. If you ask a Scouser anywhere in the world where they came from, they'll say Liverpool rather than England.

"Liverpool in the 60s became the centre of the music universe – and in many ways the centre of the universe, because I personally believe that it was music and rock 'n' roll in particular that was the greatest influence on the twentieth century. It was the voice of the youth culture. When I grew up there was no such thing as a "teenager". You had younger males and females. You didn't have boutiques, you didn't have a trendy clothing style that kids wore.

"Rock 'n' roll came and it was the universal voice, it broke down barriers all over the world, long before the Berlin Wall came down. Russia, Japan, Spain, New York, Liverpool spoke this one language which was Elvis Presley, Bill Haley, Little Richard. A youth culture was born out of this, where suddenly you wore different kinds of clothes, your clothes, whereas before you simply wore the same clothes as your mum and dad, only a bit smaller. You had your own kind of music.

"In Liverpool in the late 50s we used to feel annoyed that London always got everything first. London would get the best plays, we might see them seven years later on tour. The movies would get to us six months later. Even the records.

"Yet something special happened. We had a seaport, where the merchant seamen would bring records of American rhythm and blues. They came to Liverpool, not to London." He leans forward, reliving the excitement. "And we would go down to the docks and get these records, which were like Solomon Burke, Arthur Alexander, and suddenly this," he takes a moment to select the right word which, when it comes, all but explodes with enthusiasm, "*bible* of music was available to us in Liverpool.

"I went to the Liverpool Institute High School when Paul McCartney and George Harrison were there, and in the art college next door was John Lennon. Every classroom had a guitar. Every single year had a rock group in it. Dance halls, caverns, cellars sprouted up all over Liverpool. Tens, twenties, hundreds of them. And the fare that you would see on every stage was exactly the same. It was the Liverpool bible. It was the Liverpool hymns. Through the music, we had our own identity."

An identity which soon spread to the rest of the English-speaking world via The Beatles. Kenwright brushes this aside as almost unimportant.

"We didn't want to export that identity. I can almost guarantee you that Paul's ambition was to top the bill at the Liverpool Empire. One didn't think of London and beyond. But, as you say, it happened. And the fact that it happened to this loving, proud community made it even more of a bombshell. It was no coincidence, it was an explosion waiting to occur. We were looking for something that was *ours*."

And because of that pride, Kenwright fervently believes, Liverpool audiences are among the best in the world.

"The Liverpool audiences are very similar to those in New York. Both places celebrate success, there is very little mean-spiritedness over there.

"If you go to the Tony Awards in New York, my God do you know you've been to an awards ceremony. It's second only to the Oscars. It's *huge*. The streets are lined with banks of screaming people, you can't get near the theatre. The roads are full of police.

"They have a tenth to celebrate in theatrical terms of what we have in Britain. Yet what do we have by comparison? The Olivier Awards. Can you tell me when they were this year?"

Kenwright the actor

Kenwright started acting in *Coronation Street* at the about the same time that The Beatles became so famous. I wonder whether the birth of soap operas (of which "Corrie" was the first) also played a part in breaking down cultural barriers. His answer surprises, given that this was his big break:

"I was never a lover of soap operas and I didn't want to do *Coronation Street*. I wanted to play Hamlet. I went in to please my mum."

He is joking about Hamlet, but his self-confidence tempts me to ask if he ever had an offer. But already I have misjudged Kenwright's determination. This is not a man to wait around for anything so trivial as an offer.

"I would have set about putting it on myself if I had really wanted to. If I didn't have an offer it wouldn't have stopped me. Anyway, it never happened.

"Back then there were only two soap operas, *Coronation Street* and *The Newcomers*. Now soaps dominate the world. It's something I don't quite understand, this love of the soap opera."

Did he understand it when he was in one?

"It was very different then. Thirty years ago "Corrie" was a phenomenon in its own right. It was king. Did I understand it? No. I loved its values as a programme, though.

"On the first day I started, Pat Phoenix, who played Elsie Tanner, took me to one side. I was 19. She said, 'Listen chuck, you're a good-looking boy. You will not be ready for what is going to happen to you in three weeks' time, when this episode goes out. Can I just remind you of one thing? The graveyards are full of people who thought they were indispensable.' I thought she was mad, I didn't know what she meant.

"Three weeks later the episode went out. As a home boy I used to get on the train every Friday to come back to London from Manchester, where the series was filmed. And that week I was mobbed on the train. Can you imagine it?" His eyes widen and he throws his arms sideways to indicate the mass of people. "*Coronation Street* is huge today in that it is everywhere. Then, it was bigger and my role was one of a kind. I was the first kid in the show, the first person ever put into a soap opera to attract the girls. That was my job. They wanted a Liverpool boy with a Beatles haircut, and I looked a bit like Paul.

"The shock of this kind of fame was… I couldn't take it in! And I didn't like it, because I am quite a shy person."

So why go on and try become a pop star? It becomes clear that, whatever drives Bill Kenwright, it is emphatically not a quest for fame.

Kenwright the pop singer

"I didn't try to become a pop star as such. It is just that there is nothing I don't want to do. Two weeks ago I started a record label because, sadly enough at the age of 52, I love pop music. Always will.

"I was an actor, but why can't an actor make records? Look at any of my records – they say on the label 'A Bill Kenwright Production'. I produced them myself, I paid for them myself, I did the lease tape deal myself. I was never going to go out on the road and tour, I simply wanted to make records.

"I spent a lot of time in the recording studio. When I was in London appearing in plays and musicals I would finish in the theatre at about eleven 'o' clock, and I'd be in the recording studio all night producing. That's the side I loved, not the pop star bit." He pauses, then adds as a wry afterthought,

"Though I wouldn't have minded a hit record. A couple came very close."

So has his career been directed simply by a series of whims, I ask?

"There was never any grand plan. The only plan when I was a kid was to be a film star. I wanted to be Errol Flynn, Alan Ladd in *Shane*." Kenwright worships that film above all others, he once bought the original Alan Ladd costume at an auction. I confess that I love *The Godfather* with a similar passion, but he muses that the great mafia saga is "too dark for me".

He once memorably stated that his priorities ran in the following order: family, Everton F C, films and theatre. Is this still true?

"It's close. Certainly in terms of love it is true. In terms of perfectionism in work, theatre would be at the forefront. I have only dabbled in film, though I prefer going to the movies to going to the theatre."

I ask would he have liked to have been a big film producer, and his reply is predictably bullish: "Well, I would have gone for it if I'd wanted to. I suppose I would have enjoyed being the head of a studio, producing a large volume of films. But we have to make our decisions in life."

It seems that the inclination to produce was there even while he was acting, hence the love of producing records. Did he recognise this ambition? This provokes the first of his wonderful stories – I am to discover that Bill Kenwright is one of the theatre's great yarn-spinners.

The magic of show-business

"One of my wonderful early memories is of leaving Blackpool in the car one Sunday (we used to go there for weekends), with my parents driving. On the outskirts of the town there was a cinema on a corner. I looked up and saw that it was showing *There's No Business Like Show Business*. I pulled the blanket that was covering me over my head and prayed, 'Please God, let my dad stop and take me to see the film'.

"There was no reason on earth why he should have done so. However, half a mile down the road the car stops. We went to the film.

"I vividly remember sitting in that cinema, watching Ethel Merman, Dan Dailey, Donald O'Connor and all those stars, and thinking, 'That's the world'. In the car journey home – and I tell you this because it is the only real memory I have of wanting to be a producer – I planned to stage that film in my garden shed. I worked out where to get the costumes, the music. It's such a vivid memory. And I've tried several times to get the rights to it; sadly, it's proved impossible."

It was a man called Reg Marsh, who acted with Kenwright in *Coronation Street*, who first persuaded him to turn producer.

An impresario is born

"I was booked to act in *Billy Liar* at Oldham Rep. I got four weeks off from "Corrie" to do this play. The theatre, it turned out, had double-booked. So I put the show on myself with a friend. I used the money I had earned from *Coronation Street*; it cost about two grand. We knew nothing about producing, but we hired the sets, we got the actors, we rented a car, we hired a house, we painted the posters ourselves.

"The show got fantastic publicity because no soap actors had ever acted and produced in the theatre like this before. Reg Marsh saw it, and came up with the idea that we should start a company specifically to put television stars on to the stage during the lulls in their TV schedules. In many ways, actually, I saw it as a vehicle to get good parts for myself. Reg left after two productions, couldn't stand the strain. I stayed. It took ten years for me to get the acting bug out of my system, and slowly I made the transition to becoming an impresario."

When Kenwright tried to move shows into London he found that he had acquired the reputation of being (his own words) "a hustler from Liverpool". He explains: "When I first started producing – this is in no way knocking anyone, it is a simple fact – you didn't produce shows in London unless you were of a certain class. I had a Liverpool accent, I was very young, 23 when I had my first show on in the West End, and I wasn't ready to have doors closed in my face. Though I wasn't a very good producer, I was full of enthusiasm, full of hope and energy, but I didn't have… organisation. You learn the right way to do things in any business by making mistakes.

"The West End was run by a group of men who had run it for many, many years. It was a closed shop. I know for a fact that I and my contemporaries Cameron Mackintosh, Paul Elliott and Duncan Weldon were frowned on. Because we were hustlers.

"I can remember us having a meeting in Paul's home. None of us had been welcomed into the Society of West End Theatre Managers, or SWET as it is known. So we decided to set up our own organisation called the Society of Hustlers and Independent Theatre Producers. We were going to be SHIT. They would have SWET and we would have SHIT.

"The West End now is a far healthier place than it was then. People knock the West End because it has got a bit of rock 'n' roll next to a bit of Ibsen, next to a bit of subsidised. I love that. And if you want to do a show in the West End you could do it next week. Back then, I couldn't and neither could the others."

The drive that pushed Kenwright towards success expressed itself in other areas of his life too. He began to gamble, and remained a serious gambler for years. I ask whether the adrenalin rush of gambling was similar to the buzz he gets from producing?

"It's different. Gambling is a substitute for things. I stopped gambling the day I got married. Committed gamblers – and I was one – are basically insecure people, who have lonely lives and are single. I have no love of gambling whatsoever now."

But was there a drama in the gambling which attracted him?

"Of course. People have always said of me, give him a crisis and he thrives on it. It's the same thing – I love the drama."

A fit of the Wombles
The drama in Kenwright's career has not always been of the enjoyable kind. In particular, I venture, there were some, well, hiccups with a particular tour of a children's show early on. He interrupts me, roaring with laughter and is rather more blunt. "That's a nice way to put it! Hah! You're not going to mention the fucking Wombles are you? Jeeesus!

"I laugh about it now, but it was much more than a hiccup. If ever in my life – and I am an upbeat person – I have felt suicidal, it was at that moment. It was that bad."

I had heard that some stormed the stage in Belfast, and ask him to elaborate. Which he does, with an increasing sense of horror.

"It wasn't only in Belfast, it was everywhere. To get the rights of *The Wombles*, this enormously successful TV show which everyone was bidding for at the time, you had to procure a group of dates. They didn't want just one production. The Wombles were like pop stars: there was a finite length of time for which they were going to be big, and they wanted to cash in.

"So I suddenly found myself having to secure seven or eight Christmas dates in October and November. The theatres, of course, were full with pantomimes. I had to go to other venues, nightclubs with a stage and the like. We were due to open at

Liverpool, in a theatre club called the Shakespeare Theatre.

"Six weeks or so before we opened a guy came to see me. A real thug. He said, 'I've just bought the Liverpool Shakespeare. I'm going to close it down and renovate it and I don't want your show.'. I told him that I had to go on, everything was arranged and I had to fulfil my obligation. 'Fine,' he replied, 'You'll be sorry.' I had no idea what that meant, until we arrived for the get-in.

"The entrance was barred. I insisted that we had a contract, but was told the contract stipulated only that we open on the Monday. This was the Sunday. We needed to get in, load the set, do the dress rehearsal; but they wouldn't let us. So we opened the next day with no rehearsal. And as the kids arrived, these guys gave them Coca-Cola bottles, and encouraged them to fizz them up once inside.

"There was no barrier between the kids and the Wombles and the kids just stormed the stage, fizzing Coke everywhere. They drenched the Wombles, pulled their heads off and yelled that they were only actors. It was awful. And it hit the headlines.

"The minute that happened, all the other Wombles shows got tainted by this story. It developed into utter chaos. I didn't go to bed for about 11 days during that period. A hideous, hideous time."

Did he lose a lot of money?

"I did lose a lot, but by far the worst thing was that I had tampered with the dreams of these children. It is incredibly important to me that I give people value for money. Shows like that are often a child's first excursion to the theatre. I hold the keys to their kingdom. I've got to look after them. In that instance I let them down." His voice drops. "And that is a terrible thing to do."

The gamble pays off

The tide turned decisively for Kenwright with the first major revival of Leonard Bernstein's *West Side Story*. It was a production which came about because of a bet – Kenwright was riled when two senior producers, Richard Schulman and Clement Scott Gilbert, bet him that no British cast could ever do the piece justice. Kenwright rose to the challenge, and wagered five shillings that it could. And he was the man to do it.

"I came up against everyone. Bernstein, Jerome Robbins. They had this very valuable commodity and were afraid that a fledgling producer would screw it up. Finally they agreed to give me the number two rights, the touring rights. If I wanted to bring it in to the West End they would come and see it and then decide."

The show opened in Swindon in 1972 then went on tour and, though its producer was delighted with the production, it did not do good business. Still, Kenwright kept sending letters to New York, begging for a visit. Eventually Arthur Laurents came and decreed that it was the best production since the original.

"This was the great turning point in my career, in one aspect particularly. It was *West Side Story* that had made me want to become an actor when I was 12. It was a matinee, an Everton match was cancelled and I went to the theatre, not knowing anything about the show. The thrill that I felt when the curtain went up was equal to the best of football, the best of cinema.

"I saw this show that was about kids talking in a language I understood and doing things that were so physical, so powerful, I was knocked sideways. In the rumble that ends the first act, there was this huge wire fence across the stage with no exit. The actors ran towards it and, unbelievably, threw themselves over. At half-time I wouldn't move, afraid that I might break the spell. I came out, went straight to W H Smith and bought a brown paperback copy of the script and learnt every word. 'One day,' I thought, 'I am going to play Tony.'

"So when I produced the show, playing the lead was always in the back of my mind. We auditioned for a long time and the great news was that I was a better Tony than everyone who came in to read. Until an actor called James Smiley walked in. He had literally that week got off the banana boat from Australia. He sang "Maria" and my spine began to tingle. As he sang, my acting career flew out of the window. From that moment my dream changed from playing Tony to producing this guy who was better than me. That was a big moment. I realised from then on that I wanted to walk in the front door, rather than the stage door."

He did, however, get to play Tony once as he tells me with glee. "Everyone was injured and I had to go on. The musical director suggested that we cut "Maria". I told him *exactly* where to go."

Having finally secured the London rights, Kenwright found himself without a West End theatre. Eventually he took the show to the Collegiate, a 550 seater (now called the Bloomsbury). Had the company played to double capacity they still would have lost money. However, *West Side Story* got rave reviews and Kenwright prayed that a big West End house would pick it up.

"On the last day I made the decision to give up the show because I'd lost money everywhere. It was driving me barmy. But what a show! I directed it as well but I couldn't wait to get up in the morning and get back to work.

The luck of the Irish

"Just after I closed it, I took a call from an Irish producer called Noel Pearson. He asked me if I was the 'mad fucker who loves *West Side Story*' and asked me to come to Ireland to direct the Irish premiere. So I brought most of my own company to Dublin, and we got an Irish pop star called Tony Kenny to play Tony. There followed an extraordinary rehearsal period because this was shortly after the start of the Irish troubles. Gang warfare, tension was everywhere."

I suspect that I am about to be treated to another great Kenwright tale. I am right.

"We were due to open at the Olympia Theatre, and on the afternoon before the first night we held a dress rehearsal. The kids sat in the front of the stalls for their notes. As I finished, I suggested that we run the first act again. They groaned, and I gave in and let them go for a break. They all got up and moved away. And as they moved, a great big crack went right across the dome in the ceiling. The ceiling fell on to the dress circle, which collapsed right where these kids had been sitting. Everyone started screaming. Someone grabbed me and got me out. To this day they don't know whether or not it was a bomb.

"I found Noel in a pub and told him what had happened. The theatre was a write-off. We found the cast. The Maria started crying, this was her big break. There were no other theatres. But I was determined not to be beaten."

I ask whether he had received any threats, and get one of those impenetrable answers to which Kenwright is prone, which expose the odd shadow behind the bright exterior.

"Not exactly. I had been in a situation that I felt slightly uneasy about." He will not elaborate further and continues the story. "We had no theatre, our musical instruments had been crushed, we couldn't rescue the set. Noel found a cinema two miles outside of Dublin. The whole of the Irish theatrical community left work early that day to help us. They built a stage for us. They flew in musical instruments from all over Europe. They erected pylons for lights.

"We opened at midnight. The final curtain came down to cheers at four o'clock in the morning. The place was packed. And this is where it becomes really spooky.

"That day, on a chance visit to Dublin, were two people who had just bought the Shaftesbury Theatre in London, which had been closed for years because the ceiling had fallen in. They heard about this great rescue effort for our show and came to see for themselves. At the end – with everyone crying and hugging each other – they introduced themselves and offered me their theatre for *West Side Story*. I had been searching for this for three bloody years and here it was happening at four in the morning in a converted cinema outside Dublin.

"The show re-opened the Shaftesbury Theatre. That's the wonderful part of it. The terrible part is that it ran for six months and never had a winning week!"

Kenwright the director
As in the case of *West Side Story*, Kenwright has often directed or co-directed his shows as well as produced. Why, I ask, does he feel the need?

"There is a very fine line between producing and directing and it is one which, not to my credit, I have crossed several times and taken over productions. On *West Side Story* I was not happy with the feel of the show.

"I don't believe in airy-fairy theatre. My productions have an up-front quality to them, I don't hide and I think people recognise that as a trademark of my productions. *West Side Story* is a tough piece about the streets and that is what was urgently needed. We got it in the end – those kids were killers.

"Arthur Laurents gave me a great piece of advice. He said, 'Bill, in every great piece of theatre there has to be a tingle moment.' Go and see anything I've directed, by God do I search for the tingle moments!"

More hits

The successes started to flow for Bill Kenwright, not least a ten-year London run for Richard Harris's thriller *The Business of Murder*. In 1979 he hit gold with a touring production of Andrew Lloyd Webber's *Joseph and the Amazing Technicolor Dreamcoat* which, despite a lapse of several years while Lloyd Webber revived the piece himself in London, is still going strong. How did it come about?

"Whenever my life has reached rock-bottom, he or she up there has smiled down and sent me something. *Blood Brothers*, for instance, came at a time when I'd had nine financial flops – huge critical successes mind you – on the trot."

Since Kenwright finances all of his productions himself, without backers, I wonder how he managed to persuade the bank to loan him the money after a bad run like that. "It becomes tough. You have to put up your house and belongings for security." He pauses to insist that all of these stories

may sound romantic and theatrical but that "they are 99 per cent true".

"*Joseph* happened because John Farrow, a pantomime producer, rang me out of the blue. He needed help. He had three Christmas shows with excellent advances, but his partner had pulled out. He needed finance. One of these shows was Jess Conrad in *Joseph and the Amazing Technicolor Dreamcoat* in Brighton. I agreed to bankroll the whole thing. I lost a fortune.

"I didn't go to see *Joseph*, though I knew the musical. Then the New Theatre in Cardiff got in touch; they needed a replacement for a show that had fallen through and they would cover my costs. So I promised them *Joseph*. I went to see it and fell in love with the show."

Joseph had already caused a stir as a 12-minute oratorio for Andrew Lloyd Webber and Tim Rice. Then, Kenwright assures me, it had 'not quite worked' in its extended version as part of a double-bill at the Camden Roundhouse and around the country. He re-worked the show, repeating numbers and adding a 'Joseph Megamix' at the end, and a two-hour entertainment emerged. The two weeks in Cardiff was followed by a week in Liverpool, a week in Manchester. After a year Kenwright was still extending his original licence.

"It started off playing to only £7000 a week. By the end of the first year, we had trebled that audience. The production created its own momentum. One paper dubbed it 'The

Juggernaut of Joy'. Because 20 years ago there were no other big touring musicals.

"It remained the same kind of company. Every year this show moved into a region at roughly the same annual date and it was like the carnival coming to Rio. All the children looked forward to *Joseph* rolling into town. It became a cult."

And through the years were there, I ask, bit-part players who graduated to the big roles?

"Better. We had someone who started in the kids' choir who sang Joseph. They were a family, it was like a circus. It was totally worshipped by theatres, who knew it would sell out. They viewed it like a reliable source of subsidy."

Blood Brothers: building a show
With the *Joseph* gravy train rolling, Kenwright continued to build his empire. Hundreds of plays and musicals up and down the country. But it was not until 1988 that he decided to revive Willy Russell's less than successful musical, *Blood Brothers*. The show was to become a pot of gold for both men, and predictably it inspires some of Kenwright's most impassioned memories. He becomes positively animated, shifting in his chair and occasionally jumping up as he relives his battles to put it on.

"When I first saw *Blood Brothers* I did not want to enjoy it. In those days if you were from Liverpool you were an Alan Bleasedale man or a Willy Russell man, and I was a Bleasedale man. I produced all his shows.

"Yet I went to see this musical at the Lyric, sat in a very empty house, and I had the great theatrical experience. I thought *Blood Brothers* needed me, and I told Willy so some time later.

"The original production was too small, too simple. I felt that it required an operatic feel about it. We opened with a cast that Willy loved – Kiki Dee, Con O'Neil, Warwick Evans – but a production that he hated. So during the run, we set about changing the production.

"It toured for twenty weeks and I asked if we could bring it into town. Willy refused, he had been so knocked when it failed the first time, and didn't want a repeat. We went on tour again.

"The second tour was an even bigger success. After 16 weeks I went back to Willy, but he still would not give in. So we toured again, until finally he gave the word.

"We opened at the Albery with the smallest advance in West End history. I don't think we had £100. I made all the previews a fiver, word began to spread and it began to sell out. As I knew it would. Build it and they will come.

"On the first night, I thought that all my dreams had come true. I looked in the box and my family was there from Liverpool, I saw this show about Liverpool on stage. I knew I had a hit, and that only the roof falling in would stop it. At the end, Kiki moved downstage for her big number, and the metal bridge which was meant to fly up got stuck. Then I saw a hand desperately trying to yank it. I realised what had happened but was powerless to stop it. The side piece of the set collapsed, the bridge fell down, the cast walked forward and the whole of the back wall fell.

"Kiki just carried on. Some of the audience realised the mistake, but many thought it was simply a bold and tragic production effect.

"We didn't get the greatest reviews in the world. Yet within a week it was sold out. That was my greatest ever experience of the process of building a show."

The miracle of Broadway
Despite having been burned some years earlier, when he had taken Richard Harris's hit play *Stepping Out* to Broadway with disastrous results, Kenwright resolved to make the trip across the Atlantic once more with *Blood Brothers*. The problem previously, he reasoned, was that he had co-produced in America. He needed to be the sole producer so that he could retain control.

"I never felt confident enough to go to Broadway and mount an American production as sole producer. So I took the Bill Kenwright route. We started a new production in Liverpool, took it to Canada, and then got American Equity to allow me to take that Canadian production to Broadway. So I retained my little Liverpool family, and we were there as a team on a mission.

"We opened for previews and got a thunderous reaction. The question on the streets was *how many* Tony's we would win. The mega-agents were queuing outside the rehearsal-room door to talk to Con O'Neil. We had the buzz.

"Opening night was fantastic...until we got the reviews. The next day, everybody ignored me and whispered about how much I had lost. I went to see the theatre owner, Gerald Schoenfeld, who expressed his condolences for my failure. 'Never in the history of Broadway,' he told me, 'has anything survived the panning you got.' 'But the audiences love it!', I protested. He looked at me like I was some kind of idiot and told me gently to take it off.

"I wandered over to the box office. In New York the box office really is the hub, unlike in England, and the box office treasurer is the most important man in the theatre. I popped in to see our treasurer Herman Pearl, a wonderful man, and we discussed the situation and hit upon a decision. We would watch the last 20 minutes of the matinee. If the audience stood, I would stay. If they stayed in their seats, I and the production would go.

"The show ended, and the audience – most of them in their nineties and probably incapable of standing – did not move. I thought I was finished. Then the cast came back on for a second time and, slowly, the entire audience got to their feet.

"Every show was the same, and I took a permanent advert in the *New York Times* which read, '17 performances, 17 standing ovations' and so on. I gave masses of free tickets away, just to get the people in. Because I knew, build it and they will come.

"It started building but not enough. Gerald came to see me and this time he said, 'Son, I love this show and I really admire your guts. But I have to take it off.'. Again I resisted: 'If you take me off you will never get another show of mine.' 'You're losing money,' he groaned. 'True,' I countered, 'but I've got David Cassidy coming into the cast.' He looked dubious. 'And Petula Clark,' I added, lying through my teeth in both instances."

Quickly Kenwright got in touch with David Cassidy to offer him the part of the narrator. To his worried surprise the 43-year-old Cassidy wanted to play Mickey, a character who is an infant for much of the action. Nevertheless, he agreed. He then flew Petula Clark to New York, took her to see the show, and sat up until the early hours persuading her to sign. Next, Cassidy suggested that his brother Sean, a Hollywood scriptwriter, should play Mickey's brother Eddie. Both Sean and Kenwright agreed, but time was running out. Sean Cassidy was in Los Angeles, David was in New York and Clark had departed for Australia. They had to rehearse separately, and were only able to meet four days before they opened.

"They were a sensation. We needed $220,000 to break even, we were playing to $190,000 then. Within ten days, we were up to over $300,000. Gerald sent me the most

wonderful telegram, 'Dear Bill, last week's figures made believers of us all. I'm sorry for doubting you.' We became known as 'The Miracle of Broadway' and won seven Tony nominations."

Quite a story, but he is quick to deprecate his role: "People say that I was brave, but it wasn't that. I didn't know what else to do. How can you take off a show where they stand and shout and scream every single night? One day I'll have to take it off in London. How will I ever do it? God knows. When I was asked to give up *Joseph* because it was coming back into the London Palladium it felt like someone taking away a baby. That's what these shows mean to me."

Saving the bacon
There were, inevitably, one or two shows where the dream did not work out. All Bill Kenwright's cunning was unable to save what is generally seen as his biggest flop to date, the musical *Robin, Prince of Sherwood*. He bristles at the suggestion: "To this day I believe in that show. It is a simple, Josephy kind of show. I had lost the rights to *Joseph*, which was on at the Palladium. And I needed to fill the gap. The theatre managers asked me to find them 'another *Joseph*', because obviously they wanted the income and I wanted something to replace the show for all the kids.

"I racked my brains to find a similar story of a group of men and their leader – and it was Robin Hood! We got the show together, it had a magnificent score. The problem arose when a West End theatre became free after I'd tried it out with huge success in the provinces. Instead of sticking to my guns and admitting that this was not a West End show at all, I brought it to London.

"People go on about *Robin* as if it was one of the great flops. It wasn't, it was only ever going to run for a limited season at the Piccadilly, it didn't lose a lot of money. It was only there for a bit of fun. Then I took it on tour where it did well. It was never a disaster for me, although the critics hated it."

He begins to wish aloud that he had a musical to bring in £100,000 a week, but consoles himself with the notion that he produces the shows in which he believes. The truth is that this often leads to critical success and box office failure.

Sondheim
1996 saw Kenwright's productions of two Stephen Sondheim shows in the West End, *Company* and *Passion*, receive rave reviews but lose a lot of money. Did he expect this to happen, since – as with most Sondheim – they are unconventional types of musical?

"The thought didn't worry me, although I didn't exactly expect to lose money. I saw *Passion* twice in New York, loved the kernel but wasn't keen on the production. I would do every single solitary second of that show again, knowing that it was going to lose money. My production, Jeremy Sams's production, Michael Ball's production, Maria Friedman's production, was *it*.

"Working with Stephen Sondheim, more important, becoming a friend of Stephen Sondheim was a privilege. He's an ordinary human being and I don't want to raise anyone to god-like status. But...he's my kind of guy."

"The show came off, I had lost a lot of money, as we still hadn't done a cast album. Still, just for the hell of it, I took the Golders Green Hippodrome and we recorded a live concert of the piece. I sent a copy to Sondheim, and he phoned me to say, 'I have just heard the best recording of any of my shows.'" He bangs the table with satisfaction. "That's it."

Despite critic-pleasing shows such as these, Kenwright is still regularly criticised for the more populist shows he brings to the West End, the likes of *Elvis – The Musical*. But his reputation was boosted when in 1993 he took on one of London's most ambitious theatrical projects, the Peter Hall Company.

Highs and lows
After some highly successful productions with Sir Peter as director and Kenwright as producer, the two parted company abruptly in a well publicised disagreement.

Kenwright has slipped into a melancholy mood. He doesn't really enjoy his job, he tells me. I look incredulous, he is so full of excitement for every project. He looks sad, this is not the same thing.

"In football, if you go to an important game – a cup final, or a relegation fight, you don't enjoy it. You're sitting on the edge of your seat in a state of high tension. That's not enjoyment. I very rarely enjoy the game. I enjoy the thought of the game, the talking to the lads, the camaraderie. The actual game itself is agony.

"This game, producing, is getting worse and worse. Someone who has possibly been the greatest producer of this century, I won't say who, now tells me that he hates it. The reason he does it is that it gets him out of the house. It is very difficult. The young producers, like I was thirty years ago, come in all enthusiastic. But I know very few who, after ten years, enjoy it. There are days when I think there is a good life here. But I can't capture that and take it through the week."

What about doing less, I suggest?

"That would be even worse for me. My life can't be any one avenue, that's a certain kind of hell to me. It has to be producing plays, looking after my football team, trying to make movies, trying to produce pop records. When there is so much around, why box yourself into one corner?"

It sounds to me as though Kenwright is a man who cannot bear to give up the pursuit of his dreams. I tell him this. He looks thoughtful.

"I chase something. I don't know whether it is my dreams. The thing is, I don't like my work, but I love and believe in the world in which I work. It is just that I haven't found any way to make it anything other than the highest of highs and the lowest of lows.

I suppose I don't really want to. Happiness doesn't come into it for me. There is such a big canvas there, my fear is that there is so little time to fill it."

We talk a little more, Kenwright cheers up as he tells me of his beautiful new office building in Maida Vale, and Everton's latest struggles in the Premier League. All that will take him well into the new century. Then? He brushes his hand down a page of his diary on which are scribbled dozens of appointments – the here and now.

MATTHEW BOURNE

Dancing with the Swans:

BOURNE

Matthew Bourne's Adventures in Motion Pictures

MATTHEW BOURNE *on stage during a rehearsal of Swan Lake*

Matthew Bourne is a glorious incongruity. For this Hackney-born choreographer has not only had a string of commercial successes with his own production company (co-directing with Katharine Dore); he has for the first time managed to challenge the hegemony of the big West End musicals on their own territory, and he has done it with classical ballet.

Well, not strictly classical, as he is the first to point out. Tchaikovsky might not have approved Bourne's casting of men as the swans in his sensational production of *Swan Lake*. Prokofiev might also have spluttered a bit at the setting of *Cinderella* amongst the ruins of a world war. Yet in the midst of his innovations, Bourne is always at pains to remain true to the heart that pulses within the music. In *Swan Lake*, for instance, there is a passage where Bourne's Prince gets thrown out of a raucous nightclub. He cowers, lonely and despairing, on the pavement, until the famous theme of the swan appears for the first time, and the man-bird himself – stretching and preening – reaches out to the Prince from his own imagination. As the music reaches its climax, hope appears in the young man's eyes; he has seen a vision of beauty, and life is again worth living. The emotion in the scene is deeply moving. And that Tchaikovsky would surely have loved.

Bourne's *Swan Lake* started life in 1995, transferred from Sadler's Wells' theatre to the Piccadilly where it became the longest-running ballet London had ever seen (21 weeks), moved to Broadway, was filmed for television, won over 25 awards and, at the time of writing, has returned to Britain in the form of a national tour to culminate with another run in the West End. It became, in short, a phenomenon, affectionately nicknamed by the theatregoing public 'the gay *Swan Lake*'. It also established Bourne and his company, Adventures In Motion Pictures (AMP), as a major and flamboyant force in world dance.

Bourne's success, however, did not – as most great theatrical triumphs did not – occur overnight. AMP had been in existence for eight years by the time the swans flew, and its genesis was arduous. Bourne himself, now pushing 40, took his time settling down.

It all started at school
Bourne produced a cross-dressing production of *Cinderella* at school. Was this, I wondered, an early harbinger of things to come? The half-smile stretches a little further up the cheek: "Yeah, that was at school. I went through a period of being very much a leader when I was younger, organising and putting on shows.

"They were usually done from the memory of seeing a Disney film, or something like *Chitty, Chitty, Bang, Bang*. And yes, there was that cross-dressing *Cinderella*, though I didn't know the term then. I don't know why I did it like that, I suppose I knew the idea of men playing women from the Ugly Sisters in panto and decided to do the whole thing that way. My brother was Cinderella and I was one of the Ugly Sisters. But nobody even talked about gender back then, it was not the issue it later became."

Bourne soon began forming theatre companies, putting on variety shows at a youth club in Leytonstone where his parents worked. He grew up in a working class environment, but his parents were great theatregoers and young Matthew was brought up on a steady diet of stage and film. He used to collect autographs avidly, though he is quick to point out that he has given it up:

"I don't *now*. It's too embarrassing. But I did for several years in my mid-teens. It was a serious thing. I wrote to the stars, I went to first nights, I hung around hotels where I knew the stars were staying. I've got about 1800 autographs. It was the mid-70s, a good period for autograph-hunting. Lots of the stars whom I met then are dead now. Fred Astaire, Charlie Chaplin, I met all of those MGM people."

The first steps
Did he know that he wanted to go into dance when he met Fred Astaire? He shrugs: "Coming from a working class background, I felt strongly that dance was not something you talked about or admitted wanting to do. Even when I did begin dancing in amateur shows, I wouldn't go to a ballet class or even warm up properly. I still had that stigma which I had picked up in school."

That feeling persisted until Bourne was 22: "I'd been doing these amateur things for quite a few years and had taught myself a lot. I went to work at the National Theatre, in the bookshop and ushering for two years solid. A lot of the people there were training to be actors or dancers or singers. And as I talked to them, I realised that this is what I should be doing. I enrolled at the Laban Centre to study dance and theatre.

"I got very interested in dance as a subject. I read around it a lot, I saw everything I could. I suppose I discovered it as a more serious art form than I had realised from the musicals I had seen."

When, I enquire, did he see his first full-length ballet? "I was 19." He laughs quietly. *"Swan Lake*. The Canadian Ballet at Covent Garden, and I loved it so much that I went to see it again a couple of weeks later, at Sadler's Wells. Actually I thought it was weird. I came at it from a very strange perspective, it was completely different to anything I had been brought up with, and I liked it. I also liked the sense that it was a piece of history that had been preserved."

There is a connection, I suggest, to the films from the golden age of Hollywood to which Bourne was drawn as a child. Both styles tended to be flamboyant, even melodramatic. He agrees, in part: "They both employ broad strokes, but of course ballet comes from a rigid discipline that is very necessary. However, the thing that fascinated me about the golden age of the MGM musicals is that it was a company, and that is the parallel to what I'm doing now. It was a repertory company, housed in that big unit at MGM. Those people were trained to do what they did. If one of them couldn't dance, they were taught how to dance. If a dancer couldn't sing, they were shown how. Sometimes it was two years before they allowed them to sing on screen. And while they were finishing one film, they were working on the next one. It was a team, and they got better and better."

Was that the mission statement behind Adventures in Motion Pictures (the name itself, of course, suggests a link)? Bourne tells the story.

A new look in dance
"At the Laban Centre, choreography was my chosen subject. We were taught to try and think along original lines. Not that anything is *really* original. And that forced me to look away from the tried and tested and look into myself for the things I was really interested in. Through that I found a way of working that was mine.

"Some people see my ideas as new, but I've actually always been a bit retro in my thinking, and I reached back to that. I'm very into references, for instance. I enjoy putting in things that people might recognise, whether they know about dance or not. There is a lot in my work that I have taken from films and elsewhere. This made me a bit of an oddity. I loved figures like Alfred Hitchcock, and these are not people you discuss at dance college. I've always been a bit of an outsider in that world.

"My way of working, of searching for the populist angle within a piece is definitely not new, though. It's just not done in dance very much. Many productions of operas or plays that I've seen have really done something with the work, made you see it in a new way. I simply do the same. But there has traditionally been something so reverential about dance; as soon as you try something new everyone thinks, 'How clever!' Whereas it has been done in other areas for years."

AMP was a direct product of Bourne's college work: "I did a fourth year at the Laban Centre, which was performance based and was called *Transitions*. The students had to form a company, and we created a piece and toured it. And from that experience, we learned how to set up a company, how to tour, what it meant to perform at a variety of different venues.

"There weren't many prospects out there for work in the sort of style we were doing. So in 1987 several of us decided to start a company to create work for ourselves. Originally, there were three directors, three or four people in the company who wanted to choreograph. There were eight or nine of us in all. I was dancing as well as choreographing at this stage.

"We all went on the government's enterprise allowance scheme, which paid £40 a week in top of whatever else you might earn to help you set up a new business. And because of our experience touring *Transitions* we had made some contacts. We managed to get a date or two to perform. Our old college gave us the free use of their studio theatre for our first show. We did an unusual 15-minute piece by a guy called Jacob Marley called – wait for it – *Does Your Crimplene Go All Crusty When You Rub?* It was a strange character piece about an old people's disco in a church hall.

"Some people were offended by it, but it caught the imagination of many more. We were asked to do it in the prestigious Dance Umbrella Festival's opening cabaret evening. It was one of those nights when everybody who is important in the dance world was there. So we were seen by a lot of people. Without that break it might have taken us a lot longer to get going. We got dates from that, a few reviews, a lot of business. It was only our third ever performance, and we were already reviewed in the national press and getting offers – so that was pretty exciting.

"That's how it started, as this rep company, with me doing some pieces along with the other choreographers and some guest choreographers. The first work I choreographed for AMP was a tango piece called *Overlap Lovers*."

By 1991, though, the shape of the company had changed, and Bourne was left in complete control: "Eventually all the original members except me left. The company was doing a lot of humorous work which one of the other directors was not keen on. He was more into formal structure and stuff. He formed his own company. Others got offered more money to go and do things like tour with the Pet Shop Boys. We weren't earning anything anyway, about £1 a week for the first couple of years.

"It got to the point where I was practically the only one left, with my co-director Katharine Dore, who arrived about a year into the company. She came to advise us as part of a scheme the Arts Council had set up to give young companies administrative help – at this point we had a small grant of about £1,500 – and stayed to take over the business side, which she still handles today. We decided to go for it one more time to see if we could make it work by ourselves, and that is when it became the kind of company it is now."

That last effort resulted in a parody of the middle-classes called *Town and Country*. The critics smiled, and the work was nominated for an Olivier Award. Significantly for Bourne, he was able to take it to a conventional theatre, the Royal Court:

"Doing *Town and Country* at the Royal Court visibly moved us into theatre venues, and a lot came from that. I have anyway always felt most comfortable in the theatre. I have a real understanding of it. There has been a lot of talk of me doing film lately, but theatre is my home."

I ask whether he could make dance work on film for a mass audience. He struggles to find a modest answer, then gives up: "With the kind of performance theatre we've got, with its emphasis on storytelling, it could work. With some fine actor-dancers you could tell a story quite vividly."

Dance for the masses

Bourne's first foray into the classics occurred in 1992, when he joined forces with Opera North to produce *The Nutcracker*, which was performed as a double bill with Tchaikovsky's short opera *Iolanta*. Why, I wonder, did he steer clear of the great romantic ballets for so long?

"Simple. I had six dancers. And anyway I'd never thought about doing that. When it was put to me by Opera North it was a complete surprise, and then I realised how much I would love to do it. It suddenly felt completely right. I knew those classics, I used to go and see them all the time, and I felt that I could tell a really good story here. It is, after all, music written specifically for that purpose."

That show, in what has become a signature style for Bourne, included plenty of filmic and contemporary references. He created a magic world peopled by Doris Day clones. This technique, says Bourne, is vital to get audiences interested: "Most people are scared of dance, that they won't understand it, that they'll be confused. They need something to grab onto. Recognisable characters, recognisable images. Sometimes you can break the ice with humour. In those early days we used to find that if we included something funny, audience members would tell anyone who laughed to shush, they were so used to dance being serious."

Which is not to say that Bourne relies exclusively on humour to make his points

relevant. The *Swan Lake* famously ends on a note every bit as tragic as in the original. Bourne repeated the updating idea in 1994's *Highland Fling*, a version of *La Sylphide*, where the hero became an unemployed Scottish welder who is seduced by a horrific vampire. I ask how far Bourne is attempting to reflect society back on itself. He considers.

"I suppose that's fair. But the story comes first, the ideas come from that. And the most important aim is to make this ancient score fresh and relevant for today's audience. There was a lot of social comment in *Highland Fling*, actually. I did the whole thing about some men's treatment of women. The man leaves his nice girl-bride who does the ironing and looks after him, for this vampirish woman. But in the end he cuts her wings off with a pair of garden shears, because finally he wants her to be like the ordinary little wife back home."

Despite his success in the field, Bourne did not allow classical ballet to monopolise his time. Instead, he became busier than ever. He continued to alternate new dance, such as the Hitchcock parody *Deadly Serious*, with work in TV and stage plays. He choreographed, among much else, Yukio Ninagawa's production of Ibsen's *Peer Gynt* at the Barbican Theatre and on tour, and Sam Mendes's production of Lionel Bart's *Oliver!* at the London Palladium. I express interest in the rotation of styles – for instance, when in a musical he is suddenly forced to subdue the dance to keep it in perspective with the other elements, does that teach him a narrative discipline with which he can then inform his pure dance works? Bourne dodges the question, and suggests that he is less than happy when the dance does have to take a back seat. Finally he admits to having 'a clash of ideas' with Mendes over the volume of dance in *Oliver!*. "That," says Bourne, "made me feel that in future I'd like to direct rather than merely choreograph."

He cites John Caird (with whom he worked on the 1991 musical flop *Children of Eden*), Ninagawa and Mendes as directors from whom he has learned a great deal: "John Caird taught me how to collaborate with performers. I used to just come in and set everything as I had already planned it. Now we discuss everything, and I work with my dancers on motivation a lot more. We have a great mix of trainings from which to draw in the company. We have contemporary dancers, ballet dancers and quite a lot of musical theatre people. There's a range of styles."

The turning point for Bourne and AMP was 1995, the year of *Swan Lake*. I begin to ask whether he had any inkling how big it was going to be, when he interrupts with a groan: "Everybody asks me that!" That may be so, I counter, but this is the great mystery; can one spot what is going to be a success? "Well all I can say is that I didn't know. Everything we have done with *Swan Lake* has been a complete surprise – a run in the West End, then being a hit in Los Angeles,

winning Tony Awards and so on. However, when we were working on it we did feel that we knew what we were doing. We felt that it would work. At the same time we were all a bit worried, because this was a big undertaking for AMP. A big cast, a heavy financial risk."

Life with the Arts Council
"We had a problem with the Arts Council grant. As a small company we were given extra money to do *Swan Lake* as a one-off project for a limited time – two weeks at Sadler's Wells, a ten-week tour of Great Britain, and then we would go back to being what we were. And that was fine by us. Then, as it took off in such a huge way and Cameron Mackintosh said to me 'You must put this into the West End', it became bigger than the Arts Council could handle. Suddenly we presented them with this enormous company and there wasn't an area of money to cater for us. Plus they also had a conflict since they perceived it as being commercial, which it wasn't. We only became commercial with the follow-up, *Cinderella*."

I am somewhat aghast – surely such a big international success must have made the company a great deal of money. It is a misconception which Bourne hastily corrects: "We've never made any money from it. I mean, we've earned money to keep the company going and we've earned money as creators from it. But it has never gone into profit as such. The running costs are very big. The company includes 40 dancers, and 28 orchestra members, plus the crew. Most theatres will not put it on. They want it and then they see the costs and say 'No, thank you very much.' We have to fill something like 60 per cent of the house every night to keep it going. We couldn't ever tour it until now, and only now because ten theatres have teamed up and agreed to share the costs."

When the Arts Council saw the success of *Swan Lake* – and suddenly AMP was in the news everywhere, not least because his leading man, the Royal Ballet star Adam Cooper defected to Bourne, and dancers of the quality and celebrity of Mikhail Baryshnikov and Lynn Seymour wanted to work with him – they withdrew all funding. Was this a shock?

"It turned out to be a good thing, actually. You have to go through so many hoops to please them, it takes up an enormous amount of your time. Does it make you artistically more independent? Yes and no. You don't have to answer to anyone. But now you *have* to be commercial. You have to make it work financially. You can't do work that won't make money. Luckily the kind of work that I like to do has a popular appeal. But there will come a time when I want to do something which won't reach such a big audience. And the money from *Swan Lake* doesn't bring us enough to subsidise other things."

What about the work itself, I ask. Was *Swan Lake* Bourne's most personal work to date?

The "gay" label.

"All the things I do feel pretty personal. *Swan Lake* was the easiest, for some reason. It all flowed out of me very freely, which is unusual. There is something abut the music that I really identify with."

Yet, I observe, it has become known as 'the gay *Swan Lake*' – a term which Bourne is reputed to dislike. Nevertheless there is certainly a homosexual subplot there.

"I just didn't want it to be limited to that. I don't mind the nickname personally, but it shuts people out. There is something there to be learned about a relationship between men *without* shoving it in your face. It portrays love, and doesn't show the audience anything to make them feel uncomfortable. And maybe some audience members will come away a little less prejudiced. But those people *wouldn't* go to see it if it was called 'The Gay *Swan Lake*'. It's about labels."

Right then, the question I've been edging delicately towards, hoping he would pre-empt. The era in which Bourne grew up was one in which homosexuality was still a great taboo. I ask whether this story of a repressed prince finding his true love who is a man is drawn partly from Bourne's own experience, or from the universal coming-out experience.

"It's difficult to say because it doesn't have a positive ending, and if I was going to create something around those lines I wouldn't want it to be open to the accusation of being just another tragic gay character who ends up unhappy and killing himself. The main basis of it is about someone who, because of his position of being royal, is repressed and cannot handle his own feelings. So when, in Act Three, he is drawn to this mysterious guy in leather who invades the queen's party – and who is a real person – he projects the swan image that he has had in his mind onto this person. He wants to be like that, and he finds it attractive. And he can't handle his desire. It's that repressed English thing, which is why we set it a little time ago – it is less marked today, though still relevant. I mean, even today one of our royal princes could never be openly gay. In the 50s and 60s, though, that stricture was there in many more areas of life.

"I've never had a problem coping with anything like that myself, so it isn't personal in that respect. But I do like to comment on issues like that and I would like to do a piece that portrays a gay relationship in a more positive way. He munches his toast and laughs. "The problem is, the tragic tales make the better stories! Even if I did a gay *Romeo and Juliet* they'd still end up dead at the end!"

Ballet on Broadway

It was, as Bourne has already mentioned, the mighty Cameron Mackintosh who persuaded him to risk moving *Swan Lake* out of the dance houses, into the mainstream West End and from there across the Atlantic. And Bourne is duly grateful, though he acknowledges that the senior impresario's assistance was at times a double-edged sword.

"Cameron grabbed me at the interval of the first night at Sadler's Wells and said, 'You've got to do this in the West End. This is a musical, a West End show.' I hadn't really thought about it, but he encouraged us to look into that and promised to help. And he was always there behind the scenes. He taught us the mechanics of putting on a musical in the West End, he gave us management services for free, he gave us someone from his office to look after the show and advise us.

In London, he kept his involvement quiet. On Broadway, however, he was the co-producer and he put his name to it because he felt that would help us. In some ways it helped, in some ways it didn't. It encouraged some people because he is such a big name there and so respected. But his way of publicising the show personally, he did quite a few interviews, was to say 'This isn't a ballet. I hate ballets, you'll love this if you hate ballet.' That got a lot of people's backs up in the dance world. So all they did was come back and say very strongly, 'It is a ballet whatever Cameron Mackintosh may say.' So it had this counter-effect of people groaning, 'Oh, it is a ballet after all, I don't want to see that.'"

The show's reception on Broadway was respectable. The critics liked it, and the houses averaged around 70 per cent of capacity. While it undoubtedly created a stir, it was nothing like the *Swan Lake* fever that had gripped the public back home.

At fairly regular intervals, ballet critics have accused Bourne of possessing a limited choreographic vocabulary for ballet. He, however, emphatically denies that he is a ballet choreographer: "Others label us in that way. We all refer to what we do as shows. In a strange way we have been pulled into that ballet establishment. That is nice in a way because we have attracted a large following among ballet fans."

And correspondingly, I suggest, AMP has pulled those dyed-in-the-wool ballet fans towards the world of the West End show.

"We have been very influential in many ways, with the traditional ballet companies as well. No-one ever writes about that. All the ballet companies are now trying to do new productions of the old classics, and marketing them like shows. We started that, promoting our shows the way one would produce a musical. One of the first things we do now is to design a logo, before we have even started on the show."

Marketing mania certainly attended *Swan Lake*. Once it reached America, the trademark swan image became the balletic equivalent of the *Phantom of the Opera* mask. There were swan mugs, swan T-shirts, swan watches, swan towels. Bourne himself became a name to be reckoned with, and he is not at all averse to the sudden fame: "I quite like it! I wouldn't want it on the level of someone who gets recognised everywhere, but I like what I have and what goes with it. I've achieved many of the things that I wished for when I was younger. I could die happy now. Now *I* sign autographs!"

After *Swan Lake*

Despite Bourne's new-found status, his follow up to *Swan Lake*, *Cinderella*, perhaps inevitably failed to repeat the success on quite the same scale. As I say this, he interrupts me with a pained objection – "It's the second longest-running ballet of all time!" Nevertheless, I say, next to its phenomenal predecessor, it was perceived in the UK as coming a poor second. Was that a disappointment? He concedes the point: "Well, it was a very expensive production again and we can't really enter into that sort of thing regularly unless we can be certain of getting our money back. Financial considerations forced us to put it straight into the West End, which was our first mistake. It went on without the benefit of time to work on it before it was given full critical attention. It needed to be tried out somewhere first.

"It ran for 17 weeks, which isn't bad. In Los Angeles, however, we were able to re-work it and we got the money to rehearse for another six weeks. Two-thirds of the show was re-choreographed. I loved it, the audiences loved it, the critics loved it; it was an object lesson in how to do works in the future. Indeed, that's how we will do our new show, *Carmen*." He grins impishly.

"Actually its called *The Car Man*, as in mechanic – a different story to Bizet's opera, but the same music. And the way we're structuring that is to start off with a tour for ten weeks. One of those weeks we stop to rehearse and re-work. Only then, if we feel it has got legs for the West End, will we bring it in. So we're testing and trying it."

The Car Man will occupy the immediate future for Bourne and AMP, but he is despondent about the future of dance itself: "Ballet and modern dance are not in a good way at the moment. Most of the great choreographers are dead or very old, there is not a lot coming up, and people are relying on the standard repertory again and again. Newer talents like Mark Morris can be counted on the fingers of one hand."

What about the glut of dance shows infiltrating the West End, I ask, a threat to the dominance of the musical which Bourne himself did much to instigate.

"We're often lumped together with shows like *Burn The Floor* and *Lord of the Dance* and *Stomp*, but we're nothing to do with them. We're theatre, we're about story-telling, nobody else is doing what we are doing. You have to separate a revue from a theatrical narrative. And there still is not much of that around – it is something which is difficult to do anyway in traditional classical ballet, because the story keeps getting interrupted by all those jumps and those beautiful swishing tutus and everything.

"We have to encourage young dancers and choreographers, and I have set up a trust which does just that. One of the dancers in this *Swan Lake* company is an apprentice who is sponsored by the trust.

"The real trouble is that these shows are *so* expensive. We have made ballet about as commercial as it can get. But you can only get so commercial."

The morning's rehearsal is about to begin and I watch for a few minutes. Bourne's rehearsal style is not remarkably different from his general persona. Quiet, patient and with laid-back humour, Bourne leans nonchalantly against the wall, concentrating on the grand shape, on the narrative. A storyteller in the old tradition, intent upon taking his audience on a journey. He may have a reputation for modishness, for trickery, but his real tools are human emotions. And they remain forever contemporary. He waves cheerfully as I quietly take my leave.

The World is Full of Players

THELMA

HOLT

a truly international impresario

Thelma Holt is a one-off. A woman in a man's world, she is loved by everybody as an adorable eccentric. And it is true that she is forgetful; the time when she sat through a premiere wearing only her underwear and a tightly buttoned coat because she had neglected to put on a dress has passed into theatrical legend. Yet at least some of her dottiness, one senses, is a carefully studied weapon in her charm arsenal. Beneath the vagueness lies a cunning and a resilience fully the equal of her famous predecessor Joan Littlewood, the impresario who brought socialism to the London theatre in Stratford East.

THELMA HOLT
inside the deserted
Roundhouse, the scene
of so many of her
early productions

punished for watching this unfunny play. Marowitz's production was wonderful. But then years later, for me, the Theatre of Comedy did an even better staging. The definitive *Loot*."

Holt the producer

In 1983 she moved briefly to the Theatre of Comedy and produced the Orton play with wild success, due in no small measure to the casting of Leonard Rossiter in the lead role. This was the famous production where Rossiter died in his dressing room in the middle of a performance.

"He was...perfect. I saw every single performance except four. When I meet him again, which I am most sure I will, I know what we are going to do. *Loot*, in the author's presence, and then he'll do Lear."

Birth of the Open Space

As I picture the remarkable scene, she has whirled back again to Marowitz and the genesis of the Open Space Theatre:

"It soon became clear that I could only do the type of parts which I wanted to play alongside Marowitz. One day he suggested that we build a little theatre together. We found a space on Tottenham Court Road, put in an offer and were refused. I went on a boat to the Caribbean with my first father-in-law and while I was at sea, a telegram arrived to tell me that the site had become available again. So I replied, saying, 'Take it, I'll sort it out when I come home.'

"We agreed to raise half the money each. Charlie didn't, he tried but failed. I, on the other hand, had collateral. I had shares in my father-in-law's firm. So I sold them, and all hell broke loose. My married name was Graucob. As soon as it became clear that a Graucob was selling, everyone thought that there was something wrong with the family business! However, although I got a stern ticking-off from my father-in-law, the business survived and we did build the Open Space."

"Thanks to him, we were able to proceed. He gave me enough money so that Charlie and I could pay ourselves a modest amount, £10 a month. I did just about everything. Charlie is the kind of man who wouldn't know how to boil an egg. People used to come along and volunteer to help with the work. And at one stage I noticed that we seemed to be constantly having offers from very nice young men. It turned out that we were on some kind of circuit and the site had become a well-known hang-out for American draft-dodgers evading the Vietnam War. And they, plus actors, helped build this place.

"The first play, *Fortune In Men's Eyes*, was a tremendous success. Charlie was shrewd. He sent me to America to buy it, he correctly thought I'd do better in the States than he would. I did well, because they all thought I was mad. I made an offer to the woman who I went to buy from without knowing how derisory my offer was. And I got it!"

This was Holt's first taste of producing, and she soon found that she was a natural: "It was extremely easy. I had a book, on one side of which was our income, on the other side was outgoings. Fools rush in. It never occurred to me that it wouldn't be all right.

Delfont steps in

"On the day before we opened a bike arrived carrying £1500 from Lord Delfont, who really was the best sugar daddy I ever had. He was so generous, Bernie. He saved us for that month."

Holt and Marowitz had secured a 14-year lease, and the theatre was a critical success. After four years, however, they received an offer from an unknown bidder for the site. Holt refused to sell, and the offer kept rising until it reached £16,000, an enormous amount for that property. Eventually Holt managed to find out the identity of the bidder. It was Bernard Delfont.

"I got the lease out, made an appointment to see Lord Delfont, and put the lease on his desk.

"'A present for you Bernie,' I said, 'Save yourself £16,000. I owe you.' 'You what?' he replied, baffled. 'I owe you,' I repeated. 'You saved us with £1,500. Now give me time to sort something out, but you've got your property.' And he groaned, and said, 'Oh God, you're going to make me pay for this.'." Holt rubs her hands with glee. "He gave us a big new building round the corner, and helped us in all sorts of ways – because of course he had to! I knew what I was playing. And that was when I realised I had a taste for this."

She hastened to tell Marowitz the good news, who judged her tactic to be an act of sheer genius, declaring that, "You may not be Jewish, but you understand how to do business with Jews. You've got him for life!" And, this being Thelma Holt, there is a lovely postscript to the story: "The last time I saw Bernie was a marvellous experience. I had been working terribly hard, and decided to take a holiday. So I was on a flight on Concorde, and as I walked down the corridor I saw Bernie and Lady Delfont. He was asleep, and when she saw me Lady Delfont nudged him to wake him up. 'Bernie,' she cried, 'it's Thelma!' He slowly opened his eyes and with his waking words said, 'Thelma? I'm not paying for this am I?' He was adorable."

The theatre of risk

The Open Space established itself as a centre for risk-taking theatre, which attracted several police raids; most famously when Holt dared to show the banned Andy Warhol film *Flesh*. More important, the venue produced the early work of radical new playwrights such as Trevor Griffiths and Sam Shephard. I wonder whether the movement of risk-taking theatre has now declined.

"Well," explains Holt, "there's nothing to take a risk on. Anything goes now. There is no Lord Chamberlain to worry about, the laws of obscenity are far less stringent. There is still one huge risk – going bust. That's still there. In that, perhaps more boring sense, you risk your all when you do a play."

Still, I suggest, is it not true that stripping away the legal impediments has lulled people into a habit of not rebelling, of staying closer to what is comfortable and easily acceptable. Holt considers. "At the moment there is not much that is exciting in experimental theatre. But remember, we did a lot of rubbish. Some of the 'happenings' were rather narky, although some of them were extraordinary. At the Edinburgh Festival once I had to jump out of a giant egg, reading a telephone directory. That was one of Charlie's little plots. God knows what it was. People are more sophisticated now.

The big thing for then was that we could do theatre with a political context and now politics is probably better served on television, which is now able to show such shocking images. There are, however, always plays like the brilliant transcripts of trials which the Tricycle puts on – the Arms for Iraq production was wonderful."

Marowitz became dissatisfied with the Open Space. Holt frowns, it is a period which she gives her no pleasure to remember: "Charlie and I parted badly. He was beginning to feel, understandably, that he wasn't getting anywhere. He hadn't got a big house, he hadn't got a swimming pool. Scratch Charlie and underneath lurks an American. Success is very important to him. So he saw his contemporaries like Larry Gelbart and his old friends doing so very well, and he wasn't.

"The pupil had bought the idea more than the teacher. I was spoiled, I didn't have needs, I was looked after by a good family,

it was easy come, easy go. Possessions weren't important because they came far too easily. The business was everything to me."

Then came "The Pink Bathroom Scandal", as it became known, and Holt got out. She lowers her voice in talking of it; clearly she does not like to judge, but the episode is still upsetting.

"Charlie rather foolishly got a lot of free stuff donated to the theatre which he kept for his home. I'm rather odd, I play a terribly straight bat, which is old-fashioned, and I found that degrading. He had this pink bathroom donated under false pretences for a show. We were doing *The Merchant of Venice*, where of course no pink bathroom is required. I had no idea this had happened, and when the scandal came out it caused a parting of the ways."

Holt gave the Open Space to her ex-partner just as fortune sought her out for the next big step; the director of The Roundhouse in Camden Town was seriously ill , the place was in a mess, and Holt was asked to apply to take it over. She agreed, and the decision brought her into contact with one of the great characters of the era. If drama was what she wanted, it was certainly what she was about to get.

At the court of Robert Maxwell
"The pivotal moment came when I was summoned to meet the all-powerful treasurer of the Roundhouse. Robert Maxwell. I had been warned that this

treasurer was "barking mad". Nevertheless, I went up to Oxford to meet him with my assistant, a girl who was famous for having enormous tits which were prone to jump up whenever she was nervous. It was very noticeable, and she was terrified of meeting Maxwell. He kept me waiting for two hours without offering me a cup of tea. Just as I was about to storm out, I was shown into his office. It has since been suggested to me that this was a common Maxwell tactic.

"We entered this palatial room with a great long table, at the end of which this hulking figure stood up. No apology for the delay. He looked at me and announced, 'I'm Robert Maxwell.' I kind of knew that already, there was no-one else in the room. 'I like to start as I mean to go on, and there are three things you should know about me. I don't drink, I don't gamble and I don't sleep with women.' That was his imposing introduction. My assistant's tits went WHAM!" She demonstrates the effect of a chest thrust dramatically skyward, then continues.

"And I made one of the few off-the-cuff remarks that I have made, which settled our relationship. I said, 'Mr. Maxwell, how delightful that after 30 seconds of knowing each other we finally have one thing in common.' Notice I didn't say which of the three it was. I later found out he did gamble, he did drink. I still don't know about the women."

Holt took the job, and her staunch support of Maxwell has since been criticised in the press and elsewhere, particularly once the full extent of his financial crimes became known. She is unrepentant: "I must speak as I found. He was a crook. He was very bad and a lot of people suffered. But he never did anything to me. He was very generous, he helped me, and if I were ever to be in a trench I wouldn't mind that man with me because he was a fighter.

"I once met a taxi driver who had been in Maxwell's battalion during the war. He told me that when they first landed in Normandy they were holed up for three days. Come the nights, they would hear gunshots and everyone would joke, 'It's Captain Bob out looking for Jerry'. He was motivated, I would imagine he was extremely courageous. He was charismatic."

Holt, no wilting flower herself, crossed swords with Maxwell frequently. "We fought," she confesses, "like pigs. We had blazing rows, but generally we got on okay after that first meeting – at the end of which he said, 'Right, I'm going to give you my support which, as treasurer of the Roundhouse, you need. You've already cost me several thousands of pounds because my time is worth hundreds a minute.' He never stopped telling me that he was a millionaire. He continued, 'I do suggest however that if you fail, you accept the fact that you will be resigning immediately.' I looked him in the eye and countered, 'Mr Maxwell, if I fail, as treasurer of the Roundhouse I suggest that you resign before me.' I took to him like a duck to water."

The worst conflagration between them occurred during Holt's most successful import to the venue; the Georgian Rustavelli Company's production of *Richard III*. On the opening night there was a bomb threat and the Roundhouse had to be evacuated. Holt was in touch with Maxwell by phone, and he demanded to speak to the high-ranking Scotland Yard official who was overseeing the operation. When Holt informed Maxwell that the policeman was too busy to speak to him, her employer began to yell. Holt retaliated by calling him a 'fucking Czech spiv' and slammed the phone down. Some hours later, one of Maxwell's acolytes called. It was not that Maxwell objected to being sworn at, he explained, or the reference to his origins. What the tycoon could not understand was why Holt thought him a spiv. She explained bluntly that despite his wealth, he was always to be seen in cheap plastic shoes. The next time Holt and Maxwell met, he was wearing beautiful designer footwear.

"The most exciting place in Europe"

Holt set about making the Roundhouse a Mecca for regional and international theatre. As well as the Rustavelli, major successes included Helen Mirren and Bob Hoskins in a staging of *The Duchess of Malfi* from Manchester's Royal Exchange, Vanessa Redgrave in *The Lady from the Sea*, and a visit from the famed Citizens Theatre Company from Glasgow brought their spectacular production of Robert David MacDonald's version of *Don Juan*. Peter

Brook dubbed Holt's Roundhouse "the most exciting place in Europe". Yet the financial, and often physical struggle to keep the place going was enormous.

"It was a nightmare. The reason that I stopped acting was that when I saw the challenge that I faced at the Roundhouse – big auditorium, small auditorium, three bars and a restaurant, I knew there was no way to do both. I dumped the acting without any regret or backward glance.

"I decided to use my new career to put right for my fellow actors all the things that I had complained about when I was acting. It made perfect sense. Besides, among my contemporaries there were magnificent actresses and I was not of that quality. Why be a rather ordinary actress when Maggie Smith, Vanessa Redgrave and the rest are so wonderful? Why not just serve them? So that's what I did."

To keep the Roundhouse afloat Holt resorted to renting out space for offices and market stalls and holding all-day rock concerts. The effort was exhausting, but the theatre became a true community theatre in the best sense: a social and cultural centre for the citizens of Camden and beyond. Holt watched with delight as mothers across the class borders used to leave their children to watch the show on a Saturday afternoon while they did the shopping. There came a time, however, in 1983, when Holt could take no more.

"I went to the board and told them that I was bored. I was tired of waking up in the middle of the night to the sound of rain, getting up, putting my wellingtons on and going to bail out the Roundhouse – which is what I had to do. There has to come a time, in your forties, when it is unseemly to take the acoustic baffle down, to put it into dustbins, strip down to your knickers and get in and stamp on it because you can't afford to have it professionally cleaned. That is exactly what I and the production manager did, because nobody else would. It was like treading grapes, except that it was so dry I would have to cover myself in moisturiser. That was getting boring."

Holt left with dignity. Both the Greater London Council and the trade unions wanted the building and a bidding war resulted. The Roundhouse was sold for a huge profit, which Holt distributed among her favourite theatres – the RSC, Hampstead Theatre (which she saved), the Traverse Theatre in Edinburgh and the McFadden Pipers.

Joining Forces with Peter Hall

She moved, briefly, to run the Theatre of Comedy in 1983, where she produced that marvellous *Loot* with Leonard Rossiter. Then, in 1985 the call came to go to the National as Head of Touring and Commercial Exploitation. So successful was she that the National's artistic director, Peter Hall, asked her to take charge of an international season. Holt agreed eagerly, but soon found that the world of subsidised theatre was not always precisely that. The National's grant did not include "extra

activities" and, despite securing the services of Peter Stein and Ingmar Bergman, Holt had to raise £600,000 of funding. Needless to say, and with a little help from Robert Maxwell, she succeeded.

Holt and Hall left the National together in 1989 and she accompanied him to the Peter Hall Company. The arrangement was short-lived. "The plan" she snorts, "never happened. I was to join Peter and Duncan Weldon and produce Peter's plays. I suppose that Duncan, who financed the operation, thought that I would harness Peter to a budget. However, it was agreed that I would do two of my own plays a year with the company. That didn't happen.

"Duncan and I were a shotgun wedding. He never really saw the need for me with Peter. I and Vanessa Redgrave, though, had already got the rights to produce *Orpheus Descending*, so Duncan had to have me because he wanted that play. Then came Peter's production of Ibsen's *The Wild Duck*. After that, I wanted to do another show with Vanessa, directed by a member of the Rustavelli company. That didn't fit in with Duncan's plans.

"Peter did *The Merchant of Venice*. I like Dustin Hoffman enormously, but I did not have enough involvement in the casting of that show. And there was no reason why I should have had. I was a producer only within certain terms, but that isn't me. I am a bucket and spade girl. I mean, that artwork up there is mine." She points to an imposing poster for the Sewell *Macbeth* which hangs on the wall behind me. "Now, I could not have done that in a grown-up outfit. I'm just an out-of-work actress who does things her way."

Going it alone

Holt "wasn't having fun" at the Peter Hall Company so she left to form her own company. Shortly after her move, Duncan Weldon called to offer the office space where we now sit, so she moved the newborn Thelma Holt Ltd in with Weldon, and found him a loyal friend: "In those early days, I was no longer a member of the Theatre Managers' Association; Duncan let me put his name on my posters. If anything had gone wrong, Duncan would have been liable for every penny that I had spent. He took no security from me. He is one of two people who have acted as tremendous friends to me. The other is Bill Kenwright."

Thelma Holt Ltd opened with a production of Chekhov's *Three Sisters* starring the Redgraves: Vanessa, Lynn and Jemma. It was a great success, but Holt's gravest financial risk to date: "I mortgaged my house. I had no investors. I cried all the way to the bank, did very well and lived on it for a year.

"The genesis of that show is interesting. While I was with the Peter Hall Company the Berlin Wall came down. Vanessa and I put on a show as a celebration. Everybody that we could find was in it. You name 'em, we had 'em. Joanne Woodward, Raoul Julia, who sang *What a Wonderful World*, Christopher Reeve, who played the last

scene of *Three Sisters* with the Redgrave girls and Sigourney Weaver. And somebody suggested to me that I and the Redgraves actually do the play in London. That's where the idea came from."

Many of Thelma Holt's productions have interesting tales attached. She loves showbiz gossip, and eagerly tells me about the time she persuaded Nigel Hawthorne, an actor she loves (there seem to be few she doesn't) to direct *The Clandestine Marriage*, and then found him such a soft touch that he had "offered about 200 actors roles in this 17-part play."

She also relates with pretended huffiness the time when Janet McTeer, who won a Tony award in Holt's acclaimed 1996 production of Ibsen's *A Doll's House*, received her accolade and told the 5000 in the hall that she only landed the role after getting Holt drunk with a bottle of vodka. "Rubbish! That's an insult to me,"grimaces Holt. "It did not take a bottle of vodka, it took two bottles. There is no way that I would get pissed on a single bottle of vodka. Not with my capacity."

For love, not money

Holt's company has brought a wealth of intelligent, sometimes exotic theatre to the UK, including *A Doll's House*, a string of Yukio Ninagawa stagings including 1992's *The Tempest* at the Edinburgh Festival, and Matthew Warchus's production of *Much Ado About Nothing* in 1993, starring Mark Rylance and Janet McTeer – but throughout Holt has kept an even balance between big commercial shows like the Rufus Sewell *Macbeth* and more obscure productions from overseas. Does she need to do the former, I wonder, to pay for the latter?

"My formula is somewhat different now. When I first brought over international work to the Roundhouse, nothing had happened in that area since the days of the impresario Peter Daubeny. I felt that I needed to keep the movement alive. My main concern now, selfishly, is pleasure. I need to do one or two productions a year in the West End and perhaps a tour in order to survive. We don't need to make money, none of us care about that."

Working with Ninagawa

Her joy, she tells me, is Ninagawa. This is the great professional relationship of her life: "I met him at the Edinburgh Festival, and I brought his *Medea* and *Macbeth* to the National the following year. The first show we originated together was *Tango at the End of Winter* with Alan Rickman at the Piccadilly. In the 13 years that we have been friends, there has been only one year that we have not done a show together. I find it very satisfying and I go to see everything he does."

Remembering her impressive speech at the RSC press conference, I enquire whether Holt does indeed speak Japanese. She looks momentarily deflated: "The Japanese who were there only understood the word 'London'. I don't really speak it, though I understand quite a lot. Ninagawa is in the

same position here, he understands a lot more than anybody cottons on. People have to be very careful what they say around him. You'll be suggesting ideas with somebody about his production and suddenly from across the room comes a firm 'No!'

"Ninagawa and I have a special understanding. The other day he told his interpreter not to bother translating when he and I are together. 'She reads my mind,' he said. 'I read her face.'"

She clearly worships Ninagawa, but when I ask her why she begins her explanation in characteristically forthright fashion: "He goes for your gut. He knows exactly what to do, how far to go and when to stop. He is wildly theatrical, so visual. He uses every element, including inspired lighting, and presents this magnificent picture. And you feel that it is magic. His *A Midsummer Night's Dream* was like entering a mystical place. He is not humble, but he is constantly willing to learn. And he likes actors, he knows just how to handle them, and I like directors who like actors."

Holt also admits to admiring the vast amount of research which Ninagawa puts into every show. She admits to being 'very unforgiving of sloth'. She fervently believes that one has to earn the right to stage the classics with "a hell of a lot more work".

"You must be absolutely confident that you have the ability to make some kind of eloquent statement about the author's intention because the writer is not here. Now actually that is no problem for me, because the writer is here. I mean, I lie in bed talking to Shakespeare. I have a lot of quarrels with him."

Pausing only to blink at this unexpected revelation, I point out that Holt certainly expects her audience to work at the classics. In 1998, she staged Ninagawa's *Hamlet* at the Barbican, in Japanese and without surtitles (although for other foreign language plays she has been known to include an English introduction, read by the likes of Alan Rickman or Vanessa Redgrave). She remains steadfast:

"I wouldn't dream of surtitling *Hamlet*. The great thing about that play in a foreign language is, it's better. Because you have one of your senses missing, so you have to overcompensate with another sense. Now if you say to me, 'I have read the play quite well, but when the actor was doing so-and-so I didn't know where he was, I would simply tell the actor, 'You are not making your intention clear.'"

Certainly, I suggest, Ninagawa is a very sensory director; in that production he used delicate smells, he used silent visual activity as the audience entered. And at the end he quite calculatedly bulldozed over everything when Fortinbras staged a pitched invasion. Holt excitedly expands: "He's doing something similar in *Lear*. When he met Nige [Hawthorne] – and they were both terrified of meeting, wearing unaccustomed suits and both overawed by

the other's reputation, it was extremely funny – Hawthorne's first tentative comment was, 'Mr Ninagawa, about the storm scene, I wanted to ask you some questions.' There was a pause, and Ninagawa went, 'Ummm, no storm, no music, no sound.' And Nigel was thrilled, because no Lear can do that scene, howling against the wind effects and what have you. What will happen is that this stylised world – it is set in the Noh style – will disintegrate. Rocks will split, and fall with a Bom! Bom! Bom!" She bangs the chair with her fist to illustrate. "Lear's world will visibly splinter. We're working now on stopping the rocks from bouncing."

The Japanese actor who played Ninagawa's *Hamlet* was cast to play the Fool in this *Lear*. I enquire whether Ninagawa's sensory approach which we have discussed helps to reconcile the various acting styles. Holt emits a loud 'Hah!'

"Of course he's playing it. I'll tell you how that happened. Nigel comes to see the show, loves every minute of it, walks round and says to him, 'You're wonderful! You should play the Fool!' I told Nige that Ninagawa and the RSC are allowed to have some say. Luckily, they thought it was a good idea and it was fortunate that Nige had asked, because this guy is a huge star in Japan – far too big for Ninagawa to formally offer him the tiny role of the Fool. Yet because the approach had already been made, negotiations got under way and the deal was sealed over half a bottle of vodka. He's clever, Nigel."

I begin to notice a running theme here; many of Holt's agreements seem to be fixed up while the incumbents are "in their cups". Reluctantly I drag her back to my question, noting the mix of styles.

"Yes. And the Fool is a good character to have played by a foreigner, because he is different. It's a bit like my *Peer Gynt*, also with Ninagawa, the button-moulder was Japanese. But it worked, and we played on the stylistic differences. When we aged Peer, it was done Kabuki-style on-stage behind a gauze."

Greedy for talent

Throughout Holt's career she has championed the work of certain people, among them Ninagawa and the playwright/translator Frank McGuinness. Is this part of the impresario's role, nurturing talent? In the case of artists from abroad, giving them the space to learn about working within another culture?

"It probably is a responsibility, but I do not do it for that reason. I give a new definition to the word 'greed'. What I am greedy for is talent, though I have made mistakes. I realised what Ninagawa is, he wasn't famous when I got my mitts on him. The actress in me responds to Frank; he writes such sayable stuff. He even makes that boring Solveig in *Peer Gynt* tolerable. He has now done a new version of Strindberg's *Miss Julie* for me. So I nurture those talents. I do not have a financial target. I merely wish to please myself. And it is obsessive."

Some might view Holt as an anomaly in her profession for the very fact that there are so few women. Yet it strikes her as incidental. She suggests a reason: "Women are probably a bit too sensible for this line of work. It can be a very harsh thing to do, and women are not usually in the business of being disliked. You need a very thick skin. In my own eyes, I serve: the little mother, the little sister. I have turned it into something feminine."

For Thelma Holt, one of the few universally popular impresarios in a world of hard dealing, constant risk-taking and a ruthless search for artistic perfection, the future represents nothing if not longevity. She moves her crusade onwards with undimmed determination.

"Theatre is moving all the time, changing constantly. I have just come from casting, and it is reassuring to see that there are so many very good young actors. It troubles me that there are fewer young directors, for which one can blame the death of the repertory system. Finally, theatre is the sum of its parts. We will have good years and we will have bad years. But we will continue."

Off Message:

RAYMOND

and "The People's Opera"

RAYMOND GUBBAY *inside the*
auditorium of the Albert Hall

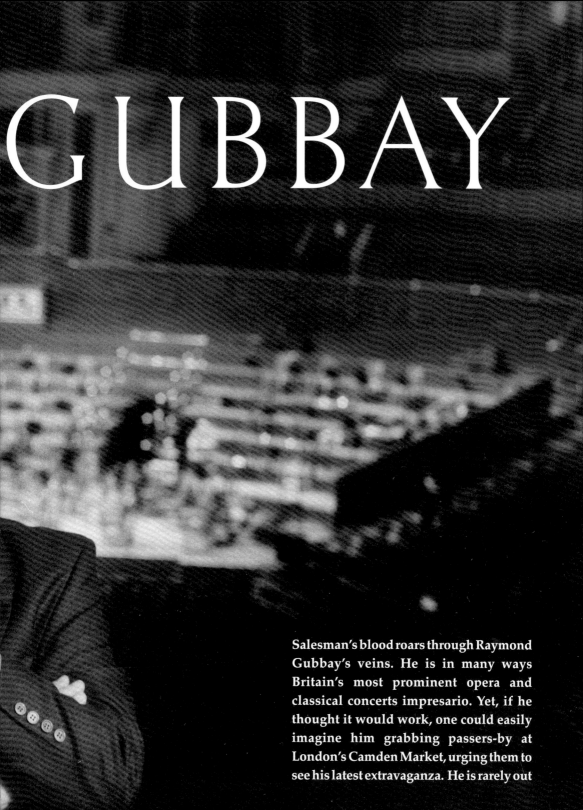

GUBBAY

Salesman's blood roars through Raymond Gubbay's veins. He is in many ways Britain's most prominent opera and classical concerts impresario. Yet, if he thought it would work, one could easily imagine him grabbing passers-by at London's Camden Market, urging them to see his latest extravaganza. He is rarely out of the papers, talking up his events or just as often raging in the letters page of *The Times* at the wastefulness of the arts establishment and the Royal Opera in particular; a ruse, the cynical might suggest, for yet more self-promotion.

The first Gubbay-produced concert was a Gilbert and Sullivan evening on 20 October 1966, at the Theatre Royal in Bury St Edmunds. It was not an auspicious start, being the day of the terrible Aberfan landslide in Wales which had crushed the local school.

If there were few laughs that harrowing night Gubbay can afford to smile now. In the year 2000 his company is due to produce over 500 concerts of popular classics (many of them at London's Barbican Centre, his favourite venue), and its current turnover exceeds £13 million. Most notably, 1996 brought a new innovation. The spectacular phenomenon of "arena opera" – the presentation of operas in enormous auditoria – had already reached this country in 1988 via Harvey Goldsmith's *Aida* at Earl's Court. But when Gubbay weighed in with Puccini's *La Bohème* at the Royal Albert Hall, he brought to the art form his customary boisterous marketing skills.

The people's opera

The Royal Albert Hall has a dignified grandeur that lent the project an air of authority without the curse of elitism, and Gubbay let it be known that he was the man to provide cheap opera for the masses. The fact that seats were actually comparable in price to English National Opera a few miles down the road did not register, so loud was Gubbay's trumpeting. It worked, and the production, critically panned but a sell-out, became popularly known as "The People's Opera" – a tabloid phrase which played on the British public's perception of opera as elitist. "The People's Opera" returns to the Royal Albert Hall every year, and every year Gubbay profits.

Music in the family

Gubbay's love of music began at home. "It came from my mother. She was a wonderful pianist, and in a another age would have gone on to a professional career. It was more difficult for a woman to do that in the 1930s, and with the war coming up the priorities were rather different. My father played the violin.

"So there was a lot of music in the house, which passed me by in a direct sense because I failed grade one piano, but it imbued me with an interest. Probably also an innate ability to understand the kind of music that I deal with; I empathise strongly with my audience, and the kind of things that I put on stem from the kind of music that I was brought up with.

"My mother was content nevertheless, particularly once she was able to bask in my career. She saw her own musical inclinations surfacing in me, albeit expressed in a different way. Both my parents died last year, but when my mother was alive I used to laugh and tell people that she hopes I might get a 'proper job' one day – in the meantime, I'll keep on doing this!"

Gubbay grew up as a Sephardic Jew in the 1950s and 1960s, by which time all the Nazi atrocities of the war were out in the open. Did that, I wonder, spur him to push for ever greater success? He considers for a moment.

"The fact that I was born Jewish had an influence on me from a cultural point of view. I'm not religious at all. But what is important in this respect is that I was brought up in an environment that was hugely influenced by the war. The vast majority of people living in and around Golder's Green had been affected. There were a vast number of refugees from Europe and guttural accents abounded.

"Many of these people had a deep appreciation of music and the arts across a wide spectrum. Moving amongst them helped to shape my own cultural tastes and areas of knowledge.

"Being Jewish does give you much broader perceptions. I don't regard myself as being English or European so much as a citizen of the world. Particularly as I get older, I can't be bothered with the self-obsessed attitude that we see in this country."

This worldly view might have given Gubbay a different perspective on the British arts scene. He agrees. "It means that one is not so insular or narrow. Coming from me that probably sounds very strange. A lot of what I do is of necessity fairly narrow, because as a commercial promoter I can only run things that work within a commercial formula; within what can be taken at the box office. So you have to separate my professional work from my broader attitude."

Yet he takes pains to remain separate from the establishment. He chortles.

"Oh, please God, yes. I never want to be part of the establishment. Respectability and I don't go hand in hand and I am very pleased about that."

In what other ways was he influenced by the 60s? A question which prompts a heady rush of nostalgic enthusiasm: "It was a period of great change. Popular culture was changing almost by the day. Attitudes changed – people suddenly liberated themselves from that 50s notion of a utilitarian, rationed, governed society.

"Crucially for me, the era brought forward a new kind of attitude to the arts. Local authorities in particular became heavily involved and were building little halls and theatres – and they needed product. The opening was there, and that's how I started, with a few singers and a pianist, wandering around the country.

"You never realise at the time how important events are. I certainly thought of the idea as temporary. I remember sitting at Golders Green station waiting to go into town one day, counting up the number of engagements I had lined up and thinking, 'I might get six months out of this.'

Before he reached that stage, however, Gubbay knew that he needed some business experience. After leaving any notion of accountancy behind, he joined Pathé News, arriving there in the week that President Kennedy was shot.

"It was the dying days of newsreel," he remembers, "when television hadn't quite got the stranglehold on regular news that it secured very shortly afterwards, so cinema news was still an important phenomenon.

"Pathé and British Movietone were the last two great cinema news agencies, so it was fascinating to observe how the process worked. They had their own team of cameramen and they received films from abroad, editing everything up. Bob Danvers Walker was the famous commentator – as a matter of fact my Dad was his accountant, which was how I got introduced. My task was to read the newspapers and suggest stories for them. The problem was that my interests were music and theatre, and theatre and television were perceived as rivals to cinema. This meant that none of my stories were ever taken up. I suppose it didn't do a lot for me, but it was a great experience."

What did inform Gubbay's later career was a spell working for the great impresario (still an immensely important figure today, and the subject of another chapter in this book) Victor Hochhauser. As his father's connections had helped him with the Pathé job, so they came to his aid again: "My father was doing some work for Centre 42, which was an organisation set up by the trade unions to promote the arts to their members. They were the original

purchasers of London's Roundhouse Theatre. Dad got to know the playwright Arnold Wesker, who introduced me to Victor Hochhauser. I went for an interview, when he asked me three questions: 'Are you a Jewish boy? Where did you go to school? Can you start on Monday?' And that was it!"

It was not a happy experience. "I got paid £10 a week to tour round the country with Russian dance companies, and later with the Red Army Choir. I stayed there for 10 months, 28 days and 12 hours."

"It was not the easiest of training-grounds. Hochhauser keeps all that he has learned clammed up inside himself. It is rather sad because he and his wife are now quite old. They have never trusted anybody enough to take some of the responsibilities off their shoulders."

No doubt the Hochhausers know that in business your strongest competitors often start as your own employees. There is a fine line indeed between letting somebody take the responsibility off your shoulders and teaching a potential young competitor all you know so that he may then eat into your market. And yet, it is true, many impresarios get their start from established and willing mentors. (Sir Peter Daubeny, for example, trained Michael White, who took Robert Fox under his wing, who passed on his tricks of the trade to David Pugh, the young producer of the hit play *Art*.)

"If you look at the roll-call of previous employees," continues Gubbay, "it is really very impressive over a 40-year period. Anthony Philips, who went on to be the Royal Festival Hall's planning manager, Stephen Flintwood who is now at IMG, there are loads of us. You could probably sit down and write 20 names without too much trouble. The late Robert Patterson was there; a huge impresario, in many ways the forerunner of Harvey Goldsmith.

"Victor was old-fashioned in his set-up. Two principals in the office, a very small staff and a lot of shouting and screaming. I did pick up a lot in spite of them not teaching me much."

Gubbay's own office is hardly grandiose. "Well this is a somewhat bigger operation because there are three directors here and all of us – myself, Bob Joley and Anthony Findlay – are also shareholders. It doesn't revolve solely around me, there are about 12 of us including people in our office in Manchester. Everybody in this business runs quite small offices."

And is that important, to keep things personal? "It is a personal business. It is a business that relies upon contacts and the ability to talk to people, to reach their level, to find out what's going on, to book the new product and develop ideas, so that aspect is crucial.

"However, we run a very open office, my colleagues and I, and everyone is encouraged to speak their piece and not feel inhibited. They are reasonably well paid and we try to maintain a good atmosphere."

With a sudden rush of enthusiasm, he continues, "It has got to be fun, you can't take this business of entertaining people too seriously. It's not like having to eat or drink, it is a luxury."

Government Funding
Gubbay still believes that governments have an obligation to fund the arts and insists that subsidy is justified. "Where the arts fall down sometimes is they appear to think that there is some God-given right for them to be given a living by the Government; everybody has to earn that privilege.

"There is always only going to be a certain amount of funding available. It is never going to be the sort of infinite sum that the arts, in their wildest dreams, would like. That then should be seen to be divided among a certain amount of companies in a fair, equitable way. That is where there are problems, and where I differ with some of the establishment."

Half-expecting a tirade, I enquire as to whether he is talking specifically about the Royal Opera.

"Well, that's a well-known *cause célèbre* which I have commented on from time to time because it has to be commented on. A lot of people in the arts business feel the same way that I do, perhaps even more vehemently, but they are inhibited from saying so because they themselves are in receipt of grants. I am one of the few who can actually criticise from the outside, who is involved in the arts but who is not afraid of what the Arts Council or government ministers might do if I step out of line. They have no sanction."

So is this an important role for the commercial impresarios – commenting from the outside, helping to keep the arts democratic?

"We are all in business to do business, and to make things happen. It is no good the arts establishment on their side or we on our side thinking that we are separate animals. We all intermingle, we all look after the same audience, we're all putting bums on seats. The only difference is that in order for them to do it with their product they need government money to make it work. In all other respects things are very similar. So we can help each other, we can comment constructively.

"However the arts has to understand that they are only part of a much wider picture. If you look at education, health, these are priorities to ordinary people and their lives. It stands to reason that the arts will never be able to usurp those other areas, to take more than what may be regarded as its fair share."

He sighs. "There have been so many instances where people have been outraged by high profile fiascos. Covent Garden is the most celebrated case where it has been a disaster, in the last two or three years in particular, but even leading to that we have seen a great waste of public money and very little accountability. Twenty-three million pounds of Arts Council money has disappeared down some black hole. That does damage to the arts generally, because people say 'Why should we give money to English National Opera or the National Theatre – look what Covent Garden has done.'"

He insists that he has "no personal axe to grind", and yet he cannot even bring himself to be optimistic about the newly renovated Royal Opera House – which he believes is "going to cost them a lot more than they think, or rather than they have admitted to". Gubbay's cynicism is faintly disturbing. The Royal Opera House has undoubtedly been guilty of chronic mismanagement in the late 1990s; yet few would dispute the artistic quality of its productions. A saving grace, some might say. Gubbay is unbending (although he "studiously avoids" commenting on their artistic standards). Yet the more Gubbay publicly rages at the perceived flagship of operatic elitism, the more it serves the purpose of his populist Royal Albert Hall shows.

Paradoxically the joint Gubbay/Royal Opera House venture *Turandot* at Wembley remains his proudest achievement, which leads me to wonder whether Gubbay the arts lover and Gubbay the businessman are occasionally at odds. And whether, to be financially comfortable in the harsh commercial arts world one has to mute one's artistic sensibilities. That universally praised *Turandot* lost nearly a million pounds, a fact which Gubbay attributes to the Royal Opera's wasteful working practices – "It was like turning on a tap and watching the money drain away.' And yet instances in this country of a promoter making large-scale opera a unanimous artistic triumph and turning a profit are incredibly rare; Harvey Goldsmith with his Earl's Court *Carmen* is an exception that proves the rule. But the rules might be bending, Gubbay himself has already mastered the account book (*Madam Butterfly* at the Royal Albert Hall made a neat sum) and one by one the critics are turning in his favour.

The critics
The press has never been naturally warm to Raymond Gubbay. In a profile, *The Independent* newspaper once memorably commented that '…[much of the music establishment views Gubbay] as the end of civilisation as we know it.' He attacks the establishment, goes the traditional argument, he claims to represent what the public wants while in reality he is guilty of 'dumbing down'.

It was the first Royal Albert Hall project, *La Bohème*, that drew the fiercest criticism. In agreement with most of his colleagues, Edward Seckerson in *The Independent* was damning in his condemnation: "Raymond Gubbay has set up his opera superstore – a kind of Opera 'R' Us. It's cheaper and less intimidating than the specialist flagships (though only marginally). But is it really a good deal – for the punters and for opera? …if this is 'opera for the people' then the people should know what they're missing. Let no one be hoodwinked by all this talk of elitism. Exciting work is happening in our national houses and, if you've a mind to, you'll find an affordable ticket. Yes, even at the Royal Opera House."

The war between Gubbay and the critics which followed that *La Bohème* culminated in a printed war of words between Gubbay and the critic of *The Times*, Rodney Milnes. They exchanged open letters, each occupying a full half-page.

"Dear Rodney," wrote Gubbay, "…I had understood only too well, having interpreted the runic symbols scattered by you over the preceding few weeks, that we were in for a stinker [of a review]. And to be fair, you didn't fail us. You perceived a threat to the operatic establishment, and what better way to assert your authority than by a total put-down in print?…You are totally incapable of dealing rationally with anything put on commercially without reaching for the vitriol. The thought of anyone trying to make money out of music seems beyond your comprehension, yet you cheerfully support unquestioningly subsidised organisations which pay out much larger amounts on artists' and conductors' fees."

Milnes' reply was unrepentant. "Dear Raymond… How nice to hear from you… My objections to your *La Bohème* were not that it was in the round, not that it was amplified, not that it was surtitled, but because by well-established artistic standards it was under-cast, poorly directed and under-rehearsed. It must be galling for you that there are journalists…to point these things out. So you lash out with a grubby personal attack…I suppose this is all about me getting caught in the crossfire of the war between you and the Royal Opera… The day you put on things matching the professional know-how… that we take for granted at Covent Garden is the day you can join that battle in earnest."

However, the very next year when Gubbay returned with *Carmen* Milnes struck against the critical flow with an astonishing *volte-face*. He loved it. "Memory suggests that Raymond Gubbay was slightly upset by some reactions to his staging of *La Bohème* last year…unkind words were exchanged in print. His *Carmen* is in a different class altogether…a real operatic experience, audience-friendly and perfectly valid on purist or any other grounds."

It was 1998's *Madam Butterfly* that finally swayed the critical balance in Gubbay's favour. This time he employed a tried and tested opera director, the Australian David Freeman, known for his avant-garde stagings with his company Opera Factory. His *Butterfly* was conceived on a grand scale. Freeman flooded the Albert Hall to create a Japanese water garden, with stages and walkways seemingly afloat. The effect caught the imagination of the critics. Tom Sutcliffe in *The Evening Standard* found it, 'painful, beautiful and very moving…not to be missed', while Milnes was again

delighted – "Each of Gubbay's arena productions is better than the previous one, and he has struck gold this year."

The impresario has often been outspoken in his dislike of the critics, whom he calls 'the vultures'. Now, I suggest, he can afford to be rather more serene. He affects not to care. "I don't give a hoot." After a moment, however, he contradicts himself.

"I say things that I mean at the time, perhaps not advisedly, but always sincerely. I don't see why they should get away with writing the crap that they sometimes do. If you have a critic like Rupert Christiansen of *The Daily Telegraph* who is *so* snobby about the whole thing that all he wants is to keep opera elitist, who has no desire to open it up to mass audiences, why should one always turn the other cheek?

"I know that he will come to this year's show (*Tosca*) and I can almost write his review for you now. He will say, 'Raymond Gubbay is an honest Indian, but he hasn't got any artistic tastes. He foists these shows on the public and opera was never meant to be done in this way and how can it possibly work when it is amplified. I can quote you chapter and verse." His fears were justified. Christiansen didn't like it.

"Surely, though," I ask, "you must expect some opposition when you champion your ventures as 'the people's opera', while ENO and the major regional companies charge similar prices for fine productions?" The businessman answers swiftly, with combative relish.

"Look, this is about going out there and getting a product sold. You can't just sit back and hopefully adopt mealy-mouthed phrases about the whole thing. You are going out to sell.

"If someone goes out to sell a product, Sainsbury's supermarket across the road here, they advertise on the telly and tell us why they're the greatest – and to an extent we are all doing that. And when English National Opera advertise their productions, they don't say, 'We're here to please you, come along and you'll have a lovely time'. They might have done that in the old days, but now they put out a punchy message; they might have a silhouette of a naked girl advertising *La Traviata*. We are all in the same business here."

So can the arts usefully do with more showmen, like Gubbay himself? "The two are linked. You cannot afford not to sell your products. The term 'people's opera' is not an expression which I coined, it was used by the press and has grown. All I can say, though, is that at the Albert Hall we get an awful lot of people who don't go to the conventional opera houses, whether they are in London or the regions, people who come to opera for the first time. The very fact that the regional opera companies would like to know where our audience comes from, the very fact that they are keen to know what our future plans are, shows the influence that all this has."

For love *and* money
Gubbay has in the past said that his ideal concert would consist of an obscure piece of

Elgar followed by a Sibelius symphony and then Dvorak. Quite high-brow stuff, compared with his own endless programmes of "1812 Overtures, *Carmen* suites and Blue Danubes. Does he ever wish that he could be free to express his own impulses more in his concerts? The response is decisive.

"No, I don't. I am governed by the box office. I am running a business and I have to separate entirely my own personal sentiments about music if it means that we are going to put something on that's going to work financially. I'll go and listen to recordings or go to someone else's concerts if I am not totally catered for by what I do. I'm doing a certain type of thing here.

"But I love the concerts that I put on. I go and sit through them. I can sit through the 1812 again and listen for the bangs and see the cannons flashing and still be amazed at the end of it when the lasers go off at the Albert Hall, it is still a great thrill to me."

His enthusiasm is genuine. And if his love of making money seems every bit as powerful a motivating factor as his love of music, it is not overwhelming. He decided not to go ahead with a reverse takeover of the record company Tring that would have seen him join forces with Harvey Goldsmith and float the company on the stock market because, he tells me, of the "lack of sentiment".

"The stock market is entirely motivated by profit. It is at the behest of analysts and specialists of various types. And you need to run this sort of operation with heart. Running things the way I do at the moment, I can strike a balance between commercial need and job satisfaction; doing something that we are all very proud of."

And this, he feels, is the secret of his success: "Enjoy what you do. All the rest flows from that. Yes, you have to have the drive to make the venture commercially successful. But you are in the business of entertainment; you have to do it with affection, you have to do it with love. If they are not there, then your audience will feel it in some strange way."

The millennium question: What would Gubbay like to see happen to the arts in the 21st century? He takes a deep breath and thinks for a moment.

"I'd like the government to continue to be aware that the arts have a hugely important role to play in people's lives. The quality of life for everyone is greatly enhanced if there is a good arts and cultural programme nationwide. Whatever the arts is allocated in terms of money, it should be allocated fairly and reasonably. We must encourage young talent, which has not always happened here. And we must take a less haughty attitude."

"I hope that people will continue to enjoy the live experience, which you can never replicate with television, or film or recordings. The experience of being there, part of an audience, whether it is a big audience in a large auditorium or a small audience in an intimate theatre, is what we all live on. It is indispensable."

A few nights later, I attend the opening of Raymond Gubbay's latest Albert Hall "People's Opera", Puccini's *Tosca*, directed by the architect of the previous year's triumphant *Madam Butterfly*, David Freeman. Keen to pose a few first night questions, I keep my eyes peeled for the impresario, but he is nowhere to be seen. I wonder whether he simply has a lot to do, or whether he is studiously avoiding the vultures.

It must be said that if this audience represents "the people" then Britain would seem to be made up of white, smartly clothed individuals who can afford to shell out £6 for a programme. I take my seat, next to a perky lady in a flowing red dress who tells me that she loves opera. Curiously, though, she "only likes the big spectacles" and has never been to a conventional opera house, scuppering the view that arena opera encourages new audiences into the theatres. This makes the responsibilities on Gubbay's shoulders all the greater. Not only is this the first taste of opera for many people, it may well set the pattern of their opera-going for the future.

The production is a success, despite huge sets that look grand and shabby at once (the statue in Act Three, for instance, towers impressively over the action, but wobbles whenever a singer comes near it). Freeman uses incense and clever lighting to create atmosphere, and draws vivid, believable characterisations from the singers. Touches like Tosca's frightened realisation that she has enjoyed the act of killing her tormentor give the show a telling psychological edge. And Susan Bullock in that role scores a personal triumph.

Then, in Act Three, trouble strikes. One of the main overhead speakers begins to snap and crackle ominously. It continues to make its off-putting presence heard for a good ten minutes. That is when I catch my first sight of Gubbay that evening. He sweeps into a box and sits down, evidently having just finished some errand. I notice him start as he hears a particularly vicious burst of crackling. He jumps up smartly and walks out. Very shortly afterwards, the problem ceases. The audience do not seem to have been too bothered, and there are frenzied whoops at the curtain calls.

As soon as the lights come up, I dive out of my seat and set off, determined to find Gubbay for his immediate after-show reaction. I head for the stage door, find nobody on guard, and sneak backstage. I turn a corner, and there he is, heading straight for me. This is my chance. I formulate my questions and prepare to get some straight answers. I am not given a chance.

"Hello-how-are-you-doing-nice-to-see-you-glad-you-could-come!" And all that without breaking his step. By the time he has finished hurling pleasantries at me, he has gone. Even now, after the glamour and tension of the first night, Gubbay's work is far from complete. There will be plenty which he will want to improve in time for the next performance, and the next and the next. The born salesman is never happy until the product is perfect. After all, his reputation is on the line.

The critics were divided about *Tosca*, with the balance in Gubbay's favour. As for his perceived arch foe Rupert Christiansen, the prophecy was very nearly accurate. Christiansen did hate the amplification, he did hate the production. The only bit that Gubbay got wrong was his opening phrase, "Raymond Gubbay is an honest Indian…" No such compliment was forthcoming.

Still, it seems that "honest Indian" Gubbay may have manoeuvred his critics into a proverbial last stand, leaving them isolated on the field. *Tosca* made money, as did *Madam Butterfly* when it returned the following year. And Gubbay will be back at the Royal Albert Hall annually for some time to come.

CAMERON MACKINTOSH CAMERON
MACKINTOSH CAMERON MACKINTOSH
CAMERON MACKINTOSH CAMERON
MACKINTOSH CAMERON MACKINTOSH
CAMERON MACKINTOSH CAMERON
MACKINTOSH CAMERON MACKINTOSH
CAMERON MACKINTOSH CAMERON
MACKINTOSH CAMERON MACKINTOSH
CAMERON MACKINTOSH CAMERON
MACKINTOSH CAMERON MACKINTOSH
CAMERON MACKINTOSH CAMERON
MACKINTOSH CAMERON MACKINTOSH
CAMERON MACKINTOSH CAMERON
MACKINTOSH CAMERON MACKINTOSH

The sun never sets on Cameron Mackintosh Productions. In the absence of the crumbled British Empire, it is Sir Cameron as much as anybody who keeps the Union Jack flying in far-flung corners of the world. The eminently recognisable posters for his productions of *Cats*, *The Phantom of the* *Opera*, *Les Miserables* and *Miss Saigon* can be sighted in places as distant as New York, Beijing, Oslo, Tokyo, Paris, Sydney – in fact, by the end of 1999, *Les Miserables* alone had played in 192 cities. There have been 31 cast recordings. Such is its popularity that President Clinton used the song *One Day*

CAMERON MACKINTOSH
outside the Palace theatre

More in his 1992 election campaign, *Do You Hear The People Sing?* accompanied television news footage of the student protest in Tiananmen Square, and the US State department used *Bring Him Home* for promotional material about the Allied troops in the Gulf War. And *Les Mis* is by no means alone. To date there are Cameron Mackintosh productions in 34 countries, and the shows have been licensed to a further 54 countries. Mackintosh has made Britain the world superpower in the production of musicals.

The anomaly is that apart from Andrew Lloyd Webber, many of Mackintosh's high profile partnerships have been with "foreign" writers. Claude-Michel Schönberg and Alain Boublil, the originators of *Les Mis*, *Saigon* and the rather more troubled *Martin Guerre,* are French. The producer's latest discovery, on whose joint shoulders are riding the hopes for his new blockbuster *The Witches of Eastwick,* is the writing team of John Dempsey and Dana P Rowe, who are American. Yet such is the influence of the Mackintosh name that the Boublil and Schönberg works were immediately hailed as "British" musicals, and the same is likely to happen to *Witches.*

One other curious fact is that Sir Cameron Mackintosh is more powerful, yet has actually produced less, than most of the other impresarios in this book. The 1999 *Sunday Times* Power List ranked him the fifth most powerful person in British Arts (behind the Minister for culture, media and sport, the Chairman of the Arts Council, the architect Sir Richard Rogers and Sir Nicholas Serota, director of the Tate Gallery).

But then, ever since he hit the big time with Lloyd Webber's *Cats*, Cameron Mackintosh has pioneered a revolution in the production of musical theatre (these days he only produces musicals). He may prefer to work on one musical at a time, with long gaps in between. Yet he has broadened the range and scope of his operation beyond anything that had gone before. For the first time, specific musicals were reaching almost as many markets as the cinema. Certainly they could now make as much money. According to the Society of London Theatre's Wyndham Report, by 1998 Mackintosh's production of *The Phantom of the Opera* had taken over £1730 million at box offices worldwide, with *Cats* not far behind at £1139 million. Both had beaten the highest grossing film of all time, *Titanic*, at £925 million.

Cats became the blueprint, and other musicals followed. Other impresarios scurried through the gates Mackintosh had opened, but though there have been one-off smash hits and the Walt Disney Company are now beginning to achieve some sort of consistency with their bold but cartoonish theatrical ventures, none has been as successful. Such is the regard in which he is held that in 1998 dozens of stars, from Dame Judi Dench and Julie Andrews to Jonathan Pryce and Michael Ball, assembled at the

Lyceum Theatre to celebrate his thirtieth anniversary in the business. The show, snappily titled *Hey, Mr Producer!* (also the title of a book about his productions by Sheridan Morley and Ruth Leon) even included an admiring piano duet sung by Stephen Sondheim and Andrew Lloyd Webber. ("Isn't he rich?" crooned Sondheim to the tune of "Send in the Clowns"; "Richer than me," responded a rueful Lloyd Webber.)

The challenge for 'Mr Mac' (as he is affectionately known in some quarters) is that now everything he touches is expected to join the Mackintosh Express: stopping everywhere.

And indeed it has been a decade since his last international blockbuster, *Miss Saigon*, which became the longest-ever running musical at London's Theatre Royal, Drury Lane, and closed there after ten years in late 1999. In the interim, Mackintosh launched *Martin Guerre* to a less than ecstatic press, closed it and opened a reworked version which did somewhat better without breaking any records, and finally opened a third incarnation at the West Yorkshire Playhouse. That *was* generally admired, and it is this version which he then opened in America. Mackintosh is nothing if not persistent.

He also lends his advice and support – often financial – to favoured projects. He gave a reported £2 million to endow the Cameron Mackintosh Chair in Contemporary Theatre at Oxford University, and students there have benefited from various professors including Stephen Sondheim, Dame Diana Rigg and Arthur Miller. The Royal National Theatre received a gift of £1 million to produce classic musicals (and even when these transfer to the West End , any profits go back to the National). He supports new writers in whose work he believes, and sticks with them through the good and the bad – as with Anthony Drewe and George Styles whose musical *Just So* at the Tricycle Theatre failed to transfer; Mackintosh sent them a note saying "two tickets to wherever you want to go". They drowned their sorrows on safari in Africa.

Rowe and Dempsey are also Mackintosh protégés, and their first musical for him, 1997's *The Fix* at the tiny but prestigious Donmar Warehouse, was a critical disaster. Undeterred, the impresario mounted a new production in Washington which was well received and enjoyed an extended run. Now he clearly hopes that these two are going to give him the new success he evidently craves. And although no amount of marketing skill can save a bad musical, with Mackintosh's flair for presentation and heavyweight investment behind it, *Witches* had as good a chance as any and caught on.

Mackintosh, who is approaching his mid-fifties but looks younger, occupies a stately building in Bedford Square. His office, reached by way of a grand curling staircase, is on the first floor. It is a large but comfortable affair, with lots of plumped up sofas and a grand piano (he doesn't play, it is there for the benefit of his composers). On the sofas are a multitude of teddy bears, which he hastens to explain are unsolicited gifts. "People just keep giving them to me," he smiles quizzically.

He speaks in a quiet contented purr, the cat who has got the cream. This is a man who has achieved his ambition and seems contentedly, but not self-admiringly, aware of the fact. That he has lost none of his drive, however, quickly becomes clear when you engage him in conversation. Touch upon a subject close to his heart and he is away, passionately and knowledgably expounding his theories and ideas.

He begins by cheerfully recalling how the 60s gave rise to a lot of impresarios, himself included, because it was tied in to the healthy state of the regional theatre: "There were places where we could go and learn our trade and persuade the local theatre that they desperately needed a revival of *Rebecca* which we could then tour. If you look at Duncan Weldon, Paul Elliott and Bill Kenwright and I, we were all touring shows out of Bristol and Guildford and all those places when we were younger. We were people who didn't have a lot of money, or indeed any money, who were able to use our wit and charm to get a show going, which was half the battle. These days very few theatres exist where you can set up a tour."

It all started early for Mackintosh, when he was taken to see Julian Slade's musical *Salad Days* at the age of eight, an experience he remembers with affection: "It was my first musical. I loved the whole idea of musical theatre, and Julian Slade was in the pit playing the piano. I went to see it for a second time, and at the end of the show I went to meet him. And instead of just patting me on the head he took me backstage and showed me how everything worked; the flying saucers attached to wires, the way the actors mimed at certain points." I ask whether that didn't that spoil the illusion. He shakes his head vigorously:

"No, no, it intrigued me! It made me realise that this was what I wanted to do."

Failed student

Mackintosh stuck to his ambition and later enrolled at the Central School of Speech and Drama. It was not a happy period and he left early. Actually, as he confesses with some pride, he was thrown out.

"It was a stage management course, and the man who ran it was a rather old-fashioned disciplinarian who shouted and ranted a lot. I always believed that you could achieve much more by sidling up to people and charming them.

"He thought I was smarmy. And also, I was obviously impatient. I had no interest in attending lectures about Euripides and he never covered musical theatre. So one day he summoned me and said, 'This isn't doing you any good, I don't want to waste your time and ours, so off you go.' I discovered three or four years later that they even got rid of Richard Pilbrow after three or four months – so if you want to be a producer get asked to leave Central!" He chuckles, pleased with the joke.

The young Cameron may not have been interested in Euripides, but these days he has a very developed sense of theatrical history: "The history of any business is interesting, particularly in our area where there is nothing new. You simply learn how the latest generation takes a new view of very old subjects."

That almost sounds, I reflect, as though putting on productions is all to do with packaging. He disagrees: "I'm talking about plots – I mean, there are six plots that have been going since the Greeks. We all know that *West Side Story* is *Romeo and Juliet*, we all know that *My Fair Lady* is *Pygmalion*. But that is not to do with packaging. That's to do with storytelling. With the fact that most of the great stories have been told and re-told over the ages. Because the basic truth that lies in the heart of each continually fascinates us."

"One of the reasons that *Les Miserables* has worked so powerfully all over the world is that Victor Hugo was a great observer of human nature. He created a lot of characters whose behaviour is recognisable in any country, in any language and in any time."

A particular strength of musicals is that – whereas all theatre tends to reflect life – musicals magnify it in a way that can have more emotional impact. "They have to be larger than life. But some musicals are just entertaining and some evoke a deeper response. That is one of the great strengths

of Rogers and Hammerstein, they always chose an incredibly touching story. Similarly, the great popular opera writers always found a story where they could simply push the buttons. Emotionally, those are the stories that keep coming back. They never lose their contemporary appeal."

From stagehand to producer

Mackintosh got close to one of the most famous musicals of them all when he worked as a stagehand at the Theatre Royal, Drury Lane – the theatre he was to dominate all those years later. His job was to sweep the stage and clean the auditorium between performances of Lerner and Loewe's *Camelot*. "The incredibly lavish sets and costumes," he remembers, "made all of my shows look very impoverished by comparison." But did he ever truly believe that one day he would have his own show on that enormous stage? He looks sheepish: "I had a dream that it would happen. I used to tell the guys backstage that I would be a producer, and they used to send me up."

Mackintosh's ties with the theatre grew still deeper when *Miss Saigon* became its longest-ever running show. That in turn has been replaced by *The Witches of Eastwick*. So the Theatre Royal is already strongly associated with Cameron Mackintosh. Is it, I enquire, an association which he would like to continue indefinitely?

"Only when appropriate. Because I do have a sense of history, I know that not many shows have run for very long at that theatre. Because it is very hard to fill, and because a lot of shows that went in there would have been far better off in smaller theatres. I have always thought that in casting shows you should cast auditoriums as much as you should cast a leading lady."

The guy who gets things done

One of his first jobs upon leaving Drury Lane was working on Emile Littler's production of *Oliver!* at the Albery Theatre. Littler, the great impresario whom Mackintosh describes as "very tight" had neglected to hire an assistant stage manager for the show. Therefore, when the stage manager succumbed to the mumps, Littler neglected to replace him, leaving the 18-year-old Mackintosh to run the entire production. He was a success, and points out an old programme which the cast had signed for him on the last night, inscribed, "To the guy who gets things done."

To his young employee Emile Littler was a very grand, unapproachable figure indeed, whom Mackintosh describes as "Godlike". The two soon clashed.

"He used to sit up in his attic at the top of the theatre. He was very old then, and had been a very important impresario, the king of panto.

"One night, when I was rushing about as usual doing lots of jobs, I didn't call the half-hour. Littler descended from his attic, and yelled at me." He playfully adopts the pinched tones of a crabby old man. "'Mackintosh, I was looking for you. You weren't in the corner for the half. It's absolutely terrible.' I said, 'Excuse me, I've

got a lot to do. I can't possibly spend all my time in the corner. And if you want the show to go up on time I haven't got time to stand here and talk!' And I marched off leaving him standing there, which was unheard of. Of course after that I was bitching about him all through the show." He begins to mutter startling obscenities under his breath, to convey the general idea.

"I had forgotten that he had a loudspeaker in his room and could hear every word I said. The notices were already up announcing the closure of the show. And the next day Littler came up to me and snarled, 'Mackintosh, I heard everything you said about me. If this show weren't already closing I would sack you!'"

Oliver!

It was while working on *Oliver!* that Mackintosh first came into contact with a character who re-emerged at various times throughout his career. The show's creator, the late Lionel Bart. Mackintosh has fond memories: "I met him on the first night. He'd just opened *Twang!* up the road which had not gone well. And he came in to watch. For some reason we got chatting, I think because I was wearing blue eyeshadow and looked very cute in those days! He asked me what I wanted to do and I replied that I wanted to put on shows like his.

"Then years later, when I revived *Oliver!* myself for the first time, Lionel was down on his luck and had sold the rights to the show. So I created a job for him, creative consultant or something like that. That's when we became friends."

Much later, in 1994, Mackintosh again revived *Oliver!* starring Jonathan Pryce at the London Palladium. The production has been to Toronto and will undoubtedly go the international route in which the impresario was by now well-versed. He went back to Bart, who had gone almost from riches to rags, and gave him part of the copyright for the show – a deal which enabled the composer to live out the rest of his life in financial comfort. And the younger man's respect for Bart is still evident.

"Lionel Bart was a legend. He was as big as Andrew Lloyd Webber is now. He led this unbelievably flamboyant lifestyle, and everything he touched in the early 60s was fantastic. He was the most important person to come into the British musical theatre since Noël Coward. And Coward took him seriously. Noël recognised his great natural talent." He frowns slightly. "That was also Lionel's problem. He didn't know how to shape it. It was instinctive. And when he was working with somebody who knew how to get the best from him, this fabulous material would just spurt out of him."

I wonder whether a strong producer might have taught Bart to harness that instinct. Cameron Mackintosh perhaps? He is hesitant: "I did think that, but that is not the way I can work as a producer. Unfortunately Lionel never really had a producer who believed in his work. In 1959 Donald Albery produced *Oliver!*, but after an unsuccessful try out in Wimbledon, he doubted it would last more than a week when he brought it to the West End.

"After a while, although Donald still presented him, it was Lionel who produced, directed and wrote – he became so controlling, he was virtually unproducable. That's why though several of the subjects were very interesting ideas – *Blitz* and *Maggie May* – they were unfulfilled."

In 1967 Cameron Mackintosh produced his first UK tour, *Little Women*. He had no money, worked from a tiny office five floors up on Charing Cross Road, and his mother was his secretary. The play reportedly cost £250 to tour, and the producer remembers "making a little money on the road".

Fingers burned

This modest success however, was more than balanced soon afterwards, by a disastrous revival of *Anything Goes* in 1969.

"Everything that could go wrong did go wrong," he groans. "I had done the show at the small Yvonne Arnaud Theatre in Guildford where it had done very well. I had originally hired the very famous costume designer Luciana Arrighi, and then one of the investors persuaded me to get rid of her costumes and replace them with catsuits from his warehouse. I was so desperate for money that I agreed to it.

"The show just wasn't a runner. It was due to come into the medium-sized Duke of York's, where it might have got by on its charm. Then it all got blown up. We moved to a bigger space, the Saville Theatre, engaged more dancers. And on the opening night, five minutes before curtain up, I sat in my seat and suddenly realised that this was

Council, who needed large-scale musical productions to fill the major regional theatres that they had recently helped acquire for local authorities. They chose *My Fair Lady* first, according to Mackintosh, because "at least it had something to do with George Bernard Shaw."

It was this string of successes that brought the impresario to the professional attention of Andrew Lloyd Webber. The two were already acquainted in a way; an argument years earlier had resulted in a drunken Cameron Mackintosh furiously chasing the composer around the Café Royal. Mackintosh grins at the recollection.

Cats is born

"Oh, I'm sure he'd forgotten all about that. In any case, he rang me and suggested that we have lunch. And as we ate and drank and talked, we realised that we shared the same feelings about musical theatre and where it was going. And we went back to his place where he played me six or seven of the settings that he had already written for a possible new show, a musical of T S Eliot's poems, *Old Possum's Book Of Practical Cats*."

Mackintosh was hooked, and agreed to produce. Initially, the pair wanted to stage *Cats* as a song-cycle for a solo star, who would sing with dancers in the background. The idea was to present it as a double bill with Lloyd Webber's "Variations on a Theme of Paganini". They touted the plan around to various ballet companies, who either hated the entire project or suggested that they drop the *Cats* half.

"So Andrew said, 'Stuff this'. He took about ten of the songs and staged them in concert at his Sydmonton Festival. During this time I tried to interest Trevor Nunn, who I knew was the only person who stood a chance of making this work on stage was Trevor Nunn. Other people thought we were barking."

Had Nunn, then artistic director of the RSC, done many musicals at this stage, I ask?

"He had never done a musical. He had never done anything in the commercial theatre ever."

What then, I ask slightly puzzled, made you feel that he was the right man for *Cats*?

"I had seen his RSC version of *The Comedy of Errors*, starring Judi Dench, and that was done virtually as a musical anyway. Trevor you could sense had the sweep of a director of the musical stage. I knew Trevor would only do it if he could work with someone whom he absolutely trusted. Gillian Lynne had worked with Trevor on *The Comedy of Errors* and *Once in a Lifetime*, and with her ballet background was perfect for the choreography. So that was the team I assembled, although it took me six months to persuade Trevor to do it. And in the end it was Trevor who came up with a storyline – that very simple idea of an outsider who is redeemed by being accepted by her tribe."

Mackintosh's adoption of the show so many people had turned down was vindicated. With a cast that included Elaine Paige, Paul Nicholas and Wayne Sleep, it opened at the New London Theatre in 1981 and became a mammoth hit, winning Evening Standard and Olivier Awards. The following year *Cats* went to New York, won a clutch of Tonys and was widely credited for spearheading a new British incursion into the stronghold of the American musical. As the new millennium begins, the show holds the London record for the longest-running musical and has just closed after 18 years in New York, the longest-running show of any kind on Broadway. After conquering America, Mackintosh exported *Cats* worldwide.

"I didn't do that knowingly. No-one thought of it in those days. If you had a big hit you could take it to New York and that was about it. We were as surprised as anyone when we started getting offers from all these different countries. Not at the fact people wanted to do it, but that they wanted us to do a replica of our production. Because that had never happened before."

And keeping all of those productions (*Cats* has been produced in 287 cities worldwide) fresh and spontaneous must be a skill in itself. He looks earnest: "It's a completely different skill. But in the event not all of our productions end up being the same. The only one of our shows which has yet to have a different staging from its original is Hal Prince's *Phantom*. About 30 or 40 per cent of the others are different. There have even been open-air productions of *Les Mis* and *Miss Saigon*."

With such a widespread empire, the responsibility of care is heavy. Sir Cameron tries not to spend too much of his time flying to other people's productions of his shows around the world. Besides, he confides, there are shortcuts. He has, for example, just approved the lead casting for a foreign, licenced production of *Les Miserables* by watching the auditions on video.

Two nations divided by Equity

The stagings he produces himself he watches like a hawk, and there are times when Mackintosh's personal attention is vital. And he can be uncompromising in protecting the quality of his shows. In 1996 he sacked nearly half the New York cast of *Les Mis*, although in typically generous fashion he offered handsome redundancy packages and invited many of those who had been fired to re-audition or move to another of his shows. He is quick to defend his action. It is the only time he has ever taken such a step, he insists, and the problem lies with a deep-rooted American system.

"American Equity works in a very old-fashioned way that still separates chorus members from principals. And you have to submit your script to a committee which tells you which roles are which. And if you play more than one part then you are chorus.

That was all fair enough back in the 20s when you had 60 people in the chorus of *Showboat* and it didn't matter very much who they were. But we were in this ludicrous situation where Javert and Valjean were principals but big roles like Enjolras, Eponine, Thenardier, were chorus! And the rules are very clear – you can never get rid of the actors.

"So the problem arose, funnily enough not with the larger roles, because they were usually proper actors who would get bored silly doing the same role for ever and left to go elsewhere. The trouble came when you had performers in their late thirties, who had been there for years and were simply no longer suitable to be playing students of 21 or 22. They were staying on, past the point when it was artistically acceptable. This is a fascinating result of the success of these shows – the problem has just never risen before."

Mackintosh's action was only one of a series of battles that he has fought with American Equity. Some he has won, as in 1991 when he threatened not to transfer *Miss Saigon* rather than sacrifice one of its stars, Jonathan Pryce. Some he has lost – in 1999 he was unable to persuade them to allow him to take the Royal National Theatre production of *Oklahoma!* to Broadway with the casting of the two leads, played by Hugh Jackman and Josefina Gabrielle, intact. The director Trevor Nunn did not have the time to rehearse a completely new cast, so the show did not go to New York. In such a situation, it seems obvious to Mackintosh that the American theatre loses as much as he does. Why then, I ask, does there never seem to be any internal pressure on American Equity to reform?

"Because a lot of people there don't want change. In the end economics will force them to change. But there is still a mentality from the American side that a hit on Broadway is far more important than a hit in London. Which is extremely curious because when you look back over decades the traffic is very one-way; many more shows have gone to America from Europe than have transferred from Broadway to here."

Les Mis

After *Cats* Cameron Mackintosh had to wait until 1985 for another hit on the same scale. It almost didn't happen. A myth has grown up about *Les Miserables* that all the critics hated it and it succeeded anyway. According to its producer, that view is both right and wrong: "There were several who liked it, but the first batch of reviews were pretty poor. There were one or two good ones, Michael Coveney liked it in the *Financial Times*, as did Sheridan Morley.

"Invariably, the British press don't really like great serious musicals. They don't quite know how to react. John Peter, who had just taken over in *The Sunday Times* was the first critic in a heavyweight newspaper to come out in support. But *The Telegraph* didn't like it, neither did Jack Tinker in *The Daily Mail*. Well, he always said that he liked the score, but by the time you got to the paragraph where he praised the music, he had already coined the now famous line about "the glums".

"So before John Peter's piece on the Sunday, we really had all the popular dailies against us. And at that point the show's future was touch and go. Then we got *abuse* from Michael Ratcliffe in *The Observer*. He thought it was terrible and was so angry, he used to go on week after week admonishing people for buying tickets, even in other reviews."

The musical started life at the Barbican as a co-production with the Royal Shakespeare Company, directed once again by Trevor Nunn and John Caird. However, it was designed with a possible transfer to the Palace Theatre in mind, where the deposit was already down. After the reviews, though, Mackintosh received a message from the owner of the Palace, his old friend Andrew Lloyd Webber: "He offered me my deposit back. I had twenty-four hours to make a decision. I decided to take the show anyway."

Once again he had defied the opinion of his peers, and, like *Cats* before it, *Les Mis* became an international phenomenon. This resilience has been a hallmark of Mackintosh's career, not least with the much re-worked *Martin Guerre*. But then, he fervently believes that musicals as an art form need time to mature.

"Few musicals get there straight away. Only the exceptions. *Guys and Dolls* was re-written 12 times. It was only on the third attempt that Abe Burrows decided to make it a comedy, before that it was to be a serious musical! *West Side Story* was nine years in gestation, and it started off as *East Side Story*, and was about Jews and Catholics. Both *Carousel* and *Oklahoma!* had considerable

out of town problems. In fact, *Oklahoma!* only finally worked properly when they got to Boston, changed the title from *Away We Go* to the newly inserted Second Act anthem, *Oklahoma!*. Very few of those shows were launched smoothly and most were shaped in long try-outs along the road."

Mackintosh is known for being an extremely proactive producer; he immerses himself utterly in the birth of a new show. Claude-Michel Schönberg once suggested that the impresario sees Schönberg and Alain Boublil as a marriage, with himself as the lover. Is that fair, I ask? He chuckles.

"They are the marriage, yes. The lover? I'm certainly the midwife. And the show is the mistress."

Phantom of the Opera

His next blockbuster followed quickly. In 1986, he resumed his partnership with Lloyd Webber for *The Phantom of the Opera*. To begin with, the plan was merely to improve an existing show, using operatic excerpts rather than a new score.

"Ken Hill was casting a version which he was writing for the Theatre Royal, Stratford East. Andrew got tipped off to it because Ken rang him up to see if his wife Sarah Brightman would audition for the role of Christine. She declined, having obviously discussed it with Andrew.

"A few weeks later, I went with Andrew and Sarah to see this version and it was much better than we had expected. We then spent some weeks discussing with Ken how to do a more lavish working of his production. He had used this idea of bringing in bits of Offenbach and other classical composers. We realised we couldn't improve on anything Ken had done and therefore decided to write our own version instead.

"At this point we heard that the composer Maury Yeston was halfway through a *Phantom*. And there was another one which was going to be done at the Manchester Exchange. Altogether there were rumours of about four or five *Phantoms* on the way. There were so many that I said to Andrew that we should put out a press release announcing our version, which might deter some of the others. So out went this press release in 1984 saying that Andrew and I were getting together as joint producers to put on this show which we were going to cobble together from out-of-copyright arias. And linking material would be written by Andrew, possibly under the pseudonym he had used for the comedy play, *Daisy Pulls It Off*.

"We worked on it during the autumn, and it wasn't until we met up with the director Jim Sherman in Tokyo that we actually agreed to make this a gothic romance rather than a send-up. And Jim turned to Andrew and said 'This is a great idea for a show. But it is an even better idea that you compose it.' Shortly afterwards Andrew decided he would write *Phantom*."

The show, in Hal Prince's widely admired production, opened in October 1986 at Her Majesty's Theatre in London. It made a star of Sarah Brightman and propelled Michael Crawford in the title role to a new-found international fame. Over the next few years the *Phantom* mask was to be seen on posters, T-shirts and mugs all over the world. The stage show's popularity shows no sign of abating and there is talk of a feature film rumoured to be starring John Travolta or Antonio Banderas.

Cameron Mackintosh was now the world's most financially successful theatrical producer, but he feels that his identity as an individual force was only secured with the success of Schönberg and Boublil's 1989 follow-up to *Les Mis*, *Miss Saigon*.

"The public kept seeing my name linked with Andrew's over two very successful shows, and they didn't really put two and two together and realise that we were different. Although there had been *Les Mis* it was a one-off, with two unknown French writers, and it was in Andrew's theatre so there was always a blurring of identities.

"And it wasn't until much later that Andrew started producing his own shows. At the same time as I was doing *Miss Saigon* he put on *Aspects of Love*, and suddenly people realised that we weren't together all the time." He becomes suddenly heated. "And you know, the press always invent something that's useful to them. They like to write about rivalries".

True enough, the newspapers started to fill with rumours of arguments and one-upmanship between the two. But, I wonder, can competitive rivalries not be creative? He grimaces: "Competition is healthy. But arguments in the theatre should be about how best to serve the piece. Rivalries about power are destructive. To be honest, these issues only tend to arise when others talk about us or what we think of each other. And people love the whole Gilbert and Sullivan thing, they love to manufacture arguments with creative teams. They did it with Andrew and Tim Rice, they do it with Andrew and me. It goes with the territory."

The making of a musical

Mackintosh adored *Miss Saigon* from the moment he heard the first act, sung to him from the piano by Claude Michel-Schönberg. Yet even in this show approximately a third was changed or developed. "We 'ad to squeeze the last drops out of ze lemon,' says Mackintosh, imitating Schönberg in a bad French accent. Then, serious again, he debates the point: "Why do shows change? One reason is when a composer doesn't know exactly what he is writing towards, it becomes amorphous and the structural unity of the work sags."

Is that, I ask, where a strong producer can come in? "Yes, but all a strong producer can do is point that out and talk in terms of reconstruction. You can't actually write the story for them."

But he can, I suggest, add to the team, as when Mackintosh brought in the lyricist Herbert Kretzmer to write the definitive English version of *Les Miserables*. He explains how it worked, and in so doing gives a fascinating insight into the genesis of a musical.

"What Herbert Kretzmer did, brilliantly, was give one voice to all the work we'd done before. He didn't change the structure. There was already a fairly complete structure by James Fenton, though it took me two years to get it out of him. Then Trevor and John Caird took what James had done, and they wrote a full synopsis incorporating his work and going back to the book. And it was that synopsis, into which of course Boublil and Schönberg had an input, that was laid down as a road map for Herbie."

The art of promotion

One of Mackintosh's great strengths as a producer is his eye for creating easily identifiable, vivid images for his shows which burn themselves into the memory. There was the green eyes for the *Cats* poster, the starving child against a tattered French flag for *Les Mis*, the mask for *Phantom* and the brilliant design for *Saigon*, an Oriental letter, a helicopter and a girl's face all at once. *The Witches of Eastwick* continues this tradition, with a demon's tail hanging from a heart. For Sir Cameron a good poster is an essential part of the marketing process: "A good poster says everything and nothing. It allows the imagination to take flight. Posters that explicitly say, 'This is what you are going to get' usually mean that you're not going to get it.

"But after you've seen the show, it should become clear that the good poster has everything in it; because it has caught the spirit of the show with something very simple. However, it is a very complicated process to make it simple.

"*Miss Saigon* was actually an amalgam of two posters. And the same happened with *Witches*. The typeface came from one design, the idea of the heart from another – and at one point it was just a heart drawn in lipstick, I've now had it built so that it has a different kind of sophistry about it, it's no longer a home-made heart."

Ironically, however, there have been drawbacks to Mackintosh's marketing flamboyance. His first night parties are famously spectacular. I mention the *Miss Saigon* celebration in which guests were sailed down the Thames, and the *Martin Guerre* party for which the host transformed Bedford Square into a 16th century French fête, complete with acrobats, lute-players, fire-eaters and a helter skelter. Grand gestures such as these, allied to those powerful logos which have become instantly recognisable in so many countries, mean that the public now expects every Cameron Mackintosh musical to be an event.

This can be a strength, as with 1991's relatively small-scale *Five Guys Named Moe*, which gained momentum from the Cameron Mackintosh name. It can also work against him.

The critics
Have people expected less than successful shows like *Moby Dick* and *Just So* to be something that they were never meant to be? (Mackintosh is adamant that *Moby Dick*, which was in 1992 his worst critical flop since hitting the big time – *The Guardian* called it "garbage" – was simply a small-scale fun show that was in too big a theatre, the thousand-seater Piccadilly.) He remains surprisingly unruffled:

"On the one hand I'm thrilled that my position allows me to lend my assistance to shows like *Just So*, which came out of my support for its writers Anthony Drewe and George Styles. And I'm pleased to see that in the work they are doing this year and next year they seemed to have reached their milieu, and are producing the sort of work people expect from them. *Honk! The Ugly Duckling* has just been a big success at the National.

"However, coming back to your point, I have had many more good reviews than bad reviews and it would be churlish of me to complain. But the thing that I find difficult is that critics will often review one of my shows and they review *me*. They are about whether *I* have got a hit. And that is painful because I am one of the few people who, firstly, cares and secondly, can afford to put these shows on. It is the author's work that counts.

"What I found with John Dempsey and Dana Rowe when we did *The Fix* at the Donmar Warehouse was that hardly anybody pointed out the fact that these guys have talent. The show itself may not have worked, but when it comes to a new writer of straight plays they will bend over backwards to find something encouraging to say about the new playwright."

What is also interesting, I mention, is that of the three versions of *Martin Guerre* which opened from 1996 onwards, it was the third and least trumpeted version which drew the best reviews. Almost as though, away from the glare of the West End, the piece could be taken on its own terms and not as "A Cameron Mackintosh Mega-Musical".

The godfather

As Mackintosh himself has implied, and Drewe and Styles, Dempsey and Rowe, the beneficiaries of various workshops for new musicals and many others would agree, he has become something of a godfather figure to the British musical theatre. Although it is a responsibility he only partly acknowledges: "I can only be a godfather to things I like. As with a real godfather, if one could choose one's godchildren, one only wants to spend time with the children one likes. And I've only ever helped with shows that are like the things I do, because if I don't like them I can't usefully contribute to them."

Is that, I wonder, the essence of good producing? The necessity to love whatever you do?

"I think so. For me, the only way I can work is to do the things that I am passionate about. I just try to do it as well as I can. And if it succeeds it succeeds, if it doesn't then you've done your best.

"What is necessary is to have an instinct. You can't teach that to a young producer.

You just have it. I've been doing this for a number of years and my sense of construction, of whether a piece works, is as developed as it is going to get. But I can't tell anyone *why* something works. And my way of working is not always appropriate. I work completely differently from Duncan or Bill, my way is to obsessively focus on a single project and examine it from every possible angle. But to be a successful producer, we all need the instinct for what makes a great show. And that is the key."

Sir Cameron Mackintosh has broken many records, he has passed many boundaries. And there are countless statistics that illustrate his success. But the spirit of his story is perhaps caught by a particular anecdote. Some years ago, while *Miss Saigon* was still playing, I took the backstage tour at the Theatre Royal, Drury Lane. A young Scottish usher showed us round the ancient hydraulic pumps and the cramped dressing rooms. He delivered his well-rehearsed patter amicably enough, though it was clear that he had fulfiled this duty scores of times before. And then we got to the stage, and as he looked around a gleam came into his eyes. "You know," he said, "years ago Cameron Mackintosh used to sweep this stage. And look at him now." He gazed at all of us, and it was suddenly clear that this man was not always going to be conducting the backstage tour at Drury Lane. "So," he beamed, "there's hope for all of us." And that, one feels, is perhaps the legacy which would please Mr Mac the best.

A Song of Summer:

GEORGE CHRISTIE

and the Glyndebourne Festival Opera

Prevailing wisdom dictates that the Glyndebourne Festival is a peculiarly British institution. Who (it argues) but an English eccentric like Sir John Christie would build an opera festival in his garden, located deep in the Sussex Downs or, as it is also commonly referred to, the middle of nowhere? Who but English audiences would put themselves through the ordeal, often on a sweltering hot day, of donning dinner suits or evening gowns and undertaking the circuitous trek to the tiny town of Lewes, near Brighton, and thence

onto the maze-like roads and byways of the English countryside, one of which leads to Glyndebourne? True enough; Glyndebourne is as British as the stiff upper lip and the Tower of London.

To many opera lovers Glyndebourne is paradise. The very seclusion of the site gives it an almost mythic or religious aura. It is a high temple to opera, where artistic values come above everything and the standards of performance, the ambition of the repertoire, and the perceptiveness of the productions are generally as good as the world can offer. For this we must not only remember Sir John Christie with gratitude, but also thank his son George, who has been chairman since 1958. It is he who has presided over the artistic health of Glyndebourne, over the regimes of three excellent musical directors (Sir John Pritchard, Bernard Haitink and Sir Andrew Davis). It is he who took the decision in 1992 to completely rebuild the opera house, replacing the old building (an outdated, uncomfortable barn-like structure) with the brilliant and universally acclaimed Michael Hopkins design. The cost of the project was immense, the dangers of it failing potentially fatal to the festival. Yet the festival's first son held his nerve, and it is for this triumph above all that he has secured his place in Glyndebourne's history.

Sir George is in fine fettle for a man approaching 65, vigorous and youthful. His study is a vast room, cluttered by books and piles of records. As a breeder of pug-dogs, my host takes great pride in showing me a large number of inanimate pugs which litter the room. There are pug cushions, on one of which sits an lifelike pug sculpture, there are stone pugs and pug paintings. Eventually, and shortly after we sit at Sir George's handsome desk, the dogs themselves rush in (four of them), fresh from their morning walk, and make for my legs. "They have no teeth of any account," Sir George reassures me, seeing my expression of mild panic. I enquire in a steady voice as to why they insist upon growling. "So would you if you had a nose like a squashed accordion," he replies, ushering them out and shutting the door.

What, I ask, was it like growing up with an opera house in the garden? He shrugs: "I never knew anything different, it seemed to me perfectly normal. When my oldest son was about six he went to a tea-party at a local house, and at the end he politely said to his hostess, 'Where do you keep *your* opera house?' In a way, that kind of attitude applies to me.

"I was actually born in a room immediately above us. I lived here until I was four, when I went to America as an evacuee during the war. I came back in 1943, settled here and have been here ever since. I suppose it is simply the confirmation of a family trend. My family have lived here for something over 500 years. It is a family characteristic that none of us seem to move on."

After the war
He remembers his time in America as "fairly wild", and returned home in time for

an important new development in the Christie legacy: "The opera house was closed during the war. It re-opened in 1946, with the world premiere of Benjamin Britten's *The Rape of Lucretia*, which we presented with Britten's involvement. Then the following year, my father and mother, together with Rudy (Sir Rudolf) Bing, started the Edinburgh Festival, and we ran that for the next three years.

"Edinburgh was really a pretext for finding money to enable Glyndebourne to continue. My father couldn't find a backer on home ground. So he decided that, if he could not find anyone to share the costs of his festival, he would go and set up a festival elsewhere that would provide the money he needed.

"The Edinburgh city fathers agreed to go ahead with his idea. It was a huge endeavour, that first festival in 1947, because after the war everyone was starved of culture. And to get together a group of the greatest musicians in the world – people like Furtwängler, Pierre Fournier the cellist, Schnabel, Yehudi Menuhin and all that lot – was a terrific artistic circus. A cultural feast, all performed at the old King's Theatre, the Usher Hall and the rest."

There seems, I note, to be an interesting contrast between the two festivals. Glyndebourne has always been recognised for its ability to nurture astonishing young singers, and in Edinburgh the emphasis seems to have been on established stars. Sir George shakes his head. "Actually no, we

pursued the same policy as far as opera was concerned. After all, at that time it was the Glyndebourne company performing at Edinburgh. However, outside of the operas, gilding the festival, were these starry concerts.

Concerts
"The economics of doing concerts are very different to mounting an opera. Concerts do not have long rehearsal periods, they do not have expensive sets and costumes. You can really get away with a relatively small expense on a concert. Mind you, the fees for artists in concerts are far higher than for opera; on the grounds that, if you are giving an opera production you will probably present eight or nine performances, so the singers come to you on the basis of a package deal. Concerts are often one-offs with minimum rehearsals, so the artists are paid more for their time. And it suits the jet-setters to fly in, give a concert for a very high fee, fly off and give another concert elsewhere in the same week for another high fee."

Has he never been tempted, I ask, to mount more high profile gala concerts at Glyndebourne, since the festival has already done one or two? Sir George answers firmly: "We have hardly done any, and I don't want to do gala performances as a rule. When you do these things, it attracts people because it is a rarity – so by definition we cannot do them too often.

"We are mounting more concerts here, but not gala concerts. Next week Mitsuko

Uchida is giving a recital. Soon afterwards the London Philharmonic will be playing with Bryn Terfel and Cecilia Bartoli singing, so that will be a pretty starry event. However, that is an LPO promotion. It is really to help them generate funds, which they badly need. They spend four months of the year at Glyndebourne as our 'house' orchestra, so there is a particular synergy to the concert taking place here."

There are more concerts planned, including collaborations with the Brighton Festival, yet Christie is adamant that the operas come first, and take up too much time for any organised concert season: "People think that at Glyndebourne we have only a short festival season, that is three and a half months long, which by the way is very much longer than any other festival that I know of. We are already going into rehearsal at the beginning of April, proceeding with the festival until the end of August, at which point rehearsals begin for our touring opera company, which takes us until mid-December. All of the rehearsals for Glyndebourne Touring Opera take place here, then we go out on the road. Once that happens, all of our technicians come with us and the house itself is emasculated in that respect.

"Then you hit the unseasonal period – mid-December to mid-March – when frankly, you would have to be mad to put on concerts here. It is freezing cold, sometimes you are snowed in. So while we do not, thank goodness, operate the same sort of conveyor belt as repertory houses, it is a long operation each year, which allows little or no room for any additional activity.

"Actually, during January and February we often offer quite major educational work. We do work in prisons, schools, we do community opera which involves up to 2,000 people in, say, Peterborough or Hastings. We do children's opera, that is opera created by children for children. The first of those, called *Misper*, was first performed two years ago and was revived last year – an amazing success. So what with all of this plus a smattering of concerts, the schedule is pretty damn full.

"We work to a kind of skeletal administration, which I am determined to continue, despite our expanding operation. I want to keep the system tight, with a lean administration doing what I call business."

A family affair

"What I call business" – not many people have their careers so predetermined as Sir George's was. He worked for a short spell in his twenties for the Gulbenkian Foundation, in charge of allocating donations to the arts (this meant that he was courted by distinguished people such as Laurence Olivier and Peter Brook, an experience he recalls with a smirk as "very satisfying"). Before long, though, the call came to join the family business. Has he ever felt restricted by the fact that it was always clear that he would take over the festival?

"No. It is not often that people are handed an extremely nice dollop of fate. I wasn't cut out to be a vet or a dentist. I very willingly accepted the inheritance and my parents were very anxious that I took it on. I had a sister, but she wasn't right for it.

"It is a mixed blessing in a way. Financially it can be a bit draining,but at the same time it can be extremely rewarding, artistically and in other respects. I've enjoyed the challenges."

Box office success
Glyndebourne is the only opera festival of international standing in this country, and one of the few in the world, that is run without government funding. At one point, in the 1960's, Sir George did apply to the Arts Council, but was turned down. He soon realised the lucky escape he had enjoyed: "I had managed to keep my independence, to which I attach great value. You are not subject to the vagaries of politicians, government, or the economy (outside of your own, as opposed to someone else's, ability to weather a recession).

"The only part of our operation which is government funded is the tour. And it receives far less than the other equivalent opera companies. The only way of measuring value for money from public expenditure is the amount of subsidy that you get per ticket sold. We are receiving £16 per ticket sold, as against Welsh National Opera, for example, who get £42. So you can see there is a huge difference."

The shortfall from the tour is made up with funds diverted from the main festival. Therefore, I suggest, sponsors of the main festival become by proxy sponsors of the tour also. Somewhat surprisingly, sponsorship does not figure over-prominently in the equation: "In a way they do. But sponsorship of the festival makes up something like 6 to 7 per cent of the turnover. It is not a major consideration. It is important, but the festival is now operating at a budget just short of £10 million, and the tour is another £2 to £3 million. We depend on the box office completely for our income."

Heir apparent
Christie has been in charge for over 40 years now, but he was only 24 when Glyndebourne called. Was he surprised when he was appointed chairman so young?

"No, my father was 53 years older than me. He died at the age of 79. For some time it was clear that he hadn't got much longer to live. I had already handed my notice in to Gulbenkian, and when my father died I came and lived here. It all dovetailed rather neatly, if sadly."

His immediate goal was, as he puts it, "not to upset the apple cart". He settled down and spent five years as an effective apprentice, watching and learning. There was an experienced administrative team already in place to steady the ship – Moran Caplat, the general director, Gunther Renert, the director of productions, and

have managed to retain control over our destiny. And I must say that the subsidised companies in this country envy us like crazy, because for the last six or seven years they have all been on standstill grants. Plus, we have sheltered from the controversy which accompanies those grants."

Enhancing the repertory
For the future, the festival will begin to explore areas of the repertory which were too large too fit into the old house. He explains: "I don't want to go into big-house repertory, I feel very strongly that the work we do must lean towards intimacy. However, we are now looking towards rather bigger works. We are going to do *Tristan und Isolde*." I raise my eyebrows in surprise, since *Tristan* is on the grandest of scales, and he hurries to make his point. "What one has to remember about *Tristan* is that it was actually originally conceived as a domestic love story, it is only because of Wagner's huge orchestration that it became so overblown. The same applies to Verdi's *Otello*, which we are also presenting. Both of these operas will be conducted by Valery Gergiev, who is very enthusiastic about coming to Glyndebourne.

"*Otello* is essentially a private, small-scale piece, which requires the interplay of subtle, complex feelings between the three major characters in a way which rarely comes off with quite the same impact in larger operas. It is only the opening scene which is big and epic. Therefore, there is room for pieces like these here." His point is made, and I

excitedly begin to run through larger works which could beneficially be "Glyndebournised". *Salome*, I volunteer, which, after all, Strauss stipulated should be played like Mendelssohn? "That is precisely the direction in which we are moving. But we are only going to do these things occasionally, it will not become the main festival fare."

There will also be experimentation with smaller than usual voices for some of these 'big sing' roles: "We will have to do that for this house, there is no way round it. At the same time, there is a type of war in this set-up, which is this: you can get singers to do *Tristan und Isolde* without the huge weight of voice that would be necessary at Covent Garden, Vienna or wherever, but why should they learn these roles if they are going to be good for Glyndebourne only? So we will have to go for singers who ideally are *tomorrow's* Tristan and Isolde."

Handing down the reins
This may well be Sir George's final major policy decision, since he has decided to pass on the Glyndebourne dynasty to his son Gus (by the time this book is published, the handover will have occurred, at the end of 2000). He is sanguine about the momentous change in his life: "I give up my chairmanship on my 65th birthday, on 31 December 1999. So Gus will take over for the new millennium. However, my wife and I will continue to live in the house and if the board will accept it, I will continue as a director of the board. Then in two or three years' time,

I will leave the house and leave him to it. So the process will be staggered. This suits him, it suits me and I feel that an abrupt break would be wrong. I feel a duty of care to all those who have put up money for the new theatre. Effectively we will share the decision-making for a while, but I won't breathe down his neck."

I march round to find Gus, the new blood, a cheerful, tousle-haired man of 36 who relishes the challenge ahead, and incidentally resembles his father to an astonishing degree. Up to now he has spent much of his career as a zoologist and making nature films (when I catch up with him he has just returned from making a documentary on buffaloes for the BBC). He has had some experience at Glyndebourne, as acting Finance Director in 1987 and more recently he has been quietly learning in the background, much as his father did all those years previously. But the festival is in his blood; he grew up in the company of musicians and singers (he used to play tennis with the baritone Benjamin Luxon) and used to sneak into the orchestra pit during performances.

Although he talks tentatively of cutting back the tour if the Arts Council refuse to up the grant, he insists that he will build on his father's legacy: "The new building is absolutely fantastic. He couldn't be handing it over to me in better condition. It has safeguarded Glyndebourne's future in the twenty-first century. What I love is that there are parts of the old along with the new.

The restaurants, for instance, are more or less the same as they always were. A lot of the audience like feeling and seeing that they are still sitting in the same place that they have so enjoyed visiting for so many years. And I'll try to maintain this as much as I can. Keep its eccentricities."

I have finished, but there are still some hours to wait until the evening performance. I decide to sit on my favourite stone bench at the end of the lake. To my right, I see in the distance an upright figure striding briskly along the crest of a hill, surrounded by yapping pug dogs. He swishes at nothing in particular with a thin cane. The sheep move away respectfully. It is Sir George, walking the turf which his family have occupied for centuries. Thanks to him, they, and their opera house in the garden, may be with us for centuries to come.

Stardust: the celebrity successes of
DUNCAN

WELDON

If life were a show, the playbill for Duncan C Weldon's particular span would read like this: "Ladies and gentlemen! The great Duncan C Weldon presents... Al Pacino, Ingrid Bergman, Charlton Heston, Lauren Bacall, Sir Alec Guinness, Dustin Hoffman, Faye Dunaway, Jack Lemmon, John Gielgud, Julie Christie, Peter O'Toole, Glenda Jackson, Peter Ustinov, Joan Collins, Raquel Welch..." And there the poster would run out of room. No single placard of a practical size could ever list all the stars who have appeared under a Duncan C Weldon banner. For Weldon is

DUNCAN WELDON *inside the Haymarket Theatre, during the run of* The Importance of Being Earnest, *where he has presented over sixty plays* famous for his star-catching ability. From his favoured London base of the Theatre Royal, Haymarket – where he has presided on and off for over 30 years – he calls, and they come: the Bergmans, the Pacinos, the Hestons (literally in this case, since Charlton brought his wife Lydia to star with him in Weldon's production of A R Gurney's *Love Letters*). Weldon provides the vehicle, the theatre and the prestige. His leading men and women usually guarantee the box office. Usually.

Weldon works from Ivor Novello's old flat in the Aldwych. Thelma Holt is just down the hall, but there is no question that it is Weldon who occupies the flashy half of the apartment. His office is Novello's old music room, a plush, circular chamber with lavender walls and ornate white engravings. Underneath the windows there is a raised carpeted platform, which now serves as a shelf. Novello's piano used to reside there, so that the great composer could gaze out across the Aldwych while he worked on his latest show. The poster quota is low; Weldon is not a man given to dwelling on the past and pride of place is given to his latest production (Helen Mirren in Donald Margulies's *Collected Stories* at the Haymarket). It rests, unhung, on the shelf, ready to be replaced by its successor.

The producer himself (though he prefers the term "theatrical manager") is fairly short, with a hedge-like brown beard. His style, when we meet, is mildly explosive and he speaks at spitfire speed. But each subject of conversation is a potential touchpaper and might easily ignite.

But without this passion it is doubtful whether he would have ended up in this career. For Weldon not only had to battle the usual odds against success, he also faced opposition from a father set implacably against his son's ambitions.

Camera shy

"My father had a chain of photographic stores, up and down the north-west of England," remembers Weldon. "Long before I left school, I started playing around backstage at the Garrick Theatre in Southport, where I grew up. In the summer the Garrick was a variety theatre and in the winter it took plays. Ironically, I used to like the variety crowd much more than I liked the plays crowd. The characters in variety were far less inhibited and more friendly than the actors. At the age of 14 I became the call boy – my job was to go around and tell everyone, "Five minutes please." I did that for a couple of years for a couple of pounds a week, and loved it.

"When I turned 17 I left school and joined the family business. I was stationed in the main shop in Wigan. Then I was forced to take a career in photography ."

Forced?

"My father didn't exactly put a gun to my head, but he insisted that I should know all about the business. So I was sent to the Manchester School of Technology to study photography. While I was there I was befriended by the head of the local Manchester Library Theatre Company, David Scace. He let me photograph his shows and I also got friendly with the well-known and distinguished actor Cyril Lukham. Cyril went to Stratford and wanted a photograph of himself in a play where the official photographer had missed him out. He asked me to come down and take a picture.

"The play was *Coriolanus*, the year was 1959 and while I was taking this photograph I suddenly found myself standing next to the actor who was playing Coriolanus – Laurence Olivier." Weldon's eyebrows shoot up as he recalls the enormity of the moment. "That was quite a shattering experience for an 18-year-old!"

What, I ask, did you say to him? He grins. "Not much. Suddenly Sir Laurence turned and asked, 'Do you want to take my picture while you're doing Cyril's?' I nearly fainted! So I did. Purely by a combination of luck – I was using a very expensive camera which I had brought from the studio – and the fact that Laurence Olivier knew how to pose for a photograph, I took two very good pictures. When I developed them I sent Cyril his pictures and enclosed the two prints of Sir Laurence, in case Cyril wanted to give them to him. The next thing I knew I heard from the head of publicity at Stratford; Sir Laurence liked the photos so much he wanted to buy the negatives.

"That led to more work at Stratford, and during the 1960–61 season, I took a lot of photographs there. It was a great year to be there, the year that Peter Hall took over. We started on the same day, in fact. Little did I know that 28 years later I would form a company with him!" Weldon was the Peter Hall Company's first backer, and in this capacity he was succeeded by Jeffrey Archer, David Mirvish and Bill Kenwright.

Weldon's father disapproved of his son's growing involvement in the theatre, and presented him with an ultimatum. "He said, 'You've got to decide what you want to do, run my shops for me or go into the theatre. But you are *not* going to ruin my business by never being there.' I decided that I didn't want to work in a camera shop all my life so I left and there was a lot of animosity. My father and I didn't speak to each other for three or four years." The rift was eventually healed, and Weldon relates the tale in a matter-of-fact tone. The pain has long since passed, it seems, and left only residual traces of annoyance.

The instant impresario
Soon after striking out on his own, Weldon became friendly with the famous Jewish character actor David Kossoff. When Kossoff wanted to tour his one-man show, the younger man asked if he could present it. Suddenly Weldon was an impresario, touring Kossoff all around Britain. It was a job which, he found, came easily: "It was hardly difficult, a one-man show with black drapes! As a kid I'd always run an amateur dramatic company, this was just a step away from that. It didn't cost a great deal

because one booked him up and down the country, one got paid and one took commission. After that, I presented Kossoff in a play, then I began doing plays without him and that's how it all happened."

Next, Weldon briefly accepted a job at the Liverpool Playhouse, to get some experience of the workings of a theatre. Already demonstrating his appreciation of the value of a star name, Weldon scored points with the management by bringing in Kossoff to act in Erik Moll's play *Seidman & Son*. Weldon also joined the cast, which included the young Steven Berkoff, but found acting "boring and repetitious".

J B Priestly calls

Leaving Liverpool, Weldon concentrated on tours until 1969, when he decided the time had come for him to set up his tent in the West End. The play he picked was J B Priestley's *When We Are Married*. David Kossoff had introduced Weldon to his famous television co-star (from the TV series *The Larkins*) Peggy Mount, and she had agreed to come on board. Weldon applied for the rights, and received a nerve-wracking message back. Priestley wanted to meet him.

"I was invited by the great man for tea. I was extremely nervous. In the event I found him a fascinating character. In fact I think he was a rather lonely man, which is why he sent for me, a young producer, to discuss casting and things like that. At that first meeting he quickly put me at my ease and asked where I proposed to get the money for his play. I

had worked all that out; it was going to cost £15,000. He said, 'Let me have a word with my agent, I might have a little bit of that.' About two weeks later I was coming down the stairs from the office I had opened in Leicester Square. There was a grey envelope just lying on the mat, with my name on it. Inside was a cheque for £15,000. It was from Priestley. That began a long friendship between us, which lasted right up to the day he died. I did a lot of his plays, and he would accompany me up and down the country to see them."

That first West End play, he points out, was done at the Strand Theatre, below the office where we now sit.

Ivor Novello slept here

"One summer night," he continues, "I was wandering across the roof because I wanted to see what the Strand looked like from up there. I stood at the edge and gazed across, and I suddenly noticed a flight of stairs. I didn't have a clue where they led, and I climbed down into these very offices. They were absolutely empty, not derelict, but no sign of life. I went back the way I came, and found the theatre manager to ask him about this mysterious apartment. 'Oh that's Ivor Novello's old flat' he replied. 'Nobody's been there for years.' A few people, he told me, lived here after Novello died, including Sir Cedric Hardwicke's widow – the actor Edward Hardwicke was brought up here – and then Zero Mostel lived here for a time. But it had lain empty ever since. I thought it would make great offices, and this was permissible as long as I kept one wing as a bedroom – it is officially a flat you see, and you were only allowed to change it so much."

Weldon fell in love with the apartment, and takes pride in showing me where Novello used to sit at his piano: "He used to look across at the Gaiety Theatre opposite. That's not a theatre anymore, but you can still see the theatrical frieze on the walls of the building." Weldon moved in with his then partner, Paul Elliott, in 1969 and there he has remained ever since. When Weldon and Elliott split up (Elliott went on to make a name as a notable producer of pantomimes, amongst other things), Elliott moved three floors down.

What, I ask, was Elliott's role? "He and I formed a company with the actor Richard Todd called Triumph Theatre Productions. Then we were joined by Louis I Michaels, who became a big theatre owner."

Into the big time

When We Are Married was Weldon's first big hit, but he also had his share of early flops. The 1972 London production of the musical Grease, for instance: "That was a *terrible* flop! It was more Paul Elliott's project than mine – he used to do his thing and I would do mine. It got very good reviews, everybody liked it. It was just ahead of its time. This was a couple of years before the film came out. Odd, because it had been a success in America, which is why we bought it."

The production was notable at least for its casting, including as it did three actors whom nobody had ever heard of – Richard Gere, Paul Nicholas and Elaine Paige. Gere, who played Danny, had understudied the role in Washington. Weldon and Elliott were impressed, and hired him for £150 a week. Did Weldon, the great purveyor of stars, spot Gere's star quality from the beginning, I ask? He answers hesitantly. "I don't think I thought of it quite in the way you put it. He was very good in *Grease*, which had a short run, but then he went to the Old Vic which was run by Frank Dunlop and it was there that he really proved himself as an emerging star."

Once firmly camped in the West End, Weldon managed to carve an immensely successful career, keeping an even balance between theatrical masterpieces. Alongside legendary productions such as Jack Lemmon in *Long Day's Journey into Night* (that cast also included the young Kevin Spacey) and Leonard Rossiter in Pirandello's *The Rules of the Game* were more populist shows like *Worzel Gummidge*. Nevertheless, I suggest, he must have had some worrying moments. He remains sanguine: "All producers' lives are like that. It can't be all good, that's not how it works. Your judgement can't always be right. Michael Codron, the producer whom I admire most, even Binkie Beaumont before him, they've all had their ups and downs.

"You can have two forms of failure. You can have a play that gets rave reviews, is acclaimed and loses money. Is that a flop? Yes, because in the commercial theatre a success is a penny profit and a flop is a penny loss. Then you can have the play that's terrible and is a flop. And then you can have the play that's terrible and is a financial success – and obviously I'm not going to name names! And then you can have a play that is good and is a success. And you are bound to have a mixture of *all* those things through a career of 40 years and 250 West End plays."

Uncertain future

If he is philosophical about the course of his own career, Weldon is determinedly pessimistic about the future of producing in the commercial theatre – it is a theme that recurs more than once in our conversation, and it clearly preoccupies him – his already fast speech and broad gestures begin to go into overdrive.

"It just gets harder. Not only are you expected to come up with the goods, but over the years it has become more and more expensive. When I started you could put on a play for around £15,000. But now you cannot mount a six-handed play with one set, and do it well, for under £300,000. And people are not going to put up that sort of money. You haven't a chance of getting it back. Flukes get it back. Well, it's a fluke to win the lottery!

"Through the 40 years I've worked in the theatre, the film and television industries have taken hold. And the youngsters that would have matured into fine actors have just followed the easy path into television. So we no longer have the pool of talent available for the theatre that was there when I started, and was even more in abundance 20 years before that."

End of the grand tour?

Surely, I argue, there are some benefits of television? It does, after all, promote fine theatre actors to wider fame and makes them more marketable when they return to the stage. He takes the point, with reservations: "TV and the cinema make people household names. Before my day, actors got famous through touring. When Ivor Novello did a musical, he spent a year after the London run going to all the cities. It would be *inconceivable* for Novello to do a show that did not then go to the provinces for that year. It wasn't just Novello either, it was all of them – Gladys Cooper, Flora Robson. Olivier would never do a play in his early days that didn't do 12 weeks on the road before London. That's how they would develop their following. There was no television to offer a shortcut.

"It *is* good that television takes a very good actor and makes them box office. But you have got to have been a very good actor before you did television to then succeed back in the theatre. What is difficult is when some kid comes from nowhere, gets into a TV series with no theatrical experience whatsoever, suddenly thinks he can do a play and of course he can't."

Weldon himself tried to bring back the touring ethic. In 1983 he even convinced the great Rex Harrison, who was starring alongside Diana Rigg and Rosemary Harris in George Bernard Shaw's *Heartbreak House*, to tour. "Until five or six years ago I would tour everything. It is no longer economical to tour. The actors don't want to." He scowls unexpectedly, "It's like pulling teeth to get them to do *four weeks*. And is it worth pushing them to tour? Because you don't make any money from doing it. The only thing that is useful is you play it in front of an audience for four weeks and polish it. You can find out about a play by playing it for four weeks in good towns – Malvern, Bath, Guildford, Richmond, occasionally Oxford and Cambridge.

"The luxury of previews has helped to kill the touring theatre in this country. Back when I did *When We Are Married*, you did your 12-week tour, and the first performance in London was the opening night! You put your set up, did a dress rehearsal in the afternoon and the critics were there in the evening! You didn't have ten days to run it in. And that was fine, because you had the experience of the tour."

The best theatre in London

Despite a short-lived merger in 1982 with the giant theatre-owning chain Apollo Leisure company (now owned by the American firm SFX) – about which Weldon, whose job it was to fill the theatres with his productions, says scornfully, "We became like a piece of machinery, having to churn out product to fill those big theatres" – and a later spell at the Chichester Festival Theatre, he has remained faithful to the beautiful old Theatre Royal, Haymarket. I ask how helpful it is to have one theatre as

a clear identity, a more or less permanent shop window for Weldon's Triumph Productions?

"What it gives me," he replies, "is the best theatre in London to offer to actors. The Theatre Royal, Haymarket is to plays what the Theatre Royal, Drury Lane is to musicals and the Palladium was to variety shows before that art form all but disappeared. I did 60 consecutive shows there over a period of 25 years. Then I left and I went to do three years, though it should have been longer, at Chichester. And now I've come back to the Haymarket."

Catching stars

The conversation turns to the actors and actresses whom Weldon has tempted to grace that stage. He refuses to acknowledge any of his casting coups as anything more than a day's work. But when the talents of a star like Ingrid Bergman are brought to the stage, is that not quite a feat? "People ask how I do it. The answer is that you get up early in the morning and you are persistent and that is how you do it. You've only named the ones who came, you've missed the *dozens* who slipped through."

Such as? "There were several who nearly came. Katherine Hepburn just slipped through the net. We were going to do *The Cherry Orchard*. Walter Matthau was another who got away, right at the last minute."

It was an achievement to bring Richard Harris back to the stage (in Pirandello's

Henry IV in 1990) – even if the production had its problems. The director David Thacker resigned.

Time and place

Are musicals much more difficult? "They're not much more difficult, they're just a lot bigger."

As are the risks and the rewards? "The risks are bigger, sure. I've just done the London production of *Rent*. But only about ten per cent of my productions have been musicals. For 90 per cent of my career I have seen a play that I want, put my hand in my pocket and put the money out; I don't go to backers. But I couldn't do that with a musical. Not when they cost three or four million pounds. You've *got* to go to backers."

I wonder whether musicals are particularly vulnerable to being performed out of their time and place. We had, for instance, already discussed *Grease* being ahead of its time, and *Rent* in Britain had nothing like the impact it had enjoyed in America. Weldon disagrees: "*Rent* hasn't worked in the same way anywhere outside of America. But plays are also prey to such hazards. Alan Ayckbourn doesn't always work in America. There was a time when American playwrights didn't work here, particularly comedy playwrights, because we didn't have the same sense of humour. But television has given us that sense of humour – the American sitcoms on TV have won over the British audience. Whereas Neil Simon used to have real difficulty having success here for instance, now

because of similar though inferior work on television, his plays can do well in England."

Is he reluctantly conceding a benefit of TV to the stage, I ask? He grimaces: "In that respect."

I ask whether he was surprised by the muted reaction to *Rent* here, a show which has been a phenomenon in America: "Oh, it still is huge over there. It was *reasonably* successful here. It ran for 18 months. That wasn't as good as it could have been, but it certainly wasn't a flop." Playfully, he adds, "We didn't have the author die on the first night, like they did, which would have been a help at the box office. Maybe if *I* had died... though Americans go for that sort of sentiment more than we do."

Vanishing stars

In 1995 Weldon was rocked by the most infamous of his few theatrical disasters. Simon Gray's *Cell Mates*, which starred Rik Mayall and Stephen Fry opened to generally poor reviews. Fry quit the production, and temporarily left London, without warning, leaving the newspapers full of the scandal, and *Cell Mates* in deep trouble. Fry was eventually sued for £500,000. When I mention this, Weldon tries to close the subject quickly with an airy, "Just one of those things", then gets gradually more agitated at the memory.

Were there any signs, I ask, that Fry was behaving strangely? "None at all. He seemed fine. Now one can say that

Stephen had a breakdown. It just happened, and became a big thing. We have full insurance on anybody's ill health. But the insurance company pointed out that in our own contract with him, let alone our contract with them, it was stipulated that if any person is ill for more than five consecutive days they must produce a doctor's note with details of the illness. And they then had to go to our doctor or the insurer's doctor to verify the opinion. He disappeared as you know, to start off with; *that* lasted more than five days."

So when was it first apparent that Fry was not coming in that day? "He left people notes. Not me, but he left them for his co-star Rik Mayall, and for Simon Gray, saying how sorry he was to do this to all of us. I only found out when one of them rang me and told me. It opened on a Thursday, he played the Friday and the Saturday night, and he did all this on a Sunday. So it wasn't till the Monday that one realised he was gone. His notices weren't even that bad."

Weldon immediately went to work to limit the damage. He put the understudy on and faced the press: "Events took over, there wasn't time for a personal reaction, because it became a massive media circus. From the contents of his letters it looked as though he might have committed suicide! Two weeks later Simon Ward took over Stephen Fry's role, by which time the play was on its way out."

When I ask whether Weldon and Fry have made up since, the answer is a grave, quiet,

"No." He pauses, then relents slightly: "If he walked in the door now I would be friendly with him. The sad thing is that he obviously was unwell. All that was needed was for a doctor to *say* so. Probably the insurance company wouldn't have queried it and that would have been the end of the situation. But they would not cough up the insurance money without that note and when they didn't get one they would only pay us provided they had the right to sue him. It was they who sued him, not me. Everyone kept saying 'Duncan Weldon is suing Stephen Fry'– *I* wasn't suing him! Eventually there was a settlement and we got paid."

The same year Weldon's touring production of *The Millionairess*, destined for the West End, was hit by dreadful reviews. Its star, Raquel Welch, was attacked by the critics. It never made it past the provinces. Weldon is irritated by the memory, but not bitter – his bank balance was hurt not at all.

"It wasn't a flop financially, she did ten weeks on the road to total capacity. But that's one of those shows that I was describing, that aren't any good but still make money. It was only me who decided not to bring it to London. To protect *her*, because I liked her, she was hard-working, professional and a nice person. She took the attitude, 'Fuck'em, we're packing out and there's queues at the box office, let's do the same in London. Who cares if the critics don't like us?'

"The critics were extremely unprofessional in that situation, because they all came to see it in Guildford. Here was a woman who had never done a play before, although she had done one musical. And we have an unwritten agreement with the critics that if you are doing a play prior to the West End they don't come and see it on the road. They wait until they're asked to see it in London. I suppose they were burning with curiosity. Mind you, they didn't come and see Ingrid Bergman when we toured her before taking her to the West End, and I'd say Bergman was probably the biggest star I have ever brought. Perhaps Ingrid wasn't as notorious.

"It was the tabloid-minded arts editors. They didn't even send the main critics. They were people who couldn't write anyway. They wouldn't have known a good performance from a bad one."

Storms over Chichester

By the end of this diatribe Weldon is quite agitated. My next topic is unlikely to calm him down – his troubled tenancy at the Chichester Festival Theatre. Troubled because it was cut short when he stormed out. I ask him to explain.

"I finished at the Haymarket, where I'd been since 1974. In all that time I had worked consistently with Chichester and had enjoyed a close relationship with all the directors there with the exception of Laurence Olivier, who was the artistic director before my time in management. In 1995 I took over the running of the Festival. I suppose I was starting to get bored in London, and it was a challenge. And in my three years there I brought the same sort of casting that I had brought to the Haymarket. That's probably why they asked me, because the Festival had lost much of its former glamour."

Weldon brought in his close friend Derek Jacobi as his artistic director: "Jacobi was there only one year of the three. He wasn't prepared to give his entire year to acting, directing and producing at Chichester. A big movie came along and he wanted to go and do that. The first year he was there a lot, we did *Hadrian VII* and another play in the Minerva studio theatre. The second year he decided to be associate director rather than in the hot seat with me. He was due to act in the play *Love For Love* but was ill, however he did act in *Uncle Vanya* later in the season."

Weldon's reign got off to a flying start, with excellent reviews and bulging houses. The Festival showed a profit. The following years were less happy. He is eager to explain the disparity, and the truth behind his abrupt departure: "That first year I made a profit of £125,000, in the second year I lost about £250,000 and in the third year I lost £500,000. What really happened at Chichester, where maybe I was wrong, though it wouldn't have affected the annual loss, was that I thought that if you could lengthen the summer season from 20 to 30 weeks you could dispose of ten weeks which is commonly known as the winter season. That is a *disaster* time at Chichester because you never get the best new shows. You get a repeat of *The Blues Brothers* or *Joseph* every year. I thought that by extending the season, maybe with one extra show to pull it out, it would work. I didn't extend it very much the first year, when I took the season from 20 to 22 weeks, and that seemed successful. 'This is fine,' I thought, and then took it to 27 and then to 30.

"In the event, we didn't do any better business. It is a fallacy to think that we actually lost any money. We lost more in the summer season at the expense of not losing as much in the winter. In other words, if the summer season had been shorter in those three years, the summer seasons would all have made money and the winters would have lost even more. We were experimenting and we saved in the winters."

Nevertheless, I gently prod, your residency ended abruptly. He frowns: "I left. I walked out." Was there bad feeling? "There *was* bad feeling, but not between me and the Board. An in-house fight had developed between the Trust and the Board. It's all about – and this doesn't just apply to Chichester, though it may apply more there than anywhere else – the fact that 90 per cent of boards and trusts in theatres up and down the country are *amateurs*." Weldon spits out the word with immense distaste. "Rank. Amateurs. They know no more about running a theatre than I do about some of the businesses they run. These are highly knowledgeable professional men, but they run furniture shops, they sell cars. And they put themselves on these boards and trusts and try to run the theatres! And they fight amongst themselves. The people doing the professional job in the theatre, from me downwards, we're being run by a load of amateurs.

"The Chichester Board was good and helpful, and they had a real interest in the theatre. But the Trust consisted of too many people, some of whom had been there from when the festival began. And several of them started to resent the Board. And I was caught in the bloody middle of it all!"

Weldon pauses to explain the set-up: "The Trust at Chichester owns the building. The Board of the production company puts the shows on. The reason for the two institutions is so that if the Board runs the company into bankruptcy, the liquidators cannot get their hands on the theatre. That's standard practice. But at the end of the day, I couldn't stand the arguments."

Weldon decided to return to the West End, the world he knows and loves, and where he as the producer has the last word. Power-sharing, one feels, is not his game. He continues, "I've worked with the top American and English stars. There must have been a hundred big stars at Chichester in the three years I was there – Kathleen Turner, Jacobi, Alan Bates, Maggie Smith, Leslie Caron.

Was the problem that Chichester was becoming a theatrical equivalent to Glyndebourne, a starry summer season which would guarantee quality and audiences? Not quite, he argues: "Glyndebourne gives around 50 performances, and when the winter comes they lock up. That's how Chichester started; Olivier ran a nine-week season, and when it ended they locked the stage door and went home until the next year. If Chichester reverted to that, the town would go bankrupt – and they didn't like me saying that, either. What has happened is that the drama of me leaving has shocked the new Board into acting on what I had always said – that Chichester must be subsidised if it wants to remain open all year long. Now they're getting £500,000 a year subsidy. If *I'd* had that, we'd have had £1.5 million towards what was eventually a total of £550,000, my losses over three years."

The maths might be a touch complex, but it satisfies Weldon, who can afford to laugh now as he is once more comfortably ensconced in the West End. And still the stars roll in – in 1999 alone, Robert Lindsay, Richard Dreyfuss, Charlton Heston, Patricia Routledge, Helen Mirren.

And this endless procession leads one to wonder what Weldon has that hot Hollywood properties will drop everything, and accept a large drop in their usual pay scale, to work for him. Charlton Heston does not hesitate: "Duncan is the most important producer in the West End, and the West End is the capital of world theatre. A lot of movie actors don't like to do stage work, for three reasons – they aren't willing to take a pay cut, they only care about their film careers, or they are scared of getting a bad notice. I've always done stage work, and I've been associated with Duncan for many years. He has great passion, an encyclopaedic knowledge of the theatre, and he cares deeply. He's a good guy to work for."

Jack Lemmon, who appeared for Weldon in Eugene O'Neil's *Long Day's Journey into Night* (alongside the unknown Kevin Spacey and Peter Gallagher), is even more effusive: "Duncan came backstage when we were doing *Long Day's* in New York and expressed his very earnest desire that we should bring it to the West End. I talked about it with the boys, Kevin and Peter, and we hesitated for – oh, about 20 seconds. Actually I'd always rather play London than Broadway because the West End has a real feeling of theatre, of family, of closeness, and Duncan epitomises all of that."

Lemmon felt so comfortable with Weldon that they became fast friends: "Duncan," he continues, "is very unusual in that you can forge a much closer relationship with him than one normally would with a producer. He is such a decent person, such a giving man – when he does favours for his actors, you don't feel it's just to keep the company happy, you feel it's because he wants to do you a favour. And he gets very involved with the production process. During *Long Day's Journey into Night* he'd attend rehearsals quite often, but he would never try to upstage the director. I think he would give him any notes privately, later on."

The commercial theatre

Clearly Weldon has the caring touch, it is genuine, and his actors – however august – respond to that. But the producer to the stars is not all smiles. He fears, deeply, for the future of his craft. His face creases with worry as he contemplates the fate of the commercial theatre, not for himself, but for those who seek to follow.

"The future is bleak for West End commercial producers. Shows are too expensive to put on, and there is too much competition from the subsidised theatre. Ultimately, there won't *be* a commercial West End. There will be closed theatres, which will either be knocked down or not as the case may be.

"On Broadway that process has already started. The Biltmore Theatre is still there, still advertising *Hair*. But over there, you see, the owners can sell or rent out the air-space above their theatre. Even better, they can move the location of their air-space somewhere else if they want, without moving the theatre! So those theatres remain, and still make money even though they are closed."

We stand up as I prepare to go. When we reach the door, he stops me, anxious that I should fully understand his anxiety. He is perfectly calm, he speaks gently. And that makes what he has to say all the more disturbing: "The last great flourish of the commercial producers has already passed. Michael Codron is probably the last of that breed still active. I have been working in the absolute, final era in which it is possible and practical to be a commercial theatre producer. It will not happen again."

As I step into the Strand, I look across at the old Gaiety Theatre, topped by the freize that Duncan Weldon had painted out – marble, mythical figures celebrating the power and the glory of the stage. Now it's an office block.

The Naked Impresario:

MICHAEL WHITE *lunches at The Ivy*

The colourful career of

MICHAEL WHITE

There is a legend that surrounds Michael White. That he is the eternal partygoer, the Peter Pan of producing who, in his mid-sixties, obstinately refuses to grow old and is to be found in a club or at a rave all night, every night. Oh, and that he will invariably be attended by one or two gorgeous female companions – much to the reported irritation of his friend Jack Nicholson, who prides himself on being with the best-looking girl at any party.

To an extent the stories are true. He does go out most ·nights, and this almost rebellious youthfulness is reflected in the shows he has produced. *Oh, Calcutta!*,

At the time, the play had already been turned down by the National Theatre, where Tynan was resident dramaturg. Soon after White announced that he would take it on, he was summoned to see the National's artistic director, Sir Laurence Olivier.

"I'm one of the few people to be ticked off by both Field Marshall Montgomery and Laurence Olivier. Olivier got very angry and said, 'You shouldn't be doing this play, in the West End or anywhere!' I told him I was going to do it, and he just got more red and more angry.

"But he was right. I shouldn't have done that. It brought no pleasure and it was wrong. Although I don't think the play was wrong. The play is really examining the question of whether there was any justification for killing civilians through mass bombing in a war. The intentions were right; it was the moment when America was destroying the Vietnamese by blanket bombing and it was meant to make people reflect on that through the example of Dresden. However, as far as I'm concerned, the whole thing turned out to be hurtful, painful, expensive and unpleasant."

Despite such setbacks, White was steadily building a reputation for innovative, visionary work. In 1963 he had discovered the brilliant student review *Cambridge Circus*: "I saw *Cambridge Circus* by accident in Cambridge on a Saturday afternoon, it was the last day of the Footlights Revue, And I remember laughing and laughing and laughing, which is rare in the theatre.

It had one of the funniest performances of all time by a 21-year-old John Cleese, one which he has never bettered. I went backstage and asked whether they wanted to come to London for three weeks, at the Arts theatre. It made John Cleese an instant star. The show moved to the Lyric."

Oh Calcutta!

One of Michael White's biggest, and most sensational (in many ways) successes came in 1969. Kenneth Tynan's "nude review", *Oh, Calcutta!* consisted of a series of songs, and sketches about sex by writers of the calibre of Samuel Beckett (a one-minute piece called *Breath*), Sam Shepard, Joe Orton and John Lennon, most of them performed with the actors stark naked. It opened at the Off-Broadway Eden Theatre and was such a success that it transferred to Broadway within a few months. A year later the show opened in London and was a great hit, running for 3,918 performances. How, I ask, did it come about?

"The truth is, I knew the fiancée of the American producer, David Merrick. Merrick was a fearsome man, and not easy to deal with. One day I was having a drink with them and my then girlfriend, and he said, 'Of course, half the people who go to the theatre just go for sex.' And at the same time as that got me thinking 'Let's do a show about sex', Ken Tynan had the same idea, so somehow the whole thing knitted together."

Like White, Tynan was a famous socialite. Had they become friends, through being part of the same party circuit?

"Yes, we were friendly. Although he was incredibly irritating on a personal level."

In what way?

"In every way. He was very tricky, brilliant but tricky, and volatile. He could be obnoxious. He was a bit like Alice, when he was right he was lovely and when he was wrong and bad he was awful. But I have great affection for him and he did write like an angel."

The original idea for *Oh, Calcutta!* was not as complex as it later became: "We had," says White, "a vague idea to do a show that was totally upfront about sex and dealt with sex in every way, with no censorship."

And then, I say, it evolved into something which aimed to be quite sophisticated. He hesitates: "Yes. No. Well, at the time it was mind-bogglingly advanced. The first scene said a great deal – the curtain went up on a brightly-lit stage and everyone was standing naked. It immediately dispelled any notion of," here his voice turns scornful, "seeing some semi-nude girl in the background in low lighting. It said, 'This is a show about sex.' And of course it was very erratic. There was much that was good and there were some dreadful things."

I ask whether people knew quite what they were in for on the first night: "The first night was great. They had an idea, because there had been so much press. There are *acres* of cuttings, more than for any show ever. There was, however, an audible gasp when the curtain went up on that opening tableau.

"The cast made it work, they were incredibly good. They included Bill Macy, Linda Marlowe and Tony Booth – Cherie Blair's father."

Even in the late 60s, however, such a provocative show was an immense risk, and the vice squad dogged his every move: "We came *very* close to being prosecuted. The Lord Chamberlain had just been abolished and the chief of the vice-squad from Scotland Yard came and followed our progress. When he finally telephoned me to say they had decided not to prosecute he said, 'If it was up to me, we would.' But Sir Peter Rawlinson, the Attorney-General, had decided that it was not in the public interest. We were lucky that there was a brand new Conservative government and they didn't want to start a major fight about something that was really abstract. Had that government been strong in power for three or four years I do not think the show would have gone on."

Sleuth

Then in 1970 came Anthony Shaffer's quixotic thriller *Sleuth*, and again White struck gold: "*Sleuth* was amazing. We opened in Brighton on a Monday night and it was *absolutely* crystal clear that it was a hit. There was never any question. And many actors and producers had turned the play down. They thought that the audience would guess the gimmick, and I felt that it didn't matter if they did."

Sleuth was an astounding success, with Anthony Quayle and Keith Baxter who also took it to Broadway, finally being made into a film starring Laurence Olivier and Michael Caine.

Who's playing safe?

Compared to these heady days, when he and his contemporaries were discovering new talents, new kinds of shows, the West End recently seems a more staid place? He agrees, but maintains that the answer is simple: "It's because of the theatre owners as much as anything. The truth is that Janet Holmes à Court, who until recently owned the giant Stoll Moss group, is a very nice lady. But their choice of material has been very safe.. Whoever decides what goes into the theatres has a huge effect. And recently it has all been *so* safe, or comedy. You need somebody more adventurous in charge and I think the new owner, Andrew Lloyd Webber, will do that and take a chance."

He would be returning a favour in kind – in 1972 Michael White, together with Robert Stigwood, took a chance on the young Lloyd Webber and his partner Tim Rice, producing their new musical *Joseph and the Amazing Technicolor Dreamcoat*.

To start with, it didn't really work. Bill Kenwright maintains that it only worked when he took a re-vamped version on tour. White has a different viewpoint:

"Bill Kenwright's wrong about that. The reason it eventually worked was that *after* we did it, every school realised that it was a perfect show for them to do. And the more schools that did it, the more teachers wanted to take the children to see a professional production. And *that's* the truth."

White almost took on *Cats*, but "stupidly" turned it down to produce a movie instead. He is, however, adamant that it would not have succeeded in the one-hour version he was planning to do and is full of admiration for what Lloyd Webber, together with Cameron Mackintosh and Trevor Nunn, achieved by extending the concept.

Another show that slipped through his fingers, and this one he still cares about after all this time, was *Hair* – "I loved that show," he groans, "I was *desperate* to do it". But he was unable to raise the required $25,000, and *Hair* made someone else's fortune.

Cult success

It was not long before White did a show that was to all but eclipse *Hair* in its fame and worldwide popularity – *The Rocky Horror Show*. "I came across Richard O'Brien through the Royal Court, which I was very involved with. They were looking for money, and Richard told me the story and played me five of the songs on his guitar, and I thought it was terrific. That's the only show I have ever done which I can always see again."

Did it have the party atmosphere then that it now attracts?

"It didn't then, but it was a great first night again. Magic. Tim Curry was fantastic and it made his name. But I was surprised when it became such an enormous cult. You can never predict things, I never believe people who say, 'I always knew'."

The film, *The Rocky Horror Picture Show,* has its own story. A horrendous flop when it opened, it seemed destined to fall into obscurity when the owner of a small American cinema happened to see it and fell in love. He played it over and over at his cinema as the midnight showing, adding drag acts to boost the attraction. Other cinema owners came to see it and realised the potential. Eventually word spread and a cult success was snatched from the jaws of failure.

Among White's other successes was the premiere of Joe Orton's *Loot*, a happy experience despite the fact that Orton was "so prickly, spiky and aggressive – I've got incredible letters from him being bitchy about this, that and the other, being nasty about *everyone*, including me." By 1974 Michael White had seven shows running simultaneously in the West End. Yet there was more to come.

A Chorus Line

In 1976 the producer brought to London what he terms "the greatest first night *ever*"; Michael Bennett's *A Chorus Line*.

"It was a very difficult show to get on here," he explains, "there was a big row when we replaced the cast, and it was a huge risk. But on the first night the roof came off. The audience *wouldn't leave*. Nowadays the audience get up and cheer at every first night and it means nothing. In those days it wasn't like that. And on that night they just would not leave the theatre. And when they eventually did, they were all outside in the side street by the stage door. There must have been 1000 people, just milling in the street like a street party. It was one of those evenings where *everything* worked."

Curiously, despite White's reputation for cutting-edge shows, there has also been plenty of family fare – after *A Chorus Line* came *Annie*, and in 2000 he produced the rock musical *Notre-Dame de Paris* alongside a tribute show to the lyricist Don Black, *Black Goes With Everything*. He answers with a lopsided grin: "I've got schizophrenic taste. But *Annie* was a terrific show. The film was awful. On stage it was less saccharine, it had *bite*. And actually," he continues, "I can't think of a single musical that has been improved on film. Not one. *West Side Story*, *My Fair Lady*, they were all better on stage. I was in New York when they sold *Annie* to Columbia for $8 or $9 million. It was the biggest amount of money ever. And they were all dancing around, naturally. But I felt then as I feel now, that the minute you spend that much money before the cameras have even turned, you're weighed down by the commercial pressures and you go the safe route. The same thing happened with *A Chorus Line*. They should have let Michael Bennett do it instead of Richard Attenborough and it would have been a completely different kind of film."

When I ask whether he prefers producing plays or films, he impassively declares, "Some nights you like Italian food and some nights you like Chinese." Certainly, he insists, there is nothing glamorous about making films, citing *Rocky Horror* as an example of a freezing cold, deeply uncomfortable shoot.

Eat while you watch

He also admits to having his share of disasters as well as success – "You can't have one without the other". The most famous failure, I suggest, was the now infamous *i*, a review show during which the audience were to be served a full dinner. White closed it at great expense, hours before it was due to open. He has an intriguing theory as why it all went wrong: "We made one great mistake. We should have done it as a snack theatre – this sounds trivial but it isn't. The concept of having a full dinner was much too difficult and took up too much time. The show itself was an enjoyable entertainment. If we'd just served hot dogs or pizza it would have been fine. It was all too elaborate.

"I went on television to announce that I was closing the show, and caught the presenter completely off-guard. He said, 'You mean you're postponing?', 'No, we're not opening,' I replied. It was a great moment. I've got it on video somewhere.

"Princess Margaret was supposed to be coming to the first preview. And there was a policewoman in the lobby who wouldn't leave until Buckingham Palace ordered her to. So she stayed there, even though I told her there would be no show and no Princess Margaret!"

Avante-garde? Non!

In 1993, Michael White had hit a relatively barren period – an unusual position for him – at one point he even had to sell his house to cover a loss. Yet he bounced back in style

with the Gershwin musical, *Crazy For You*. An old-fashioned, all-singing, all-dancing extravaganza, I wonder whether he was now moving away from the avant-garde.

"There is no avant-garde at the moment," he replies, "I haven't seen anything in the last 20 years apart from Pina Bausch, and one or two others, which could be called avant-garde. People like Mark Ravenhill and Sarah Kane aren't avant-garde, they're just tough, contemporary, like Quentin Tarantino and *Trainspotting*. If there is an avant-garde it's in the worlds of dance and art now, more than in the theatre."

White's last attempt at something which most saw as an aspiration to avant-garde theatre (or else another shot at creating a *Rocky Horror*-type cult hit) was 1996's *Voyeurz*, a musical about a girl's lesbian experiences starring the "lipstick lesbian" pop group Fem 2 Fem. The reviews were merciless: "The show is nothing like as sexy as it thinks it is and is often naff beyond belief… Voyeurs will leave *Voyeurz* feeling not so much bored stiff as bored flaccid," wrote Charles Spencer in *The Telegraph*, who confessed that it made him want to "punch Mr White on the nose". Similarly, David Benedict in *The Independent* found it "shoddy…the choreography makes you long for the steamy eroticism of Pan's People."

And it was not only the critics, the gossip columns too were full of delighted tales of the West End's latest bomb. Nigel Dempster in the *Daily Mail*, for instance, merrily reported the fact that Andrew Lloyd Webber and his son left after only 25 minutes. Suddenly White was seen as the chief pornographer of the West End, leading the last charge of the dirty mac brigade.

"I liked *Voyeurz*," protests its producer. "We got stuffed because the composer didn't deliver the music in time for it to be widely played, which would have been a tremendous help. And also the show had definite faults, but I enjoyed it."

Was it ironic that in trying to tap into an issue of the 90s, lesbianism, it backfired all the more heavily in the press for being a newsy subject?

"Yes but I only get upset because we lost a lot of money from very nice people. But I was trying to evoke the atmosphere of a club in that show. It should have been done in a club not in a theatre. I would still like to come up with a show staged or set in a club. A club is a very theatrical setting."

As he has touched upon the subject, I enquire about his own love of the club scene. Is it important for a producer to stay in touch with fashion? "No, but it does keep you abreast of what's going on. And I actually like nightlife. I like the music, I like the atmosphere and a lot of people of my generation don't."

Serious money

White, the natural partygoer, is also a natural optimist. The theatre business has after all, over a span of more than 150

productions, been good to him. But even he worries about the future for those who follow him: "Today it's all much, much harder." He frowns, pained. "Just – *everything*. The cost; when I started you could open a play and do very little in the way of publicity. If you got good reviews the play ran. Today, you're *besieged* with advertising, marketing, you need so much money. And because of that it's all getting more corporate."

Does he worry, I wonder, about the American companies like SFX which are starting to try and buy up theatres in Britain? He puffs uneasily: "I can't knock SFX, they're my landlords. But I always feel that theatre works best when there's a dictator. Rightly or wrongly. The minute you have committees of any kind deciding group activity, it generally doesn't produce great work. And it's very telling that the film company which has been most successful recently is one which is run by one person, Harvey Weinstein of Miramax. You have to have one person with a vision and you go with them."

What is Michael White's place in this increasingly corporate theatre world? Might he relive his early dream of becoming a novelist after all? He leans back in his chair and ponders, before answering, quietly: "Yes."

Down, But Not Out:

The giant steps of

HARVEY GOLD

By any standards, Harvey Goldsmith has had an eventful life. He talks big, justifiably so. He has, after all, been harnessed and hoisted high above the stage of the Hammersmith Odeon by The Who, pinned against a wall by a furious Miles Davis (who lost his temper when Goldsmith offered him a watermelon, unaware that the fruit is a symbol of slavery) and has promoted in his time acts as diverse as The Beatles, Bruce Springsteen, Madonna and Luciano Pavarotti. He moves between the glamorous and unpredictable world of rock concerts and the glamorous and often equally

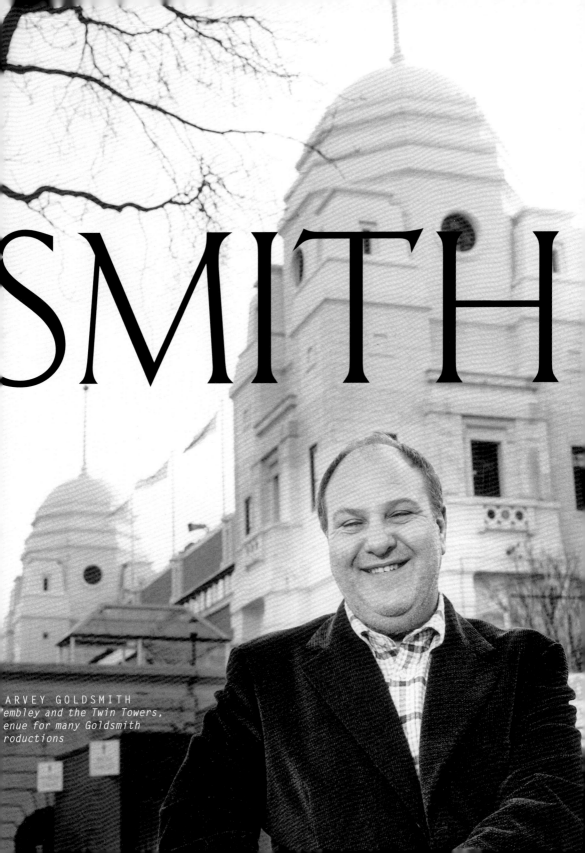

SMITH

unpredictable world of classical music and opera. His innovations are well-known – rock extravaganzas such as the 1985 charity spectacular *Live Aid* and the introduction to this country of arena opera and giant classical recitals such as *Pavarotti in the Park*. Never before in Britain had either genre been staged on such a scale. Because of all this, Harvey Goldsmith is probably the best-known impresario in the mass market.

All the more dramatic then his recent fall from grace and the collapse of his company. It happened with all the flamboyance and explosive spontaneity of one of his own events. On Thursday 30 September 1999, *The Guardian* carried the following headline:

"Goldsmith Empire Faces Final Curtain: The Eclipse of An Impresario". The receivers had been called in to Harvey Goldsmith Entertainments Ltd. and its parent company, Goldsmith's Allied Entertainments Group.

Total eclipse

The news vividly illustrated the precariously tipping see-saw which every impresario must straddle, with massive financial stakes at one end balanced by potential high rewards at the other. There had been an accumulation of factors, but in the end it was one failed concert spectacular that shattered Goldsmith's equilibrium. He had organised a high profile festival in Plymouth to celebrate the August eclipse of the sun. Expected audiences of 25,000 failed to materialise, and in the event only 7000

turned up. The company faced an estimated loss of £750,000. The game, it seemed, was up.

Those who thought so, however, underestimated Harvey Goldsmith and the loyalty he commands from so many of his performers. By November he had established a new company, Artiste Management Productions, and was already planning British tours of Sting, Jools Holland and the band Black Sabbath. He had taken a savage knock, but survived to fight another day.

When I meet the impresario, though, this crisis is some weeks away and to all appearances it is business as usual. He occupies a large but unostentatious building in the heart of London's Camden Town, minutes away from the famous street market.

Goldsmith is approaching his mid-fifties. He joins me at a table, facing the glass wall so that he will not miss anything that happens on the rest of the floor, and orders two cups of tea from his waiting secretary. Gravel-voiced with a cockney accent, he tells me about his youth, growing up in North London. Despite a great love of jazz, he decided to be a pharmacist.

"I went to the college of technology in Brighton to study pharmacy. Very early on in my university career I arrived late for a Friday morning lecture, and as I was the last one in, I got elected to be the pharmacy rep to the student union. This was a post which nobody ever wanted, because pharmacy was a six days a week course and we had to work bloody hard.

Butter wouldn't melt...
"So I went to my first student union gathering and said, 'Alright, where is this big social life that is meant to be going on here in Sussex?' They looked at me in surprise, and I decided that we could do better. I suggested that we open up a club. The president of the union asked me who I was. When I replied 'Pharmacy' they all laughed because no pharmacy rep had ever turned up to a meeting before. But he said, 'Do it.' So I did; I opened a club in the college called 'Club 66', named after the year it opened, and it became a huge success."

What was different about it, I ask? He shrugs: "We got bands in. We took over the common room, darkened it up and did things a little bit different from just having a bar in a room. We put candles on the tables, bowls of nuts and crisps and stuff and made a bit of an effort. Within about three weeks this place was packed to the gunnels. I was the king down there because I was the only person in the history of the student union who had ever made a surplus, which went to subsidise the football and rugby. I put on all sorts of gigs. I remember one rag ball I put on which featured John Mayall's Blues Band with a young guitarist in it called Eric Clapton. We became friendly and he came to stay with me and introduced me to a load of different acts.

"I got more and more involved in the student union. At one point I was vice-president and was going to run for president but my professor warned me off, apparently my studies were suffering."

The student, however, was becoming tired of lectures. He decided to take a break, and headed for America. It was the turning point in his life: "I went to New York and bought a $99, 99-day Greyhound bus ticket. I went from one end of America to the other. That was an incredible experience. I saw more of America than I've ever seen since. I just went where the bus took me.

"I ended up in San Francisco. As we were going over the Golden Gate Bridge, going Downtown to the bus depot, there was a whole gathering going on in this park. It looked interesting, so I went to have a look. It was a concert with The Grateful Dead playing. Somehow or other I got backstage, met the band, they befriended me and I suddenly realised there was more to life than pharmacy."

Learning on the hoof
Had meeting The Grateful Dead taught him anything about the business side of putting on concerts? He laughs: "This was the 60s. There wasn't a business side! It just happened. It was a whole different form of music emerging for the first time. There were two organisations which were mounting all these concerts. And they were advertising these events with a new form of poster-art which I had never seen before. I managed to do a deal with both of them to

represent them and sell their posters in England."

How, I ask, was that managed? The reply is vintage Goldsmith: "I told them I was the biggest poster distributor in Europe."

In this case, however, the great bluffer had been out-bluffed. He joined a poster-company called "Big O Posters" which had recently opened in Kensington Market: "I came in as junior partner, very full of myself, and proudly told the guy who ran it that I had an exclusive arrangement with the people who did these posters. He burst out laughing and told me that everyone who came back from San Francisco had a deal with these guys!"

Nevertheless, Goldsmith was happy with the company and took time out from college to work with them. He never went back. He continues: "We were working with International Times and a publication called *Oz* magazine. We were keeping *Oz* going by publishing the posters in the middle as a pull-out, then the magazine got busted for obscenity. We published the first few issues of *Time Out*. I still had one finger in the music side of things, which was more explosive than ever, and I met The Stones and The Who, Jimi Hendrix and all the bands that were happening. So I began to put on benefits to help *Oz*, and our place at Kensington Market became a bit of a Mecca. People used to hang out – Rod Stewart, Ronnie Wood, Roger Taylor and Bryan May from Queen. It wasn't a business, you didn't know what you were doing. Every day you just woke up and followed your path."

After a year, he was recruited by the pop singer Manfred Mann to help run his London office. Some time later, Manfred Mann casually asked whether his young employee "did touring". 'Oh yes,' he was assured. "Well, tour me," said Mann.

Fun in the park

Thus he learned how to tour, and then teamed up with an old friend from university, Michael Alfandary: "We lobbied Camden Council to let us do something for the local kids – there was nothing around, you see. The council gave us the Camden Roundhouse and told us to produce a festival. So we put on two weeks of events at the venue. Then the council gave us Parliament Hill Fields and suggested we do something there. So we came up with the idea of putting on these free concerts. The council gave us £250, and somehow we made it work. The crowds were phenomenal. We had 25,000 for one, 30,000 for another. I began to realise the real business potential.

"Next, the Greater London Council came to us and said, 'We've got this place called Crystal Palace. So you think you could do something there?' We came up with a series of garden parties, as we called them. The first was with Pink Floyd. They were an instant success and we started to make good money."

Talent spotter

Part of that success was due to a keen eye for spotting new talent. Harvey Goldsmith's discoveries over the years have ranged from Harry Connick, Jnr to Bryan Adams. Is this, I enquire, a talent he has always had?

"You've got to have it," he replies firmly, "You need an eye for the talent and an ear for the music. And you've got to be able to pick out talent that can transmit what they're doing. The edge of the stage is a barrier, and the magic of an artist is how they jump over that barrier and get to an audience. And when you see an act that can *reach* an audience, you know there is something you can do with them. I spend as much time watching the audience as I do the band. That's what makes a star. And the trick of what I do is picking that talent out at an early stage and then nurturing them along and making it work. Picking up the positive energy of it – when you know something is moving along a positive route.

"The last element is timing. Artists have a kind of inbuilt clock in them and somehow I know when the alarm bell goes off, when it's starting to happen, and that's my secret."

He began to tour the acts from the Crystal Palace show, backed by the producing company John And Tony Smith Presents. This, he recalls, is where he really learned his trade: "I started putting on event after event. And I learned the whole gamut of the business, from being a roadie upwards. We became so successful that we soon found ourselves in conflict with John and Tony Smith, our original backers! Because John was touring The Beatles and The Stones and all these other acts. So we all merged and

formed a company called John Smith Entertainments. After a while, we found a new band called Genesis, and Tony Smith left to become their manager. At the end of 1975, the others went to manage bands and I just carried on promoting, which was all I wanted to do."

What was it about promoting, I ask, that was so captivating?

"I like the idea of moving around, working with different artists. I didn't like the idea of working with one act who would be in your face 24 hours a day. It's a marriage, when you agree to manage an act."

Crazy for you
In January 1976, Harvey Goldsmith Entertainments was launched: "I set up shop at 7 Welbeck Street. The first band I promoted was called Lynyrd Skynyrd, who were an extraordinary bunch of people. Fantastic musicians, but completely and totally crazy. One of them was found one night at about two in the morning running stark naked down Marble Arch with a meat cleaver, trying to kill a cat because he thought it was a lion."

Paradoxically, in the crazy society in which he moved, it was the steady Goldsmith who stood out. This, he explains, endeared him to the artists: "I was Mister Normal in a charmed, surreal world. All the acts liked me because they were completely off their trolleys all day long, and I was the one who would bring them back to reality and nurtured them through it. It was very bizarre. They trusted me to grab them back from the brink and help them stay on an even keel. So I was accepted within their community."

Empire building

Harvey Goldsmith's empire continued to build, turning over millions of pounds every year (according to figures obtained from the British Library, by 1997 his company had reached profits of over £1,817,000 and promoted an average of 200 shows a year). Goldsmith, who by now had the title "impresario" written in his passport, continued to add to his list of artists. Queen, Elton John, Paul McCartney and many more knew that they could rely on him to put on and sell a terrific show.

Apartheid row

Then, in 1985, Goldsmith hit his first spot of trouble. He and his partner Ed Simons sold their business to the South African company Kunick Leisure. This was during the height of apartheid, and there was an enormous outcry from the entertainment world, including many of Goldsmith's clients. Stevie Wonder cancelled a planned UK visit, George Michael even changed his managers because they were about to join Harvey Goldsmith's organisation. Even today, he is still puzzled and angry: "I was in no way supporting apartheid, even implicitly. It was the complete reverse, but somehow or other the business took a different viewpoint. What actually happened was that a guy called Sol Kersner, who had started Sun City, was as upset

about apartheid as anybody and wanted to get out. So the investing with us was a way for him to try and get away. We were part of the *anti*-apartheid movement, but suddenly everyone began accusing us of supporting apartheid by forging business links with South Africa. Someone even did a hit song about Sun City and the whole issue. Kersner got maligned, even though his was the only major entertainment organisation that had equal rights for everybody *and* he was trying to escape. But nobody would listen. We had to buy ourselves out of Kunick and sever the links."

Pavarotti

In 1986 Goldsmith flirted with the world of classical music for the first time. The situation came about almost by accident: "In the summer of 1985 I booked Earl's Court for Bruce Springsteen, who at the time declared that he would never play open air as long as he lived, and he then decided to play Wembley Stadium! In the meantime I had paid for Earl's Court, and was stuck with finding an act for it. It suddenly struck me that classical music had never really had a voice, and I thought about some huge orchestral extravaganza or something. Then I heard about Luciano Pavarotti, who had just done his first big arena concert. I knew that I had found my act. There was a history of opera singers becoming great stars. Caruso had set the pathway, then there was Maria Callas, Tito Gobbi, Mario Lanza on film, and Pavarotti knew this and realised that he could also become such a star. He was a larger than life character, he had a great voice, and he projected a warmth across the stage that I'd never seen before or since. You could sit in the back of the hall and feel enveloped in the warmth emanating from this man.

"It took me a year to persuade Pavarotti to come over. When he finally did come, he played Wembley and scored a *huge* success – it was that concert which really started him on the path to fame in that side of the industry."

It seems somewhat surprising, particularly in that era before such ventures became common fare, that a leading opera singer would easily entrust his concerts to a pop promoter. How, I ask, did he win the singer's trust?

"His manager initially sent me a curt telegram wondering who the hell I was. I said, 'Here's x amount of money that I think you could earn and I think he could be a huge star in England outside of the opera house.' Unbeknownst to me, he was having enormous rows with Covent Garden and didn't know what to do about his career in England, and this became the answer. The money sorted the details out. When we met we became instant friends."

Does Goldsmith like classical music or opera? He is uncharacteristically slow to answer:

For the love of a good tune

"I like classical music. I like certain very stirring parts of classical music. I was always intrigued by opera, because opera to me is the culmination of all the art forms. It's the best music, the best singing, it includes ballet, there's a strong story, the whole thing melds together. I was fascinated by it."

Goldsmith likes the "best bits" of famous works. In this he represents the man on the street for whom he caters. But is that enough? As he remembers, when he announced that first Pavarotti concert he faced outrage amongst the opera-going public that "stopped just short of threatening letters".

After the success of Pavarotti, however, the impresario was keen to expand his classical operations. He went to the agent Mark McCormack and suggested a new enterprise, Classical Productions Ltd. This would bring to the UK a previously unseen phenomenon: arena opera.

Arena opera

"I knew that if we could make a big arena feel like a theatre, we could open up opera for a huge amount of people who can't get to see it. We could literally open the doors, stop opera being closeted in these small, closely-knit, very elite environments. And there was a much bigger audience for opera than anyone had ever thought. In Europe, of course, Verona and other big arenas had been putting on opera on a massive scale for years and I thought that if they could do it, so could we.

"It had to be done in the centre of town so that people could get there, and the only building available was Earl's Court, which is not an easy building in any sense. It's designed for exhibitions, not music. But I knew its pitfalls – I put on an acoustically horrendous concert with The Rolling Stones there in my first year – and I felt I could handle the space. So I struck up this partnership with Mark McCormack and we announced a staging of *Aida*. Much to my amazement we sold 122,000 tickets; maybe more people were going to see *Aida* in one week than had ever seen it in total before! And it was sung in Italian!"

Despite the exaggeration, this *Aida*, which Goldsmith imported from Verona, did open up opera as a mass entertainment concept. The critics were unimpressed, though, and the promoter is inclined to agree: "It was a rather drab, if spectacular, production. For our next project I suggested to McCormack that we go ahead and produce our own. We trawled around and analysed it and concluded that *Carmen* was the best bet. It is the most popular, it has got music that anybody can understand and, as I said at the time, it has got a hit in each act."

This production, set in a bullring, starred Maria Ewing and was a triumph. It is, I start to say, often cited as the greatest example of arena opera… "Ever!" he finishes. In this country, I add. He shakes his head vigorously: "*Not* in this country. I'd say in the *world*. I met the director Steven Pimlott and the designer Stefano Lazaridis and took the pair of them to Earl's Court one day when it was empty and we sat upstairs in the gallery. I said to them, 'I want to make

this huge barn intimate.' We sat there for four hours and talked it through, Lazaridis started to doodle, and I suggested that we put everything in the middle, to draw everyone's attention into the centre. Out of that came this extravaganza which is one of my proudest moments. I did a lot of research and got totally immersed in every aspect of the production. Casting, choice of orchestra, the look of it, how it all worked, the marketing, everything. We created a real spectacle and it was incredible."

No expense was spared. The toreador Escamillio had a full retinue, a carriage and horses, he and Don Jose had their Act Three fight on a huge rope-bridge suspended high above the action, and just in case the audience might get bored, they were treated in Act Four to an authentic Spanish flamenco troupe. The whole enterprise cost approximately £4 million. It toured the world, and was a success everywhere. I ask whether it ever turned a profit.

"It did, not a lot. It was a hugely expensive show. Also, we decided to televise it and Sky had just started. Rupert Murdoch was looking for a vehicle with which to get brownie points from Margaret Thatcher. He realised that if he put on something classical he would thwart everybody who denounced him as a devil who was going to change the face of television for the worse. He therefore acquired the live television rights, which Thatcher even picked up and used in a speech defending him. It helped him sort the whole BSkyB business out."

Star turns

Carmen was one of many classical ventures to come. I wonder whether the opera stars he has dealt with were as fussy as some of his pop acts had been?

"Not at all. Just the same as the great rock 'n' roll stars, they had their quirks and madnesses. But I didn't change. If you get stuck into these guys they'll drive you completely doolally and if you pre-empt what they want and give it to them they can't argue. Also, they realised that they were suddenly being promoted as superstars, which they have never got with the Royal Opera, where they were just performers who lived or died by that night's performance. And they had never seen 20,000 people a night before. We were making them into stars. And they became stars."

While he has been working in opera, I suggest, the industry seems to have come to increasingly resemble the pop world.

"Of course it has. To me it's very simple. I'm in the entertainment business. It doesn't matter whether I'm working with Boyzone, The Rolling Stones or The Three Tenors. It's entertainment. What was happening was that the classical world was not entertaining. They were too much into themselves, there were too many egos. I gave the artists an escape valve. McCormack and I allowed the classical singers to become icons for a mass audience."

Pavarotti in the park

A newspaper article once quoted Harvey Goldsmith describing his idea of hell as waking up on the morning of an open air concert and seeing torrential rain outside. Then, in 1991, came *Pavarotti in the Park*, a giant free concert in Hyde Park, and the heavens opened. Had his nightmare finally come to pass? He laughs.

"It certainly was very strange. The night before, at about nine o' clock, I was walking around with the St John's Ambulance people and the fire brigade, deciding how many more water stands we were going to put in because it was so hot we thought a lot of people would pass out. When I woke up in the morning I looked out and said, 'My God, look at what's happening out there.' Ever the eternal optimist, I kept saying that it would blow away soon. It didn't, it just kept on and on.

"I spoke to Pavarotti about it; 'Look, whatever happens the stage is covered so you can still perform.' He was very worried that there might be no audience. When we got there, the audience was just incredible. Tens of thousands had turned up. The atmosphere was *unbelievable*. Luckily it was warm; if it had been cold and wet it would have been horrible.

"A few minutes after the concert started, and remember we had the Prince and Princess of Wales and 90 per cent of the Cabinet out there in the front, I looked out and I could see a lot of jostling going on. People had umbrellas up and the audience behind were yelling that they couldn't see. I knew that I had to deal with this. I rushed onstage, passed Pavarotti in the wings and hurriedly said, 'Hope you don't mind, I've got to make an announcement.' He thought I might be about to stop the concert.

"Before he could say 'What the hell are you doing on my stage?', I raced past him and made the following statement, 'For the convenience of all and the inconvenience of some could you please put your umbrellas down?' And there was this roar of approval from the audience. Everybody but a bunch of Germans and a bunch of Italians put their umbrellas down. Even the celebrities in the front!

"I shot back offstage, passing a puzzled and frankly miffed Pavarotti for the second time. He then walked out onstage to continue and the audience went BERSERK. His eyes lit up and the whole thing took off from that point. That made the concert, no question. He was unstoppable after that! People still come up to me at airports and other places and prod me, saying, 'I was there, that day in Hyde Park, I remember exactly what happened and it will live with me always.'"

The Three Tenors
Goldsmith's association with Pavarotti developed still further when he began to promote The Three Tenors. The act, consisting of Pavarotti, Placido Domingo and Jose Carreras, had been a sensation at the Caracalla Baths in Rome in 1990, and more concerts and a world tour followed.

From the beginning, Harvey Goldsmith was an admirer: "We were going to get involved with the original Three Tenors concert. In fact I did in the end, helping them to sell the TV broadcast, which was extremely difficult at first, particularly in America. I had The Rolling Stones on at Wembley Stadium that night, and while that concert was going on, I had a big screen set up behind the stage to watch the Three Tenors!

"Tibor Rudas, who was looking after Pavarotti, came up with the idea of reviving the act and we got fully involved with it then, both in Dodgers' Stadium, then we did Pavarotti in New York's Central Park and then The Three Tenors here in London."

Did he find, I wonder, Domingo and Carreras to be natural showmen in the league of Pavarotti?

"They lived up to his standard. For all three of them it was a real buzz, they enjoyed trying to outdo each other. Friendly rivalry."

Now, a decade after they first joined forces, all three tenors are nudging retirement age and impresarios around the world are already hunting for their successors with a ruthlessness that irritates their English counterpart: "The Three Tenors and the various female divas came through naturally. The problem now is that people are being pushed too hard, they are being forced through and that is wrong. There are no boundaries and there is no fixed entry point, talent comes from wherever it comes from. You can force it up to a point, but then the talent itself has to take over.

Clouds on the horizon

At the same time, he believes talent must be sought out and encouraged. To this end, he sought in 1992 to create an annual National Music Day. In that first year 1,500 music groups across the UK applied to take part, from schoolchildren to Eric Clapton and Elton John. Never given enough government subsidy or commercial sponsorship, it was doomed to failure and stuttered to a halt after several years. It was a project close to its creator's heart: "It was an umbrella to tell everybody in Britain that there is a lot more to life than the pop charts, and a stimulus for people to think about and create new ideas. The industry didn't accept it at all. They couldn't see it, for them it was too unfocused. I just wanted everyone to go and listen to music, to try it and also to participate. There was to be music in every nook and cranny. We never had the resources to fix it in the calendar. However, we had five or six years of growth where we got up to something like 2,500 events in one year."

In an ominous warning of what was eventually to follow, Goldsmith's business was beset by financial troubles in 1996. The company had begun to produce films and scored a success with the virtual reality thriller *Lawnmower Man*, starring Pierce Brosnan. Then came *Lawnmower Man II* which lost the company a reported £1.7 million. This, allied to a legal dispute overseas and a downvaluing of his film library, meant that Harvey Goldsmith was in some trouble.

"I wasn't personally involved in the movies at all," he explains. "It was a string which we were trying to develop alongside the concerts. The problems were due to a set of unrelated circumstances – we produced 12 or 14 films in total. *Lawnmower Man II* was a disaster because, firstly, the costs went sky-high. Then our leading man, Pierce Brosnan, got the James Bond part and we did not want to stand in his way and make him do the sequel. We parted with our distributor in America. It all added up and yet we were too far gone to stop production."

Flatley, yes!

Goldsmith began to fight back by capitalising on the latest entertainment phenomenon – Irish dance: "The *Riverdance* thing came up. I was asked to go and see it and get involved right at the beginning, but was unable to get up to Ireland. Suddenly it turned and became big and I had missed it. Then I went to see it in London and met Michael Flatley and his co-star Jean Butler and I said to both of them, 'When you're ready, come and talk to me.' Six months later I got a phone call from Michael's manager; he had left *Riverdance* and was unsure exactly what to do. I told him that I would create a show around him. So we developed *Lord of the Dance*. From those two shows, the whole dance idiom started to

MICHAEL

CODRON

Ask any of the theatrical impresarios in this book who among their peers they esteem the most and the reply will often be Michael Codron. Duncan Weldon is quite voluble on the subject, Bill Kenwright hints at the fact heavily, and once a year Thelma Holt reputedly asks Codron to marry her.

The reason is that Codron oozes not only style, but integrity. Ever since, aged 27, he had his first hit – Bamber Gascoigne's comedy revue *Share My Lettuce* – Codron

has picked and chosen his productions with finesse. He has never been a flashy producer in the manner of Weldon or Cameron Mackintosh. He does not spend vast amounts on marketing or lavish first night parties. Instead, he has focused his efforts on finding and nurturing a generation of new writers. The first major author he discovered was Harold Pinter, whose play *The Birthday Party* he produced in1958. It was a famous flop at the time, but

Codron kept faith with Pinter and *The Caretaker* followed two years later.

There were many others after Pinter: Alan Ayckbourn, Joe Orton, John Mortimer, Tom Stoppard, David Hare, Christopher Hampton, Michael Frayn, Simon Gray. During the 1960s and beyond Codron ushered in a multitude of fresh, original voices to the West End. They challenged and overthrew the rather polite, conventional old order. Not, one might add, without a fight. In 1964 Peter Cadbury of the powerful ticket agency Keith Prowse joined Emile Littler, president of the Society of West End Theatre Managers in producing a list of "dirty" shows. In pride of place was Codron's production of Joe Orton's *Entertaining Mr Sloane*. In a fury, Codron resigned from Littler's executive. He received powerhouse support from Laurence Olivier and Kenneth Tynan at the National Theatre, and from Peter Hall at the RSC. When the dust settled, it was Codron who was left standing.

And he remains standing, though he is now 70 and his rebellious new playwrights have themselves become the established order – braving out the gunshots from young pretenders like Mark Ravenhill and Patrick Marber with their unflinchingly explicit new plays. Still, Codron is guardian of his writers' mature work as he was of their emergence. And, one senses, until Ayckbourn himself (Codron's most prolific playwright feeds him at least a play a year) lets up, Codron will stay at his post.

Codron conforms to the stereotype of the impresario in that he chain-smokes cigars – several burnt-out cigar butts lie in the ashtray on his desk, gazed at by two miniature crocodiles. He invites me to take a seat among the gathering of ornamental reptiles in his office.

Love of new writing

Michael Codron has emphatically not played safe during most of his career, but he has almost always backed winners.

My first question is, as we sit down and dine, when did he first decide to combine his keen business sense with his love for theatre? Codron's face is impassive: "How do we know that there is a love of theatre? You are presuming that there has to be. You might better phrase it by saying 'when did I decide to make theatre my profession', yes? And then grow to love it."

So did that love come later? "I don't want to disillusion you, but love didn't come into it. It seemed to me that I had a feel for the business, I had a liking for theatre. But I've never been as passionate about theatre as other people you may be interviewing. It is my business, but if you came to my home you would see no evidence of what I do for a living, unlike other people who have their posters up and scatter mementos around the place. I do like people in the theatre, I'm at home in the theatre, obviously, but it's not an over-riding passion. I know Duncan Weldon and Bill Kenwright are much more passionate about it. I am, however, more interested in writing. I do like specific writers, and I do believe that new writing for the theatre has some sort of purpose in society.

The beginning

"I had done a lot of theatre when I was at St Paul's School and at Oxford. But I never expected to make it my living and I didn't see how one could do so."

Codron originally joined his family textile business, which he was eventually expected to take over. He remembers it as "a bit of a disaster". Soon he left, with a letter of introduction to the famous bandleader-turned-impresario Jack Hylton: "My mother's cousin's husband vaguely knew Jack Hylton, and he gave me this letter of introduction which said, "Don't give this man a job, he's already got a perfectly good job in his family business." Nevertheless, I got in to work for Hylton, because he was producing a play – more of an oratorio, Honneger's *Joan of Arc* – with Ingrid Bergman, who lived with the Italian film director Roberto Rosselini. And Bergman was touring the United States and had sent a list of costumes in Italian to Hylton. So Hylton asked me if I spoke Italian. I lied and said yes. I *kind* of spoke it. And I was taken on to translate the list, becoming the office boy. That's how I began."

Codron soon found himself in a rather embarrassing situation with the great Bergman. Being, in his own words, "a rather sensitive lad", he decided that the Bergman show needed a curtain-raiser. So, with Hylton's blessing, he found a production of *Giselle* by Ballet Rambert which seemed ideal. Madame Rambert was interested, and Codron brought her to Bergman's suite at the Savoy Hotel, so that the two could meet: "I knocked on the door, and she shouted that she wouldn't let us in until her expenses were paid. So I had to leave the bemused Madame Rambert standing in the corridor, run to a phone and call the office." Someone, it transpired, had forgotten to allow for Bergman's salary in the budget. Money was hurriedly sent to the hotel, and Codron and his illustrious guest had to wait. When it arrived, Bergman insisted that Codron kneel down and feed the ten pound notes individually under the door. "Eventually she let us in," he remembers, "She was drinking neat gin, which was a terrible shock for someone who was young and had idolised her."

Salad days

Codron soon had an impact on Hylton's business, when he persuaded the older man to take on Julian Slade's musical *Salad Days* (a production which inspired the five-year-old Cameron Mackintosh). Not a man who enjoys gazing into his own past, Codron sighs. "Is this all going to be going back into the beginning of the century, James?" I hasten to assure him that I will be moving along swiftly. He nods approvingly.

"I knew Julian Slade," he says, "because he used to write shows at Cambridge, and I was at Oxford and we used to go and see each other's productions. He put *Salad Days* on at Bristol; I thought it good enough to recommend to Jack. Jack put it into the Vaudeville Theatre. We thought we might get a year out of it, and it ran for five."

It was also successfully revived recently. "At the Vaudeville, and I then owned the Vaudeville. There we are – full circle!" Codron adds.

Breaking in

In 1957 Codron struck out for himself, "much too early" in his own opinion. Unable to afford an office, he worked from home:

"Jack decided to move on to television, and there was less and less for me to do, since much of my job was to go around and look for plays. I came across a play called *Ring For Catty*. Jack was going to produce it with Richard Attenborough starring. When Attenborough dropped out, Jack decided to drop the show. I, in my arrogance, asked to produce it myself. And that is how I learned to do it.

"You know, when you are working for someone else, the decisions you have to make are so different to when you're working on your own. It was quite a shock. I had no office, I had no staff, I began from scratch."

Ring For Catty, a hospital play which starred Patrick McGoohan, was performed at the Lyric Theatre on Shaftesbury Avenue. Codron was 25 and the show did not do well.

Next the fledgling producer attempted a play called *A Month of Sundays*, which he describes as "my attempt to do a good old-fashioned H M Tennant sort of piece". However, his investors proved to be 'very disreputable people' and let him down with the finance. Codron found himself in deep trouble with the bank and had to be bailed out by his father securing his overdraft. He remembers the humiliation well: "My father said, 'You're not cut out for this sort of thing. You've got one more chance to show what you can do, and then if you fail you'd better come back and work for me.'"

Much was therefore riding on Codron's third solo effort, an innovative review that he had spotted at Cambridge. It was Bamber Gascoigne's *Share My Lettuce*. The show opened in Brighton with Kenneth Williams and the unknown Maggie Smith heading the cast, and – once it reached London's Lyric Theatre, Hammersmith – was an enormous hit, establishing Codron as a force in his own right. From there he attracted the interest and support of the legendary literary agent Peggy Ramsay, who began to send Codron all her new plays and introduced him to a flock of brilliant young authors. When, in the 60s, he took over London's Arts Theatre and mounted a play every four weeks, he became increasingly reliant on Peggy Ramsay's steady supply of scripts and authors.

A producer to watch

Tom Stoppard, who later became one of Michael Codron's most bankable playwrights, and first met him when he interviewed him as a journalist in 1962, remembers Codron being the producer to watch: "Binkie Beaumont had dominated things for so long, and Michael Codron – along with one or two others – changed the face of the West End. He struck me as young, interesting, enterprising. The new face of commercial producing."

Beneath the laughter

Many of Codron's big successes, from *Share My Lettuce* onwards, have been comedies, whereas one tends to think of a man who champions new writing in a rather serious way. He answers with an observation that Alan Ayckbourn once made: "I pose as a serious producer but underneath I am, as Ayckbourn said about me, 'a vulgar man with an impeccable streak' – or is it the other way round? I love comedy, and comedy itself can have a serious impact."

And somebody like Ayckbourn who uses comedy to unearth serious issues or emotions, would therefore seem to be a perfect fit?

"Yes. I was at the cutting edge of the whole movement of, if you like, black comedy. There was no such term before I began to do the plays by Joe Orton and Simon Gray. All of a sudden people began saying, "These are black comedies". These writers wrote comedies which were, in my view, serious plays with comedic elements.

"Even when I did Terence Frisby's *There's A Girl In My Soup* there was a lot of unrest in the gallery. The gods were very powerful then, the gallery first-nighters were an extremely retroactive bunch. They always wanted Ivor Novello or Noël Coward or those very well-made plays. They didn't like what I was doing at all. And because at the end of *There's A Girl In My Soup* a girl sleeps with a man who is much older than her and then doesn't marry him, it was generally regarded as 'another of Michael Codron's dirty plays'."

Shock of the new

When Codron heard that Mark Ravenhill had written a play called *Shopping and Fucking* he reportedly called the event "the end of civilisation as we know it". Has he not now become a reactionary?

"I said it ironically, it is a line from Alan Bennett's play *The Old Country*. But you might be right, I may well have become a reactionary. I read *Shopping and Fucking* when it was considered for the Peggy Ramsay Award, and we all thought it was going to do well, but we didn't want to give it a prize. I like Kevin Elliot's and Jonathan Harvey's plays much better."

Codron himself never considered that Pinter's *The Birthday Party* might be part of any new style: "I didn't think of it as new wave at all. I was astounded when it was regarded as something rather obscure. It seemed to me just like a well-constructed play with something mysterious happening. In fact, looking at it now, if it is badly done there can seem to be something of the repertory theatre about it."

But certainly, I argue, it changed the frame of reference for audiences. "No, there was a movement. There was Beckett. Pinter may have been the first British writer in that movement."

A new style of writing is destined to fail initially, while playgoers adjust to the change. Perhaps *The Birthday Party* was a sacrifice to that rule.

"I think it probably was," he replies. "In a very drastic way. I'm trying to think of a modern parallel. One might say Sarah Kane who wrote *Blasted*, if one believed in her talent. That's why one doesn't know if these sensational writers are just going to stutter out."

"I was discussing Joe Orton with someone last night, and I wondered what would have happened to him if he had lived. What he would have become – what does that style of writer do when there is nothing left to shock?" Young firebrands soften up as they get older. He agrees.

"Yes. *I've* softened up. Of course you do, you must if you are of an age. The great danger is in looking back, which is why I won't revive any of my plays.

"All I was doing was putting on plays which I liked and which I thought were conventional. What must have happened was that my taste was one step ahead of the public – it was nothing more courageous than that. And they took it, in the main. That was part of the trick."

A writer's producer

Yet Codron was far more proactive in shaping the plays themselves than he admits. It was he who persuaded Orton to change the ending of *Entertaining Mr Sloane*. Do writers always trust his judgment, I ask?

"It varies. Alan Ayckbourn has usually, by the time I come to do it, already directed it and tried it out at his theatre in Scarborough. It would be difficult to get him to change much. Simon Gray and Michael Frayn, on the other hand, write and rewrite, as does Tom Stoppard.

"The writer is the person in the whole team that I am closest to. And it is mainly a question of getting the right team. Probably your fate is sealed before you even go into the rehearsal room. When you are lucky, you often know on paper that the chemistry is right and unless something catastrophic happens things usually work."

According to Alan Ayckbourn, Codron is the quintessential writers' producer:

"He's a good reader of scripts," comments Ayckbourn, "There are some producers who don't really read the play at all. They like the idea, or the idea of the principal casting. Michael is deeply concerned about the scripts. He phones you up and asks if he doesn't understand things."

Yet there are certain actors, notably Michael Gambon and Felicity Kendal (who has appeared in eight of his plays), who have prospered in several Michael Codron productions. Is he, I enquire, an actors' man as well as a writers' man?

"Yes," replies Codron, "but there are other people who are much better at it than I am. Duncan Weldon especially. His career has been based on finding the right vehicles for the right stars. And he has done very well. I work a different way. I find a play I like and then go to actors, stars, who I like and often ones with whom I have worked before."

Stars, he believes, are a necessity. "There will always be the freak exceptions, but in the main you must have stars. How ever many pats on the back you want to give me for new writing, if you look back, I have always tried to get a star. Because the public wants to see actors working with good material. And if you don't have a name, they wonder what is wrong with the show and why haven't you managed to get a better cast?"

New faces

He breaks off to ask me whether I plan to include some younger producers in the book – "You should, you know" – and commends to me his former employee, Richard Jordan who he believes "is a young Michael Codron". I promise to talk to him. But several other impresarios, Duncan Weldon in particular, are very despondent about the future of commercial producing. Weldon thinks that the age of the great impresarios is over. Codron smiles, and says mischievously: "There are two things that strike me about Duncan. One is that he has more energy and enthusiasm than any producer I know. The other is that he is always sounding the death knell for the commercial West End. It is a great way to discourage the young competition though, isn't it?"

What about Codron himself, I ask? Are there any new directions that he wants to explore? Is there is anything left to achieve? His answer is typically self-aware: "No. I'm keeping going, a little beyond my sell-by date now. In the sense that it's getting more difficult for me to find plays that I like and that appeal to the public, because that public has whittled down somewhat. Again, for everything I say there are exceptions, because you can get *An Inspector Calls* which goes on and on because it was done in an extraordinary way. But for a play now, the audience has dwindled.

"When I used to do, say, any of Tom Stoppard's plays, *The Real Thing* for example, a hit would keep going. Now you're lucky to get six or nine months. Mainly because the actors won't stay. The first thing an actor asks you is 'What's the release?' Because there's so many other things to do, there's also the competition from the National, where they do three different plays six times a week rather than the same part eight times a week, which is much less stimulating. That's our main competition.

"But I will stay on, hoping that I can still do one or two plays a year that my writers still want me to do."

Nights to Remember:

ALAN

ALAN SIEVEWRIGHT *in his famous "salon" surrounded by his stage designs & Oliver Messel chairs*

SIEVEWRIGHT

From the late 1960s to the early 1980s London was home to an extraordinary operatic series. International stars would fly in, give a single concert performance of a work so rare that Britain – and sometimes the world – had not heard it for decades, and then make an equally quick exit to sing their umpteenth *Tosca* or *Carmen* on the standard circuit. Thus was the city treated to Joan Sutherland and Marilyn Horne in Rossini's *Semiramide* at the Theatre Royal, Drury Lane, Montserrat Caballe and Tatiana Troyanos in Donizetti's *Roberto Devereux*, Placido Domingo in Ponchielli's

La Gioconda, the first ever performance of Puccini's *Turandot* with the original, complete ending and much, much more. A few of these events were recorded, some spawned a lasting legacy, pieces which were then taken up by other opera or record companies. Together they constituted, as Bernard Levin once noted, "a treasury of operatic performances (those who saw them) will never forget".

The man behind these spectacular evenings of discovery is not a household name. Yet this does not matter to Alan Sievewright. He cares little for public recognition; what delights him are the friendships he has struck up with the singers he so admires. Domingo, Carreras, Horne, Caballe, Sutherland, the great bass Ruggero Raimondi (a Sievewright discovery). It is to the greater glory of talents like these that he has dedicated his professional life.

In terms of volume, fame and profit it is true that Sievewright has done less than the other impresarios in this book. He has never followed the standard repertoire, preferring to be different and to produce works which do not interest the mass market impresarios, who might need greater turnover. He treads his own path, slowly and with care. He lavishes the same attention on his Maria Callas exhibition as he would on a concert of *Medée* with Grace Bumbry, the all-star *Fanfare for the New World* concert he mounted in Liverpool for 15,000 people in 1992 (with Sir Peter Ustinov and the King and Queen of Spain),

or Mozart's *Il Re Pastore* with a promising but unknown young cast for the British Lebanese Association in 1999.

The unsung pioneer
It was Sievewright who first re-introduced the idea of a stage upon a stage in his production of *Les Huguenots* at the Royal Albert Hall in 1968, an innovation which has since been used at Glyndebourne and elsewhere.

Starting out as a designer, he spent three years in the 1960s working for Warner Brothers at Pinewood and then Elstree film studios. The atmospheric flat where he lives and works above Hyde Park Square is "in the Regency French style".

The size of the ivory-white doors grabs your attention first. Approximately twice a man's height, with large golden handles, they tower imposingly over the visitor. Inside, there is no diminution in scale. Sievewright's abode is dominated by a vast lounge. It has been for years a kind of musical "salon" where the muses of art and music mingle with the famous and the merely inspired at Sievewright's soirées. It's shadowed interior is crammed full of operatic artifacts – dizzying collages of Maria Callas memorabilia, photographs of the great stars, costume and set designs in gilded frames.

Music in the blood
Sievewright is an affable man, content to make things happen when he feels like it, rather than make a fortune. Physically

large, his passion for opera is limitless and he enthuses about it in appropriately dramatic tones. One is reminded of Orson Welles. He speaks as a diva might sing; declamatory, sensitive and full of affection. There is no question that opera is his world.

And he grew up watching those stars from an early age. As a boy soprano and a more than passable pianist (he once gave a recital at the Royal Academy of Music), he was drawn to the world of music.

"I started to go in and out of the theatre regularly from about the age of eight. That gives one a head start of about ten years on one's contemporaries, who tend to get into opera and ballet in their late teens. I stood through the five hours of Wagner's *Götterdämmerung* when I was eleven. When you start early the barriers are broken down. You realise that this is a living art form. Everyone says it's dead. Well, if it is, the corpse won't lie down. And operas keep coming along and holding their place in the repertory – Britten's *Peter Grimes*, and more recently perhaps Jonathan Dove's *Flight* and John Adams' *Nixon In China* will last. But I love and want to present *Troilus and Cressida* by William Walton – but with *great* singers!"

He remains proud of the traditions of opera performance in Britain, but rueful because as a nation we do not appreciate them: "We have had wonderful pioneers in this country. Ninette de Valois, an amazing woman who created the Sadler's Wells Ballet, Lilian Baylis and the people who were new in my youth – Margot Fonteyn, Robert Helpmann and Maya Plisetskaya (Sievewright presented her in America in the 1990s at a performance attended by Madonna). We've done a great deal of useful exploration. It was Glyndebourne who blew the dust away from Mozart's *Idomeneo*." He points to a wall where reside two of the costume sketches for that production, signed by Oliver Messel and by its star Birgit Nilsson. "But the English always look at art as something which has nothing to do with real life. The Italians, by contrast, look at a tie and realise that it has been designed, and that *is* art."

Glamorous nights

After studying art and design, Sievewright won his contract with Warner Brothers and had what he describes as 'a very glamorous three years', working at the end of the studio system. During that time he was spotted by the designer Pierre Balmain. This led to a spell working in Balmain's studios in Paris. One day, Ginette Spanier, the house's famous *directrice*, told Sievewright that she had a surprise for him: "We arranged to meet for lunch outside the house of Christian Dior. She walked with me around the corner and pressed a doorbell. The door opened and there was Marlene Dietrich. I was being taken to lunch at Miss Dietrich's flat, we were eating in the kitchen and Dietrich was doing the cooking, liver. The first thing she said to me was, 'Do you like typewriters?', I thought I was going to get a boiled typewriter for lunch, but it turned out to be liver in the kitchen!" Later he found that she had an amazing collection of typewriters. It was the start of a long friendship, which lasted for six years, and he remembers her with tenderness. "Her knowledge and love of music was quite formidable. She started life as a violinist and would sometimes talk extremely interestingly about Beethoven."

Dietrich introduced him to a wealth of famous figures, such as Noël Coward, Lena Horne and many others. Dietrich's daughter inscribed her biography of her mother to Sievewright, "To Alan, how many memories we have together".

Other influential figures who made an impression were the conductors Jascha Horenstein, whom Sievewright convinced to buy a new 'midnight-blue' dinner suit, and Leopold Stokowski. Stokowski, he had been advised, would be charmed by the presence of a lovely woman, so he brought his attractive friend (later his producing partner), Denny Dayviss, to a party where the great maestro was holding court. Stokowski, he remembers, was so taken with Dayviss that he immediately came over to talk and dismissed anyone who tried to interrupt. These, he attests, were 'among the wonderful people whom I had the privilege to see and sometimes know, and who taught me much and influenced my taste'.

Ad hoc opera

In 1968 Alan Sievewright, together with his partners, Denny Dayviss and Michael Scott inaugurated their rare operas series. "The idea," says Sievewright, "really came from Alan Oxenberg, who had created the American Opera Society in New York. He put on star-studded concert operas at the Carnegie Hall – Callas went and did Bellini's *Il Pirata*, things like that. And we decided to do the same, with Caballe."

The first venture was Meyerbeer's *Les Huguenots,* starring Joan Sutherland and Martina Arroyo, conducted by Sutherland's husband, Richard Bonynge, at the Royal Albert Hall. The opera was semi-staged, with the singers all in evening dress on a raised stage behind the Philharmonia Orchestra. Sievewright, with the flair of the designer, created "simple gothic panels" for a set and provided Sutherland with an enormous throne – an authentic prop once used by Sarah Bernhardt. It was a success, and was turned into a commercial recording (Decca). This was swiftly followed by Marilyn Horne's British concert debut at the same venue. The team quickly got into their stride and over the next seven years mounted a further 23 shows.

The second production was Donizetti's *Lucrezia Borgia*, with Caballe and Raimondo, at the Royal Festival Hall: "Although she had previously sung here at Glyndebourne, it was that *Lucrezia* that made Caballe's name in England. She looked marvellous in this dark blue satin with this long coat edged in mink; she wasn't as big as she got later, God bless her. She acted, and was very dramatic. And we got Richard Bonynge to conduct, and because of that Joan Sutherland was in the audience with me and decided that she liked the opera. But she always said that the best Donizetti singer she ever heard was Montserrat that night."

The drama is in the music!

Sievewright, who believes that opera productions should emphasise the music before everything, claims that the audiences themselves enjoyed the chance to see the singers without the distraction of a tricksy production now out of control: "The performers were free to focus on the texts and the music. You know, the idea that singers didn't act until Callas is rubbish. Even if you go as far back as Giuditta Pasta, the acting is in the voice. You can intellectualise as much as you like. The intellect is terribly important, but it mustn't get in the way of the *meaning*. What needs to be said is all in the music." Then, as an afterthought, "And if possible there should be some sort of dramatic entrances and exits."

Stunning debuts

As well as introducing works to the British public, Sievewright brought about several important debuts. One of these was the British debut of the sensational soprano Elena Suliotis, in his 1968 *Nabucco* with Boris Christof and Cappuccili. Suliotis arrived, the press groped for hyperbole and, it seemed, a new star was made. But several years after her dramatic entrance, Suliotis abruptly exited the scene, never to

be seen on a professional stage again. It is commonly believed that she destroyed her voice by using it recklessly. Yet, I suggest, she was a singer who embodied Sievewright's ideal of dramatic conviction. He agrees, but believes that the press are wrong as to why she stopped: "Marilyn Horne said to me of Suliotis, 'This is the one truly dramatic singer of our time.' Most people don't understand about Suliotis. There were reasons for the problems she encountered. One day I said something to her. She didn't respond. I repeated myself, and it was only the third time that she turned and replied. What I didn't know until some years later was that she had been born with defective hearing on one side. She could never have the corrective operation because it might have damaged her further.

"Suliotis suffered from the pressure of being dubbed the new Callas. However, she had a firm technique – her singing teacher also taught Alfredo Krauss, Carlo Bergonzi, Renata Scotto and Fiorenza Cossotto, all of whom had extraordinarily long careers. Suliotis had a glorious six years. Then she hit a vocal crisis, which all singers have, and lost her confidence."

Although he is adamant that it did not happen to Suliotis, he does feel that singers today are thrust into the spotlight too fast and encouraged to do the wrong roles too early: "The impresario must be careful. There is a tremendous danger of causing singers to burn themselves out. Although much is in the *way* one sings. My dear friendship with Birgit Nilsson has taught me a lot. I once heard her say at a masterclass I arranged at Covent Garden (1992: Sievewright also presented an evening with Birgit Nilsson at the Donmar Warehouse in that year), 'It's not when you sing the heavy roles, it's how lightly you sing them."

Nurturing new talent
Sievewright has done his share to nurture young singers. Denny Dayviss had seen the young Jose Carreras in Spain and brought him over for his international debut in 1971, a concert of Donizetti's *Maria Stuarda*. However, it was, as he remembers, one of the later shows that rocketed Carreras to fame in Britain: "Denny went to see Caballe's first Norma in Barcelona. The Flavio came on, he's only got about two lines, and that was a young singer whom Caballe's brother Carlos had discovered, called Jose Maria Carreras. When he came over, it was clear that Denny and Carlos Caballe had been right. The press predicted that he wouldn't last more than two years.

"Jose's big moment came when Montserrat wanted to do Donizetti's last opera, *Caterina Cornaro*, in 1973. It was the single performance of the opera in this country ever, until I put it on again in 1998 with Julia Migenes and Bonynge. It was to star another Spanish tenor, Giacomo Aragall, because he was the only tenor in the world who knew it and had already done it at the San Carlo Opera House. Forty-eight hours before curtain up Aragall was ill. Jose had

flown over to see his great friend Caballe. And he said to me, 'I think I can do this'. So he went on. Montserrat's presence meant that all the record companies were there, in case they wanted to record her in it. And that's where they all noticed Carreras, who was a sensation!"

An evening with…
By 1977 Sievewright and Dayviss decided the time had come for a change and went their separate ways. Sievewright produced a high profile recording of Stravinsky's *The Soldier's Tale* with Glenda Jackson, the Irish actor Micheal MacLiammoir and Rudolf Nureyev (in his first acting role) for Argo Records. Then he hit upon a new idea. A series of celebrity interviews, conducted by Sievewright himself, in front of an audience entitled *Encore! An Evening With…* It was a project close to his heart: "The evenings were a cross between *Desert Island Discs*, with musical excerpts, and *This Is Your Life*. I was greatly encouraged in this by Placido Domingo, who thought it was a great idea. Far from being a sort of lecture, they were celebrations of great careers, like marvellous parties. The guest on stage was Dame Eva Turner. The first one I gave was in Wyndham's Theatre with Placido and it was a whacking great success. And many of my old friends came to support me. Ava Gardner sat in a box, Dame Alicia Markova came, and the audience enjoyed seeing these people. That's an old eighteenth-century idea, filling your boxes with famous celebrities, which is an added bonus for the audience.

At that time Birgit Nilsson was at the height of her fame and was singing *Elektra* at Covent Garden. She told me that she would come. Placido didn't believe me when I told him. In the second half Domingo said, 'I'd like one day to sing *Tristan und Isolde* with Birgit Nilsson.' And suddenly this voice from one of the boxes piped, 'Well hurry up!' I turned a spotlight on the box and it was Birgit, and she had brought the great conductor Carlos Kleiber with her.

"After that I took the Albery Theatre for Joan Sutherland. There were several more, including Victoria de los Angeles, Carreras and Ricciarelli, some of which we broadcast on radio. It climaxed with the *Evening with Elisabeth Schwarzkopf*, which was just phenomenal. At the end, Schwarzkopf asked me how many men worked on the event. There were five in the crew. She took five £20 notes from her purse and asked me to distribute them among the crew. An interesting lady."

Finally, in 1982 Sievewright and Denny Dayviss decided to produce another of their rare opera seasons. The venues for these series have been (not exclusively) the Theatre Royal, Drury Lane (ten productions, including *Jose Carreras and Friends* in 1991, with Agnes Baltsa, Katia Ricciarelli and Ruggero Raimondi). The first was Puccini's *Turandot* with Sylvia Sass, Franco Bonisolli, Barbara Hendricks and the London Symphony Orchestra, hardly rare, though less commonly performed than is the case today. However,

Sievewright included the full original ending by Puccini/Alfano – who had completed the opera after the composer's death, but had seen his work reduced to a bare minimum by its first conductor, Arturo Toscanini. Sievewright discovered this ending in Milan and gave Alfano's full completion its world premiere, at London's Barbican Hall, which was the first time ever that an opera had been staged there. Critics wrote at the time that it was unthinkable that the opera should be performed again in the standard version. It was a success which influenced many subsequent productions, and he followed it with performances of *La Gioconda* and *Medée*. (*La Gioconda* had been a success for Sievewright once before, with Sherrill Milnes in his British debut in 1969.)

A man of many parts
After its second brief flurry the concert operas series went dormant once more. Sievewright busied himself with successes in other, related areas. He mounted a tremendously successful Maria Callas exhibition at the Royal Festival Hall. Then he collaborated with the documentary maker Tony Palmer on a television profile of Callas, for which they both won awards. That heralded a move into television, where he has remained (though not exclusively) ever since – these days in partnership with the television producer Chris Hunt's Iambic Productions. Together they filmed documentaries on, variously, Robert Helpmann, Puccini, Caballe, Carreras and Dietrich, and more awards followed for him.

Online Classics

Now there is a new way to bring the singers he loves to the public. The internet beckons, and Sievewright (as artistic director with vast experience) and Chris Hunt have launched a service which will send video and audio performances of opera, ballet, classical music and opera across the World Wide Web. Called *Online Classics*, the early signs are good – big-name associates include Trevor Nunn and the Royal National Theatre, Jessye Norman, Montserrat Caballe and Jose Cura – and the company initially floated (albeit in the heady dotcom days when every new site automatically seemed to net a fortune) at a value of £7.2 million. Sievewright has entered the big league.

Together with one or two rival companies, *Online Classics* is establishing itself as a pioneering force in the use of the internet for not just opera, but all the performing arts. "It represents what I have always believed in," says Sievewright, "quality and access." Meanwhile his partner, Chris Hunt, is effusive in his praise: "Alan has a great eye for quality. He never accepts second best, he is more adamant about that than anyone else I know, and artists respect him for it. He has a special place in their affections. I mean, this man has brought me to people like Pavarotti, Domingo, Carreras, Caballe, and these people have genuine affection for him." Hunt also notes Sievewright's knack for spotting upcoming talent before most other people: "He recommended Roberto Alagna, Angela Gheorghiou and Jose Cura before they were remotely famous".

Back to basics

Despite his burgeoning presence on the World Wide Web, the impresario returns to the stage for projects or artistes that fire his imagination – recently he presented a one-woman fully-staged show showcasing Julia Migenes, a soprano he adores, and produced *Il Re Pastore* at St John's, Smith Square in London. It received ecstatic reviews from the papers, with Hilary Finch of *The Times* declaring "Mozart doesn't come much more authentic than this". He has also presented in the USA, Japan, Belgium, Australia and Greece (big shows with new stars, e.g. Olga Borodina, Dimitri Hvoroftovsky and more). And who knows when he might exhume his much-missed concert opera seasons in London? Of one thing he remains certain: "Opera *is* a medium for the people. I sat back at the top in Covent Garden when they did Luc Bondy's new *Don Carlos* production a few years ago. And a lady tapped me on the shoulder and said, 'Oh, Mr Sievewright, never though I'd see you sitting up here. Seen *Don Carlos* before have you love?' I replied that I had. 'I've already seen this production four times you know,' she proudly told me. You see, they don't interview *her*. Or the bus driver who had a whip-round to donate to the Royal Opera House's development scheme. In Vienna if you talk to a taxi driver he'll tell you who is in the cast of the opera that night. But there are taxi drivers like that here too. The sad thing is the press never talk to the real people. Only to the people with a champagne glass in their hand."

Looking back, Alan Sievewright is sanguine about his life and career. He has followed his own credo: "I have always tried to know my own limitations but have remained ambitious. I have an enormous respect for other, greater people's talents. I *love* to be in awe of what a director or designer has done in a theatre. I enjoy knowing I couldn't do that, but I can help encourage these people to do their best work."

He will, he says, continue his ad hoc routine of picking the things he wants to do when he wants to do them. And he will never court the limelight: "Fame is the great danger to everybody. If you prostitute art, the money will come. But you'll get an old parade of *La Bohème, Carmen,* and a few others. You'll *never* be able to see *Il Re Pastore,* Bellini's *Il Pirata* or Rossini's masterpiece *Semiramide.* Schwarzkopf turned to the audience at the Duke of York's Theatre when I did an evening with her and said, 'You do this because you love it. He loves it.' And it *is* that."

Perfectly Composed:

ANDREW

LLOYD

WEBBER

ANDREW LLOYD WEBBER *attends the first night of The Witches of Eastwick at the Theatre Royal Drury Lane, a theatre the Really Useful Group now owns.*

and the Really Useful Group

At the butt-end of the old century, Lord Lloyd-Webber of Sydmonton pulled off an astonishing coup. The world's most famous composer of musical theatre had for years also been one of its biggest impresarios through his producing company, the Really Useful Group (which in recent times has produced mainly his own musicals around the world). Then, as 1999 drew to a close, and against fierce competition from home and abroad, the theatrical peer managed to engineer a joint purchase (with NatWest Equity Partners, now Bridgepoint Capital Ltd) of Stoll Moss, the UK's largest and most prestigious group of West End theatres. With the London Palladium, the Theatre Royal, Drury Lane and 11 others, constituting one third of the theatre seats in the West End, firmly in his grasp, Lloyd Webber was now more than ever before one of the great forces in world theatre.

Superficially, the facts make him seem a veritable business genius. That one man could manage a sprawling production empire, buy Stoll Moss under the envious noses of competitors like Cameron Mackintosh and the mighty American Schubert Organisation, and still find time to compose blockbuster shows is an amazing feat (although one might make a case that with *Aspects of Love, Sunset Boulevard,* and even the steady but hardly trailblazing *Whistle Down the Wind,* the Lloyd Webber *oeuvre* has become less critically successful since he became his own producer). But this is a misleading view, as Lloyd Webber is keen to make clear when he telephones me the day before our interview. He is anxious that I understand that he is "highly reluctant to be viewed as an impresario". He is, he explains, really just a figurehead for The Really Useful Group and stays as far away from the business side of things as possible. And there is truth in this. But when we meet – when he tells me how close he came to losing his company and how only his prompt action saved it – it is clear that, now at least, he keeps a strong paternal eye on what he still likes to call his "family business".

A compelling interviewee, Lloyd Webber appears intriguingly nervous and confident at the same time. One feels that he doesn't much like being questioned, but he has very strong beliefs and does not hesitate to state them. His eyes tend to dart, his voice is energetic. He begins before I can.

"The Really Useful Group has now, finally, come back to what it really should be. It is there to exploit the copyrights that it owns. And it's unique among all the other names that you've got in your book because it actually owns the entire copyright of all of those shows. With other producers, the rights revert back to the owners, but with us they don't because we own everything right down to the last button on the last costume of all of them. With the exception of *Evita* and *Jesus Christ Superstar,* which Tim Rice and I get back at the end of next year, and we want to keep those for ourselves."

The company runs now, he continues, in the manner he always hoped it would. "It's got a fabulous managing director in Bill Taylor, who stepped in after Polygram was bought out. In a way, I have never been involved in the business side at all. What will happen is that they will consult me on creative matters. For example, on my new musical *The Beautiful Game* I will choose what theatre we go to because that's a creative decision; but I won't enter negotiations with the theatre owner about what rent we pay."

A musical family

The Lloyd Webber family was always eminently musical – father William was also a composer, and brother Julian is a famous cellist. But the emphasis in both cases is classical, and Andrew writes rock musicals. He brushes the difference aside.

"My father was very catholic in his tastes about music and he really liked anything as long as it was good. So a lot of different kinds of music cohabited in the house. He liked the fact that I enjoyed what was going on in contemporary pop. I really liked everything, but I happened to be a child of the rock 'n' roll age and so it never seemed to me unnatural to draw on the influences that surrounded me at the time. Actually, there did seem to me to be something retro about musicals in those days. But there was no reason why one couldn't absorb everything around one.

"I'm still doing it now with *Beautiful Game*. I love Hindi pop a lot, and there's a tremendous amount of affinity between the percussion of the Hindis and the music of the Celts. It's all basically the same. So I've used a lot of percussive patterns, put it on Celtic instruments and the result is extraordinary. The thing is, musicals have always got to be a little bit of their time."

Did he start out to search for a new style? And did an early meeting with one of the masters of the established style, Richard Rodgers, have a great impact?

"It did because I was a great fan of his. I adored Rodgers and Hammerstein, unfashionably in those days. When I was about 15 or 16 the chattering classes considered them to be *rubbish*. Mention *Carousel* and people would choke in their coffee. Because they were considered to be sentimental slush. *The Sound of Music* was appallingly reviewed in London. My Aunt Vi's best friend was Vilda Hope, the famous director of *The Boy Friend* and lots of other shows, and she was very shocked when I told her I liked *The Sound of Music!*"

Structure and style

Was he in those early days seeking to take musicals a step further? He shakes his head: "No, neither Tim Rice nor I sat down and consciously decided to do that. But I did think that it was easier for me to dramatically control an evening if they were through-sung in the main. And with *Jesus Christ Superstar* of course that is the case. I saw it again the other day in Dublin and realised that the fact that it is through-composed is its greatest strength. It doesn't let you off the rollercoaster anywhere along the line.

"It happens that *Beautiful Game* has got a lot of book in it. It has got to have a bit, because I can't start doing all of these Northern Irish accents singing very fast, sorry! But yesterday Ben Elton and I were discussing the dialogue in exactly the same musical terms of rhythm and structure."

Paradoxically, I suggest, although it employs rock music, *Superstar* is structurally operatic.

"For that reason, yes. I learnt very early on from playing scores at the piano. The original stage version of *The Sound of Music* for instance didn't miss a trick. Even down to how the reprises were done, down to how the scene change music was done. It's all *so* precise. And if you look at the greatest scene of musical compression in opera history, the Café Momus scene in *La Bohème* – I mean, Puccini manages to get *everything* in there through sheer, absolute technique. I realised that very early, construction is the most important thing in any musical. And the musicals of mine that have worked less well have not been as well constructed as the others. It doesn't mean to say that the tunes are any worse, but the actual rhythm of the piece is not quite right."

Company matters

Soon after *Superstar*, in 1972, Rice and Lloyd Webber created their first company, Qwertyuiop. The name, Rice's idea, came from the top line of a typewriter.

"I can't remember what it did particularly," recalls the composer with a grin. "In fact I don't think it ever did anything, except a letter to *The Times* when the letters of the typewriter were being changed to say that as directors of Qwertyuiop we were appalled at the turn of affairs! I don't think it even traded. It was just a funny name for a company."

Five years later came a more serious effort, the Really Useful Company (as RUG was then known). However, admits Lloyd Webber, the original idea was "far more mundane" than a fully-fledged production company.

"It was just a small company that was set up with the intention for it to do one or two little things and then be sold. One of those little things that we had done was to buy the rights to *Thomas the Tank Engine*, but in those days nobody could see a future for the project. Although part of an episode for a proposed TV series was animated to my music it was like banging a head against a brick wall. But it was a good idea – look at *Thomas the Tank Engine* today! Of course my option on the rights lapsed years ago. *Thomas the Tank Engine* also explains the name of the Really Useful Group because Thomas and the other engines had to be really useful all the time.

"Furthermore I realised that if I could persuade Brian Brolly to join the company I could perhaps, when my exclusive contract with Robert Stigwood ended, set up a fully fledged theatrical producing company that would produce my works and those of others to my standards. We decided that my services as composer and producer would be contracted to the company on a totally arm's-length basis. This is still true today. John Cohen as my personal lawyer negotiates the commercial terms with the Really Useful management as if I had no shareholding in the company."

Brian Brolly was persuaded to come on board, and brought new, wider ideas: "Brolly had come from working for Paul McCartney. And he suggested this idea of making the company fundamentally about copyrights. Because he had been trained by John Eastman, Linda's brother, who had made McCartney buy loads of rights – so Paul McCartney now owns the songs of Buddy Holly, the Frank Loesser catalogue, things like *Annie*. McCartney frankly is far more of an entrepreneur than I am. People don't realise the extent of what he owns. The most *amazing* catalogue of copyrights.

"And Brolly was the London end of the Eastman enterprise before he came to join me. He was also the guy who had got MCA to record the *Superstar* album when nobody else would do it. And he came to me and said, 'We have to make sure that we own all our copyrights from now onwards.' So he made sure that with *Cats* for example, we owned it. As far as Cameron Mackintosh is concerned, he is the producer in London and certain other territories but he does not own the underlying rights.

False move
"Then siren voices said that we should let the company go public and it could start to do lots of other things. That was a foolish move. I was no longer part of the company once it had gone public, but I soon saw that it was doing so many things it knew nothing about that I feared it was haemorrhaging and I felt that I had to come back."

It is a curious anomaly, considering the extent to which his work is identified with RUG that while the company was public, Andrew Lloyd Webber only owned 30 per cent of the shares. To raise the money to buy back the remaining 70 per cent, he was forced to sell the 30 per cent he already owned to the recording giant Polygram and

cede to them effective control of the company.

After Eastman, the buyback of the company and the Polygram deal was managed by RUG's managing director Patrick McKenna. So straight away the composer went hands-off.

"I've always been managed by other people," he replies. "Up to 1978 I was managed by Robert Stigwood and David Land. Brolly came in fairly soon after 1977 and the transition to the new business manager was pretty seamless."

Mirror, mirror on the wall
So were the marketing innovations – the *Superstar* album being released before the show, for instance – his ideas or did they come from the business side?

"The *Superstar* recording was the only way we could get it heard because no theatre producer would touch it. The person who influenced me most in all of this was Robert Stigwood, because Stigwood was the one who invented this practice of producing musicals around the world, with *Evita* and *Superstar*. And I remember sitting down with Cameron Mackintosh when we were planning *Cats* – who at the time had only done some successful revivals and a couple of original things, but I liked him a lot – and saying, 'Look, you've got to take on board that if *Cats* works we've got to take it abroad very quickly.'

"I personally told him everything that Robert Stigwood had told me. Cameron at first didn't want to do it in New York. That's why he's not the producer there – he's on the billing, but the Schuberts produced it, though Cameron's contribution cannot be overestimated. Of course once he saw what has to happen, he did a brilliant job with it. But it was Robert! It is in a lot of people's interests to rewrite history. But I tell you Stigwood is a brilliant, underestimated figure in all of this. He had something like 18 productions of *Superstar* up and running by 1972 – although I have to admit now I come to think of it that I disliked that staging, which was another reason that I set up RUG."

To be fair, Mackintosh has never taken credit for the idea of exporting musicals. What he has done is to do it on a broader scale that had been tried before. But people sometimes make the claim for him, and this seems to slightly rile his old friend. It is, however, far from the great rivalry that sections of the press like to perceive in their relationship.

Over the years, I say, RUG has diversified into productions outside of the Lloyd Webber portfolio. One of the most successful was the comedy play *Daisy Pulls It Off* by Denise Deegan, for which the composer wrote a song under the pseudonym of Beryl Waddle-Browne (a witty anagram of Andrew Lloyd Webber).

"In the case of *Daisy*," he recalls, "the director David Gilmore rang me and asked me to look at it in Southampton. It just so happened that I had a gap in what I was doing at the time, and I went. I agreed to put it on, but I only gave them one piece of advice, which was that they do it as though it was a musical, not as a play. And they did, and it worked.

"We have also done quite a few other things, and we will again. But at the moment the boys are so overstretched with a myriad projects. *Jesus Christ Superstar* opening on Broadway in May, *The Beautiful Game* here, a new production of *Phantom* has just opened in Mexico, another in Antwerp. We've gone from having to let people go a few years ago to looking around all the time now for good new people. Just now, we are probably in the process of getting up and running three times as many productions as any other company!"

The empire strikes back
In 1997, Lloyd Webber's relationship with Polygram came to a head in a crisis which could have led to the destruction of his company. Whereas in 1994 RUG had enjoyed reputed profits of over £46 million, by 1997 they were losing to the tune of a reported £10 million. It was time for a divorce.

"I began to realise the possibilities open to Polygram. They had the right to move to control the company in 2002 and obviously the lower the company's value at that point, the cheaper. They would have got majority control over all of those copyrights, some of the greatest copyrights in the world. I do not know to what extent they had this in mind, but I kept saying to them 'There's something wrong here.' However, it seemed as though they wanted me to have as little to do with the company as possible."

Lloyd Webber, who did not even have an office in the RUG building, began to pry further into his own affairs. He did not like what he found.

"I had not appreciated that we were investing in a lot of our productions, something David Land told me never to do, and I do understand about the economics of musicals. We had invested heavily in things like *Sunset Boulevard* in Australia – not every musical is the same animal though, and the company lost a lot of money."

The composer confronted Polygram who did agree not to move to control the company during Lloyd Webber's lifetime. Then however, Polygram was bought by another company, Seagram, and enough was enough.

"I got Elton John's manager, John Reid, to negotiate a buyback on my behalf. And the impossible happened. We got it all back.

"I think I'm the luckiest man on the planet, because we approached Seagram at just the right time." He pauses, then adds, "It's a very complicated story."

Does he ever feel pressure, I ask, having to write to satisfy the commercial needs of RUG? It appears not.

"If I had wanted to go and be a hermit, I could have done. There was never any commitment to write in my contract, I've never been under any obligation at all. The problems with RUG merely arose when it was pushed in wrong directions. After it went public I voiced my disapproval, but wasn't in a position where I could stop it."

I wonder whether he ever resents RUG distracting him from his composing, but again he denigrates his role: "I had to do something about it, but I never got myself into any of those things and I didn't really get them out. Other people took over and did it."

Fame is blame?

For a man who dislikes being associated too closely with the producing side of his business, Lloyd Webber has often come in for criticism for decisions that were nothing to do with him. RUG is in trouble? Lloyd Webber is losing his touch. Faye Dunaway leaves *Sunset Boulevard*? It's all at Lloyd Webber's behest. This clearly frustrates him.

"I so frequently read in the papers things which I'm supposed to have done which I have not. It's only because the company is so hugely associated with me because it has produced all these works of mine. Although today, I must say, the spirit of the company is completely different and they *would* refer major things to me.

"But when, for example, Faye Dunaway left *Sunset Boulevard*, it was not a capricious decision by myself alone. I was not even part of the company at the time, but I was asked to have breakfast with the creative team and the American producer. Everyone was very worried – and I know that both Trevor Nunn and the musical director David Caddick had her best interests at heart. It was felt that it was difficult to go forward. But the baggage of the decision stuck to me. And I wasn't even supposed to be in LA at the time, I only went there because my *Requiem* was being performed in the midwest. I took the plane back and there was a phone call from her waiting. I hardly knew her, but if she was that upset about it I suppose I should have called her back and called Trevor and everybody. But I had just got off the plane and I was absolutely knackered, and I decided to deal with it in the morning. The next day of course she had given a press conference and it was all over the media!"

Caught on camera

One new area where RUG are having great success is the filming of the Lloyd Webber shows. Both *Cats* and *Joseph* have been released and been snapped up by the thousands, in video shops and supermarkets alike (Alan Parker's Oscar-winning feature film of *Evita* was not Really Useful-produced). At the time of writing, the *Cats* video has sold more than four million copies. In the pipeline is *Jesus Christ Superstar*, and there is talk of *Sunset Boulevard* with Glenn Close. How involved in this, I ask, does he get?

"It seemed to be logical. When we got the company back, we noticed that in the *Cats*

film agreement we had with Universal, who had been talking about making an animated version for ages. RUG had reserved the video rights for the stage show. So I said, 'Why don't we just do it?' That went very well, and so we decided to do *Joseph*. And we have discovered that for a fraction of the price of a movie, you can do really good pieces of work today.

"And all these videos are on DVD. Whether or not they're shown on the big screen is becoming irrelevant, since DVD is obviously becoming the formula of the future."

He would, he concludes, like to see all of his work on screen in one form or another. His *Beautiful Game* collaborator Ben Elton is currently at work on a screenplay for *The Phantom of the Opera*, to be directed by Shekhar Kapur.

Bricks and mortar

Soon making the headlines was the newest, potentially most influential side of Lloyd Webber's business. His is not the only production company to own West End theatres (Cameron Mackintosh has effective control of five), but the venues he has acquired are by far the most prestigious. And this makes his power to shape London theatre immense. Theoretically, if he doesn't like a show he can block it getting onto any of his stages. The previous owners, Stoll Moss, were often criticised for refusing to take risks, for playing safe (which of course, in theatre, is a dangerous practice indeed). When Lloyd Webber's purchase –

a joint venture with Bridgepoint Capital Ltd – was announced, the general feeling was that at last the theatres were in the hands of someone who understood how theatre works, that you have got to experiment.

The buying process itself was a typically skilful piece of manoeuvring, as the composer is keen to tell me. At the time, Lloyd Webber needed money to clear the £60 million debt he had incurred in getting back the RUG shares. The first idea was to sell the Palace, a theatre he already owned. One of London's prize venues, it was old and in disrepair (despite the fact that Lloyd Webber had already spent a small fortune on renovations, it needed many more), and a buyer had already been found. Then came word that Stoll Moss was up for grabs.

"When Stoll Moss became available," he explains, "Bill Taylor thought there might be a way that we could put together venture capital and sell the Palace and our interest in the Adelphi and the New London theatres into the Stoll Moss consortium. And that is what we have done, sold those theatre interests into the consortium and we have ended up with 50 per cent of the company – because the venture capitalists are sort of buying my name. They are obviously going to be very strong about what happens and so one will have to deal with the company at arm's length, and also Stoll Moss is a long-established company with long-serving employees and so you can't just steam in there and dictate.

"However, the chief executive Richard Johnson had already resigned, so we had to find a replacement. That has given me the moment, more quickly than I expected, to put my own stamp on the company. And I have appointed Andre Ptaszynski, somebody who is well respected by West End producers, which is terribly important. There is a lack of a real bond between Stoll Moss as was and other West End producers, and that we have to change."

Caring landlord

The deal does, however, give him the chance to indulge his other great passion, besides theatre and art – food. "I've told the catering people," he announces with a gleam, "that they have to pull themselves up or we're off! I've leapt into *that* one, let me tell you!"

He returns to his former theme: "If you ask me what the community wants me to do about Stoll Moss, it'll be in the area of making it accessible and making producers feel that they're understood and that their plays will be given a sympathetic approach, as opposed to the very hard-line approach that there has been before, and if necessary given a break. I said all this on a TV interview and one of the venture capitalists rang me and said, 'You can't say this!' I simply told him that the way to run theatre as a business is *not* to run it as a business."

So, I add, as a composer whose early successes depended on producers taking risks with – to say the least – unusual subjects for musicals, will he actively encourage his theatres to take risks? "Yes!" he replies with vigour, "My wife has already given the bank a long lecture. She told them that theatre is a very small community, and if you don't get someone in control who is welcome in the Ivy, you might as well have 13 buildings with nothing in them. I'd say if anyone's involved in the entrepreneurial side it's my wife. And Bill Taylor is very keen to use the clout that the theatre group has to get internet theatre ticketing properly organised."

Good housekeeping

Ever since his company sailed so close to financial disaster, one law that Lloyd Webber has laid down as a producer is that of economy. When he was creating *Whistle Down the Wind* he stated his intention to keep the costs down – no small task these days when the cost of a big musical hovers around the £4 million mark. Did he succeed?

"Yes, we did make it reasonable. It breaks even at around £108,000 a week. We did it for £2.3 million which is quite good. All that happened was that whenever anyone asked for something I said no. Of all the musicals that came to London that year it's the only one that's still there, and that's because it is running at a sensible rate.

"What's so irritating is that had I really been on the case, *Sunset Boulevard* would be running now! It had been planned to break even at 85%! I mean, you do your figures on the basis that 85% is the most you will ever do, and if you exceed that, well, eureka. But

you *must* work on the principle that 85% is all you will achieve."

Is this now the standard for all future musicals?

"Yes, I'm screaming at them all about *The Beautiful Game* at the moment. Actually," he continues happily, "this side of things I *do* enjoy. I decided to take some radio ads for *Whistle Down the Wind* and see what happened. Within a week or two we had taken an extra couple of hundred thousand at the box office. It proved my point that these shows are music-driven, so what is the point of all these stupid posters up and down the escalators in tube stations? So I stopped them on *Whistle*, and they all howled, 'You can't, we've done this on musicals for ever!' Of course, that's the point.

"That's the side of producing I do enjoy. I do feel that I've got a role there. Whether that's an impresario's role I don't know. But not the other side; I couldn't employ a cleaner!"

But a caterer?

"Ah," he replies, a determined look on his face, "we *will* get that right."

He talks about the complexities of his catering plans: "I went to the Royal Opera last night," he confides, "and learned that they are all having 35 and 40 minute intervals. Because everyone has such a good time in the new Floral Hall that they can't get them back into the theatre. They're taking all this money at the bar, but at the other end everyone has to be paid overtime. You don't think about these things! Perhaps the way is to offer them things afterwards and not give them too much in the middle of the show."

So there are areas in which Andrew Lloyd Webber does get very involved with the business side. And however he may protest his deliberate isolation from it, the tactical running of his company seems to fascinate him. He may once have lived or died by his advisers, and he still relies on them greatly, but since buying his company he has toughened up and been forced to play a part. Lloyd Webber the businessman is nobody's fool, and since his business is theatre – the one thing he is most passionate about – he is very serious about protecting its interests. Good news for the West End?

Taming the Beast:

BRIAN

McMASTER

and the Edinburgh Festival

The Edinburgh International Festival is many things to many people, and it can never satisfy everyone. How then can one measure the success of its director? The statistics outline the vast scope of the job. For its annual four-week span – the 1999 festival included 12 opera, 24 dance, 36 theatre and 53 music performances – simply overseeing a smooth operation is something of an administrative triumph. It is in many ways the biggest impresario's job of all; the director must be at once ringmaster, innovator, scheduler, negotiator for (including lectures and talks) over 160 events.

Brian McMaster has had his triumphs. Thanks to him, Britain has become familiar with the work of Mark Morris, Robert Lepage, Yukio Ninagawa, Baz Luhrmann, Peter Stein, Harry Kupfer and Goran Jarvefelt. Some of these were discovered during his tenure as managing director of Welsh National Opera. He is widely credited with turning that solid regional company into an internationally respected ensemble. Most of the stars were brought to these shores through McMaster's ingrained combination of (artistic) ambition and tenaciousness. A somewhat shy man upon first meeting, there is nothing bashful about him when the hunt is afoot to secure an admired artist. Famously, he once made a beeline to Stockholm to secure the services of the great soprano Elisabeth Söderström for WNO, and sat stubbornly on her doorstep until she agreed.

Brian McMaster discovered classical music in his teens when he heard a snatch of *Madam Butterfly* on the radio. From then on, music became his passion. After he graduated at Bristol University he made a game attempt to enter the world of legal high-fliers, training as a solicitor. It was never going to last. The opera was playing an increasingly major role in his life. His legal training behind him, he submitted to the inevitable, and joined the Arts Council's arts administration course at London Polytechnic. His stage was set.

"The course was designed to foster the next generation of arts administrators, and this was its first year. I was there at the same time as Nicholas Payne, now the head of English National Opera. It was great, because being the first, they didn't really know how to run it. So we were able to control the course and learn exactly what we felt we needed to learn. It was a big success and most of us now are in pretty important jobs."

He began his working life as an office boy at EMI records in 1968. "At that time the classical department was very small and nobody there was particularly interested in opera. That meant that I could become involved in casting for a lot of the major recordings which we made. One thing I did – it's a terrible recording – was on the Otto Klemperer *Marriage of Figaro*; I cast Kiri Te Kanawa as the first bridesmaid and Margaret Price as Barbarina. At that time Te Kanawa was just a student at the London Opera School."

EMI duties often took McMaster to Eastern Europe, where they regularly recorded the ultra-famous conductor Herbert Von Karajan. While in East Berlin he was exposed to some of the great German artists; he remembers the theatre productions of Felsenstein having a particular impact.

"This was all firmly behind the Iron Curtain, which could get quite scary. I remember being terrified once because one of the people in the East German recording company asked me to bring some Beatles records (EMI were recording them at the time). I had to smuggle them in, a really nerve-wracking experience."

From EMI, McMaster was head-hunted by English National Opera, where he took up a post as controller of opera planning: "I assisted with casting and organised all the rehearsals and that sort of thing. On my first night in the job, there was a performance of Wagner's *Die Walküre* conducted by Sir Reginald Goodall, with the fantastic Australian bass Clifford Grant. Cliff decided to play a joke on me. He did all his warm-ups and preparation somewhere else, and only turned up backstage two minutes before the curtain went up. By this time I was in an absolute panic and had been searching for him for ages. And he strolled past me and walked on stage as if there was nothing amiss."

To Wales
Despite this fraught start, McMaster 'survived' his ENO tenure, and in 1976 the call came to take over Welsh National Opera. Did this come out of the blue?

"Completely. I knew they couldn't find anyone to do it, but I never expected that they would ask me." He adds with a twinkle, "But then they *were* desperate."

He arrived at his new company to find his old friend Nicholas Payne already there as financial director, and a music director with whom he was to form an extremely rewarding partnership, Richard Armstrong. However, his first few months were a baptism of fire, literally: "I was faced with a crisis. I started in July and there was a production of *Orpheus in the Underworld* planned to open in December for which no director had been selected. I had to find someone to stage it urgently, and did so with a conspicuous lack of success. I picked the Frenchman Louis Ducreux.

"In addition to this, about a week after I arrived there was a fire in the scenery store, destroying all of our scenery. As it happens, this was in many ways extremely fortunate for me personally, I was able to start with a clean sheet. As a matter of fact, various people thought I had bought a box of matches too many!"

This clean sheet meant that McMaster was able to quickly bring in the cream of European directors. His first move in this direction was to hire the German, Joachim Herz, whose work he had seen at the Komische Opera, to direct *Madam Butterfly*. Harry Kupfer soon followed with *Fidelio*, and McMaster's reign culminated with Peter Stein's universally lauded Verdi productions, *Otello* and *Falstaff*.

And so to Scotland

In 1991 Brian McMaster became director of the Edinburgh International Festival. It is interesting, I suggest, that both WNO and Edinburgh are international organisations, yet are expected to balance this with a responsibility to the respective regions. It is a situation of which he approves: "It is a healthy tension to keep. It is particularly relevant now, as Scotland is about to open its parliament, and everyone is concentrating on nationalist issues. However, there is a danger, that all this nationalistic fervour will lead to artistic narrowness. You can see it in Canada, you can see it in an extreme form in Catalonia.

"But there is something really exciting in Edinburgh. It is a challenge to develop the local and regional identity at the same time as the international side, so that – if you get it right – they grow together. That's what it's all about."

There have been those who have accused McMaster of not bringing enough Scottish focus to the festival. His predecessor in the job, Frank Dunlop, was one, and another was Professor George Steiner – who gave an infamous inaugural lecture criticising the festival in 1996, its fiftieth anniversary year. In different ways, McMaster is dismissive of both: "Frank Dunlop has never seriously criticised me and I admire what he achieved tremendously. George Steiner did a fantastic job for us in our fiftieth year; thanks to him the Edinburgh Festival was on the front page of every newspaper. It was publicity which may have encouraged some people to come to some rather more serious events." Steiner also suggested that the festival should embrace the sciences as well as the arts, a notion to which McMaster's response is that there is no need, since a science festival already exists.

The hot seat

"When I left university I suddenly realised that I was going to have to go to work for the rest of my life, and that was a horrible day. I sat around with some friends and we discussed what careers we should pursue. My dream, I told them, was to end up running Welsh National Opera. Unfortunately, I got that when I was only 30. So the next job was going to have to be something special, and it was. There is nothing quite like running the Edinburgh Festival. A major experience.

"I first came to Edinburgh in 1961, Lord Harewood's first festival when he mounted the complete (with one exception, the opera *Moses and Aaron*, which I later made up for) works of Arnold Schoenberg. I don't know whether we would we would survive if we tried to do that now."

Has the festival changed much since? He thinks for a moment: "There are several answers to that question. There is an exciting way in which it hasn't changed since its inception in 1947. The basic structure is still the same, which shows that the festival's originator Rudolf Bing got it right.

"It has, however, gone through various developments. Frank Dunlop had to deal with a very difficult one. The old Labour council told him that the elitist Edinburgh Festival must become more populist, in a way that the Labour party itself, new and old, has done. That was a very difficult experience to come through. After a while, the council gradually realised that something like the festival actually talks to everybody and has relevance. Hopefully the country at large will come through that identity crisis too."

The "anarchic" Edinburgh Fringe

The Fringe is an enormous explosion of small-scale performance events which is separate from, and yet an irreplaceable addition to, the main festival. McMaster has mixed feelings about it.

"Now the Fringe *has* changed its character. That is a continual process. At the moment it is large and vibrant and sometimes hugely exciting. It is less of a motor for new writing and new developments in theatre than it was. Universities were all doing new plays, enormous numbers of young people were directing and actors were acting and many of them went on to become well-known. That's not quite true now. But it will come back. It has been a phenomenal breeding ground for comedy for a few years now."

In 1998 the Fringe moved back a week, so that it ran entirely during August (whereas the main festival still stretches into the first half of September) to avoid the risk of cold weather. McMaster, who believes that having the Fringe start earlier than the Festival dissipates the power of both, was given just under a year's notice of the move, and the decision still rankles: "I am firmly against the move. The Edinburgh Festival used to be the last two weeks of August and the first two weeks of September. There are an awful lot of orchestras, conductors and dance companies on holiday in August can't come then. As it is, there are a large number of companies we cannot present. If we followed the Fringe and moved fully into August, there are a lot more that we would never get.

"That is not to say that I think we should seek closer ties with the Fringe in a creative sense. It is anarchic. That is what defines it. Therefore, you cannot shackle it artistically by seeking to impose any sort of structure, and it would be wrong to try."

Funding

Funding the Edinburgh Festival has never been easy. Over the years, I say, John Drummond and Robert Ponsonby both resigned as directors of the festival for financial reasons. What was the funding like when McMaster took over?

"Inadequate," is the concise reply. "It still is. We got it up a bit, rather a lot actually, and it has declined since." The Edinburgh council gave the festival £1.3 million, a figure that has now fallen to £1.1 million, and the Scottish Arts Council provides £700,000. The majority of the funds, as McMaster explains, are donated by private and corporate sponsorship – around £1.5 million. Effectively, the Edinburgh Festival has to be run as a largely commercial operation.

This raises the spectre of corporate entertainment. Has it been a struggle to stop the festival becoming the exclusive domain of the sponsors? McMaster frowns: "Many of the Scottish financial institutions support us, and that all adds up to more than we get from the city council. That says quite a lot. They do use performances for entertainment. That can sometimes introduce new audiences, because a lot of the people that they bring don't have the habit of going to the theatre or a concert and some of them are attending for the first time. And a lot of these corporate sponsors are passionate about the arts. Many of them put time, money and love into the orchestras and companies that they support. I don't see it as quite the negative factor implied by your question."

But do the sponsors hog all the seats? He insists that there is no problem: "It is now June, and there are only five concerts already sold out in this year's festival. That is all. And that's what I like. Also, the tickets for the festival are unbelievably cheap. I hope that one can get in for roughly the equivalent of the three shillings that I used to pay. The whole festival experience is unique and special, so I certainly don't want performances to become inaccessible."

Artistic policy

When McMaster took over from his predecessor, Frank Dunlop, it was generally perceived that he was being handed a mixed bag, artistically. Dunlop had been praised for refurbishing the main Edinburgh theatres, but trounced in the press for trying to popularise the festival too much with shows like *Treasure Island*. His successor refuses to criticise: "That show brought pleasure to a lot of people. I talked about the structure of the festival being the same since 1947, which it is. But within that structure it has changed enormously. It responds to two things. One, the subjective tastes of the festival directors – each regime has a distinctive flavour, and that subjectivity is the key to the success of the festival. It is one man's personal taste, and that is much the best way of doing it. When I am asked which is my favourite event in a year, I always reply that I want to see all 150 performances. That is why I chose them and it is the only honest approach.

"If you are blatantly subjective," McMaster argues, "not everybody will agree with you, but at least the programme will have integrity. That is what the festival's first director, Rudolf Bing, did, and every director since.

"You have got to analyse what a festival is, what it should do. One of the things that we try to do, and Edinburgh always has, is to fill the gaps in the provision of repertoire at a particular time and responding to that era. Schoenberg was unknown when George Harewood featured him in the festival. That was fantastic, to come here and hear all of those pieces, particularly in the 60s, when they sounded really difficult. Only something like the Edinburgh Festival can do that."

McMaster himself has certainly taken some risks. Robert Lepage's five-hour play *The Seven Streams of the River Ota* and the Peter Stein's enormous (seven and a half hours long) *Oresteia* are cases in in point. "It is suicide not to take risks. We have never taken risks like we have this year, though."

One of McMaster's tastes is for programming themed series of events. In one of his first years, for instance, he scheduled a Beethoven season which included all of the composer's symphonies and piano concertos as well as a *Fidelio* day (which featured Beethoven's earlier version of the work, *Leonore*, as well as other music associated with the opera). It is a policy of which he is proud: "That's a practice which dates back at least to Lord Harewood. It's one thing that a festival can do really well. We programme 150 concerts in three weeks. Not much work gets done in Edinburgh outside of the service industries during that time. People come and see what we put on. And I don't want anyone to come to only one event; you come to a lot, that is the idea. Therefore one needs to programme through that and give the experience an extra dimension. In the old days, the festival would often concentrate on the work of one particular country, and the government of that country would donate a lot of money. That funding has dried up, so it doesn't happen that way any more."

Surrounding the events is a programme of informative talks, an area which McMaster has deliberately expanded and, he tells me, it is so popular that he is about to turn it into a year-long programme. With education of classical music and the arts whittling away, this is an increasingly important role for arts institutions to fulfil. "I have got a fairly radical view of this. The new building that we are moving into has a fabulous new auditorium. But Edinburgh already has a fantastic number of auditoria. The reason for the new one is to create a 52 week-a-year educational space. It will be used to educate everyone who has an interest, from schoolchildren to people of my age and older.

McMaster explains that the world is changing drastically: "Poeple retire earlier and live longer. There is lot of government-speak and Arts Council-speak about how we have got to care for the audience's education and get them to enjoy the arts while they are young, which of course is perfectly true. But the fact that the biggest audience for the arts is older is not surprising. There is a period in people's lives when you cannot, whatever you do, attract them out, because they are at home looking after the kids. But with earlier retirement and the greater part of the population being over 50 there is the massive audience for the arts. We should give in to that. It is not regrettable, it is desperately important.

Another McMaster idea was the late-night concerts, which have proved a conspicuous success. "They had been around before, we simply developed the idea. The amazing thing about Edinburgh is that you will have what you think is a groundbreaking idea like that, and then you look back through the archive and discover that it has been done before."

One facet of the festival which he has been credited with re-energising to thrilling effect is dance. Yet McMaster was not initially a dance fan: "When I took over in 91, I didn't know much about dance, and the art form was in a bad way. And there wasn't anywhere where the major creators could be seen, in London or anywhere, that was promotable. This presented Edinburgh with an opportunity; a responsibility.

McMaster believes that the most exciting developments in the arts world are happening in dance.

"Mark Morris was astonishing, because even in his first year, 1992, he attracted a large audience. About the same time I was doing some work for the Arts Council, and their director of modern dance was very depressed, because both London Contemporary Dance and the Ballet Rambert as it was then (it later relaunched as the Rambert Dance Company) had just folded for lack of audiences. Actually, I think it was a lack of creativity which led to the poor audiences. I brought the lady from the Arts Council to the Playhouse here when Mark Morris was playing and showed her the packed house, and I asked, 'How's that for an audience for modern dance?' She was gobsmacked.

"That was Mark's first year, and he built a great following. From there on grew a huge audience for dance in Edinburgh all the year round. The dance audience from London are now regular visitors, and there is more dance in Edinburgh during the festival than in any other city. Building that relationship with Mark Morris is one of my proudest achievements."

One of the criticisms which McMaster has faced recently is that the festival has become too predictable in its programming, that the same names crop up each year. Presumably it is the result of building an audience and a workbase?

"Of course. However, this year we have got the most radical programme we have ever put on. The whole feel of it is fresh and new. In the dance programme, for instance, all of the names are new, and first-time visitors to Scotland.

"William Forsyth was, of course, at Sadler's Wells in London, but one of his major pieces, *Artefact*, is being done by Dutch National Ballet, who were here last year with a retrospective of Hans van Manen, whom the press thought not worthy of much interest, and I think the project proved them wrong. Because that was a hit with the audiences, the company are able to return this year with this incredibly difficult piece by William Forsythe. Normally it would be hard to fill the seats for this work. But since the audience know Dutch National Ballet from last year, they've booked for it. They don't book for what they don't know. So there is the strength in building relationships with these companies.

"The festival creates an atmosphere where everyone feels they have the freedom to create. Andras Schiff has said about a series of Schumann recitals which he gave in 1999 that he could not have done them anywhere else in the world. No promoter would have taken them on."

So the director of the festival is in a unique position, because to take great risks and build from them. McMaster is not sure just how much licence he has: "It remains to be seen whether we get away with this year's programme or not. But at Edinburgh you are at least free to try."

How much of the director's job, I ask, is involved with originating new work, as opposed to bringing in artists or productions from elsewhere? There is no straightforward answer: "It depends on what you mean by originating work. I can go to Scottish Opera and say, 'You want to be in the Edinburgh Festival? Then do Smetana's *Dalibor*.' Or I can put it another way – 'Luc Bondy has always wanted to direct Verdi's *Macbeth*. Shall we try to persuade him?' I am able to have an influence that way. They can tell me where to go, but they usually don't.

The theatre programme is the one which McMaster finds the most difficult, and at the same time the most interesting, to select: "What should the theatre programme be? I don't want to compete with established companies with very firm identities like the Traverse, or even the National Theatre or the Royal Shakespeare Company. A lot of our audience is shared, at least the most curious or hard-core elements of their audiences will be here in August. It's an interesting question. There are people in Edinburgh who think I should just book the RSC because they don't ever get to see that company. Actually, they can go to Newcastle and see them there.

Things were easier when McMaster first arrived. The work of some of the great European directors had never been seen in Britain. Now it is hard to find anything new. But despite his penchant for adventurous productions, he rejects controversy for its own sake:

"I've never set out to be controversial. By some definitions today, I'm very conservative. My radicalism now is trying to get theatre back to the text, but expressing all that in a fresh way. There seems to me a genuine creativity that one tries to project and there is a fake posturing which is the trap many fall into.

"The wonderful thing is that I can do what I believe here. And now the responsibility grows with the advent of the Scottish parliament. It will be exciting to see what we can do in the new Scotland."

THE

LILIAN & VICTOR HOCHHAUSER
entertain inside the Coliseum Theatre,
at the first night of Boris Godunov

HOCHHAUSERS

Without the Hochhauser's, life for balletomanes would have been much less bearable in the second half of the 20th century. The glories of the Bolshoi and Kirov ballet companies, brought to the West by the Hochhausers, have been unbeatable for excitement in dance. In the 60s names like Ulanova, Maximova, Plizetskaya and Kolpakova among the women were household names in ballet households before any of them had appeared in Britain. The men included Liepa, Lavrovsky,

Vasiliev and Soloviev. They were already stars here, by word of mouth, before ballet fans had even seen them. And they lived up to, if not exceeded expectations. Even today, seasoned ballet goers pine to see the likes of Soloviev virtually flying in the *Bluebird Pas de Deux*. And Plizetskaya's "boneless" rippling arms which drew a corporate gasp from a Festival Hall audience as she glided on stage from the wings in *The Dying Swan*. It was encored twice. And there were more phenomenal events to follow; Nureyev, by all reports, hovering high above Covent Garden stage in *The Corsair Pas de Deux*, dancing with the considerably older Margot Fonteyn, whose career gained a new lease of life with their internationally fêted partnership. He had defected from the Kirov during a visit to Paris.Makarova too, then Baryshnikov, defected from the Kirov soon afterwards. These were living legends and the Hochhausers alone, in those days, offered them to an audience feverish with excitement.

The publisher of this book declares an interest as a great admirer of the Hochhausers. He has given me a good Hochhauser story. It occurred during the writing of this book. Hochhauser is always "on duty" at the theatre on his own opening nights, standing in the lobby of the theatre to greet his audience, attending to their problems; the genial, concerned host. My publisher, spying the elegantly besuited figure in the foyer of the London Coliseum one night (where he was presenting the Bolshoi Ballet in their latest London season), decided to introduce himself and explain that he was publishing the forthcoming volume about the Hochhausers "and the other impresarios". The Hochhauser right eyebrow shot up impressively. "*Other* impresarios?" he exclaimed in his heavy Czech accent. "Very funny!" He walked away chuckling.

Certainly there *are* other impresarios, yet perhaps none of them retains the mystique of Victor Hochhauser, who seems to have always been there, bringing great international companies such as the Bolshoi and the Kirov to London for generations. One should say the Hochhausers, since Victor's wife, Lilian, is a vital part of the operation. There are some who attest that, though it is Victor who (almost alone among his colleagues now that Lew Grade has died) cuts the classic image of the old-fashioned impresario – always expensively dressed, courteous yet remote, a formidable conversationalist (if only for the energised speed at which he talks, commandeering the discussion like a general deploying his troops) – it is Lilian who actually runs things. My visit to the Hampstead mansion in which they live and work rather persuades me to this view.

The house is set back from the main road like a fortress, with the door to their offices hidden around a corner and down corrugated iron steps. The Hochhausers occupy separate offices and, despite my request to the contrary, I am to talk to them individually rather than together. I am directed to an ornate chamber, decorated by large posters in golden frames, and dominated by a stately wooden desk and a luxurious leather armchair.

As I wait, I reflect on the man I am about to meet. His contribution to the daily artistic life of Britain has been immense. It was Victor Hochhauser who managed to lift the Iron Curtain as far as Russian artists were concerned; far enough to export the likes of Rudolf Nureyev, Msistlav Rostropovich, David Oistrakh, Natalia Makarova, Sviatoslav Richter, the Kirov and Bolshoi companies. Indeed, practically all the Soviet artists who visited Britain from the mid-1950s to the mid-1990s were able to do so because of the Hochhausers' machinations. Without them, it is questionable whether this artistic exodus (literally in some cases, since there were several notable defections to the West) would ever have happened. Or perhaps it would have happened much later, by which time we might have missed out on an entire generation of performers. However, Victor Hochhauser is not one to undersell himself, as I am about to find out. The door opens and through it bustles my host, a small, man with quick, restless movements. He sits in the armchair, peers unflinchingly across at me with a vaguely pleasant expression on his face, and says in a challenging tone, "So who else are you doing in this book?"

Once we get past his displeasure that Raymond Gubbay is to be ranked alongside him ("I'm not sure that I'm happy about that – he used to work for me you know"),

he relaxes and tells me, with quickfire ebullience, the remarkable tale of his life.

Born in Czechoslovakia to Jewish parents in 1926, his family fled Hitler shortly before the outbreak of World War II, arriving in England. He graduated from the City of London college and then attended a local *yeshiva* (a college for Jewish studies). Hochhauser had inherited a love of theology from his grandfather, a very distinguished rabbi. Soon, however, he discovered a new talent.

In 1945, Victor joined his school social club, and was asked to raise funds. He did so in a fairly extraordinary manner. He drums the table with satisfaction as he remembers: "I put on a concert with the famous pianist, Solomon. My first concert."

Suitably impressed, I ask how, as a mere schoolboy, he was able to get the legendary musician. He repeats my question excitedly: "How did I get him – exactly! My father met his father, who introduced me to his distinguished son. I asked Solomon to do this concert and he agreed! Not only that, I got the Whitehall Theatre for nothing. I was able to raise a few thousand pounds for the school. It was a sensational concert. Solomon was one of the finest pianists we ever had."

"After the war there was an enormous pent-up interest in music, of which people had been deprived for years. An impresario named Harold Holt had a series of Sunday afternoon concerts. In 1946 I had the *chutzpah* to ask him whether he would let me have the young Yehudi Menuhin for a concert at the Royal Albert Hall. He was shocked that I, an upstart competitor, should have the temerity to ask for his biggest money-spinner. However, he let me have him. He had this fantasy, which people don't any more, of trying to help the next generation. He even gave me a reduction; instead of a thousand guineas, I only had to pay a thousand pounds.

"Holt remained a competitor, but he was also a friend. He didn't care that I might affect his business as I became more successful. He was South African, very rich I believe and wanted to help me as a young refugee. After the chance he gave me, I managed to have Yehudi regularly for 40 or 50 years."

From that first Menuhin concert, Victor Hochhauser became a regular name above posters at the Albert Hall. With Holt's help, he presented all the great names of the day – Eileen Joyce, Harriet Cohen, Louis Kentner, Mark Hambourg, even the matinee idol tenor Mario Lanza. He and his wife, who joined the business soon after they married in 1949, also pioneered a series of 'ballet for the masses' at the old Empress Hall. Stars such as Alicia Markova danced in front of audiences 4000 strong. These were the early precursors of the opera and ballet arena spectaculars later produced by Raymond Gubbay, Harvey Goldsmith and occasionally Hochhauser himself.

The new impresario was a quick and sure success. So much so, that he began to look for fresh territory to conquer. And that is

when he fixed his gaze upon the Soviet Union. His interest was first aroused when his father returned with tales of a bright new Russian talent: "In the early 50s, my father went travelling in Eastern Europe to see what had happened to the rest of our family. He couldn't find many." He pauses, mouth pursed. "He did, however, tell me about a wonderful Russian violinist whom he had seen, called David Oistrakh. He heard this fellow and told me that here was the next great star.

"I wrote and wrote to the Russians about Oistrakh. There was no answer. Eventually, after Stalin died in 1952, relations between England and Russia eased up a bit and I finally got an answer – 'Yes, you can have an Oistrakh. But it turned out to be the son, Igor, who was 21. He came in 1953 and was a great success. Then, finally, David came the next year and became a very good and close friend."

With Stalin gone, Hochhauser found that the Russians were suddenly eager to do business: "After the death of Stalin, the whole world was interested in the Soviet artists, who were the greatest – from the ballet companies and the orchestras to the pianists and chamber ensembles. And none of whom had ever been seen, except by travellers to Moscow. When things opened up, the Russians realised that this was good publicity and also, of course, that they could make an enormous amount of money without having to produce anything new. They simply had to send their artists around the world. And so Oistrakh,

Gilels, Richter, Rostropovich, Galina Vishnevskaya, the ballet companies and the rest, were launched internationally. I was there at the beginning and picked up all these people and ran things by myself without any interference for about 20 years."

When I remark on his skill in getting to the Russians first, Hochhauser is disarmingly ingenuous, and demonstrates a flash of the political perceptiveness that doubtless stood him in good stead in his negotiations with both sides: "Like everything else in life, it was to a large extent luck. Nobody else thought of the idea. The timing was right. The British government also realised that there was something to be gained by creating a new kind of a relationship with the Russians; one which may not be strictly political, but had a political perspective in that it opened up a new channel of communication. So it became very important to them in a diplomatic role."

The political dimension

To Hochhauser's delight, the diplomatic significance of his work with the Soviets was formally recognised by the Anglo-Soviet Charter of 1956. The agreement, negotiated by the prime ministers of the two countries, officially sanctioned the exchange of cultural and scientific personalities and projects. Hochhauser's Russian channel now had, it seemed, the political stamp of approval.

The political aspect, however, remained a double-edged sword and Hochhauser was always vulnerable to any diplomatic changes in East–West relations. I put this to him, and he fires off an answer heavy with bitterness: "Not only was I vulnerable, but I got it from both sides. The Russians tried to use the arts as a political tool, refusing to send the artists – for example, in 1971 when Britain kicked out 105 spies from this country – but I also got into trouble with the Jews for bringing the artists." The incident to which he refers occurred in the 1970s, when he was barracked by the Anglo-Jewish community for dealing with a Russia that was hostile to its own Jews. This is a particularly tender topic for him, even now.

"Although I had been bringing artists here for over 25 years, the greatest artists and many of them Jewish, the Jewish people wanted to use this to highlight the plight of the Jews in Russia. They probably had a point when it came to the Red Army Ensemble, but it certainly had nothing to do with David Oistrakh, who was a noble personality, or Richter, who was very far removed from politics, or Rostropovich, who eventually came to live in London, or Shostakovich, who was a great friend to the Jewish people. In any case, I believe that the way to deal with issues is not to cut off relations, but rather to encourage this sort of movement."

I mention the play *Taking Sides* by the English playwright Ronald Harwood, a piece which debates the moral case of the great German conductor Wilhelm Furtwängler, who elected to stay in Germany during the Third Reich. It raises to go and bring him here by train from Italy or wherever he was playing at the time. We used to have these wonderful conversations on the way over.

"He was a painter, he appreciated films, he appreciated architecture. He would have been a great artist in any field that he chose. As a pianist, in my view, he was unique.

"Richter had to practise an enormous amount, and often I would sit in the next room and listen. The night before he was due to come here on the last visit, about five years ago – he had been ill and had a massive bypass – he fell in Paris and broke his knee. He never recovered and he never played again. The knee led to something else, his heart wasn't very strong and so forth. But every month I used to visit him, until he died. He was a great treasure in my life."

The Royal Ballet

In the year 2000, the couple promoted the Royal Ballet in its own home, the renovated Royal Opera House. That a subsidised company had allowed itself to be presented by a commercial impresario caused an indignant flurry in the press. Mrs Hochhauser is unrepentant: "We first worked with the Royal Ballet in 1998, when they didn't have a home because Covent Garden was closed and we had the London Coliseum and offered them a season. We found that we got on extremely well.

"And there is a certain edge that we as commercial impresarios can bring to a subsidised company. They are cushioned, after all, and we are not. We don't have any kind of sponsorship. We *have* to make it go. That means that we bring a sharper edge to it. And they like that, they find a sense of excitement about it – the artists as well.

"We were asked to bring a company to the house to fill the weeks after the Royal Ballet's regular season, and who better than the Royal Ballet? And we will put on a different kind of repertoire with them, geared to the tourists and summer visitors."

Where next?

The Hochhausers have been mining the riches of hidden worlds for more than 50 years now. Are there, I ask, still lands yet to be charted? She is uncertain: "It's always more and more difficult to find new things. Especially when countries have been opened and the novelty of bringing something new has worn off. But there are other ways of broadening the existing type of attraction. I mean, if I want to bring the Kirov, I can suggest to them new or unusual works that British audiences would like.

"That's my goal now. I want to enlarge the wonderful and existing companies that I have forged relationships with – and they do listen to us – and suggest to them ways of presenting things, older things, newer things. The most important thing is that I also remain very receptive, I'm willing to listen and hear and take advice. And I'm still excited. I still have tremendous enthusiasm for what we do."

The phone, which has been ringing every minute or so for a good ten minutes, rings again, this time with a particularly irritated tone. It seems that Mrs Hochhauser is late for her lunch appointment. She picks up the phone, as she has done every minute for the last ten, and slowly and with great emphasis says, "I…know…I'm…on…my…way." This time however, she means it, and we both rise to leave.

As I wander back down the snake-like drive towards the road, I pause and look back at the house. It is all so wondrously tranquil. A passer-by would never guess that inside this grand but quiet old residence live a perfectly contented, gracefully aging couple, happily working together at their business. A business which has, in its way, shaken the British Isles.

There are some who have already made an impact.

Sally Greene

All eyes are on the ex-actress Sally Greene, whose previous hits include the long-running Reduced Shakespeare Company. Her new venture, Old Vic Productions, will try to succeed where others did not in establishing a permanent theatre ensemble. Greene relishes a challenge and is no stranger to adversity – when she decided to close a play starring Nicol Williamson early (the box office receipts had been irrevocably damaged by Williamson's tendency to walk off mid-show) the actor yelled across the footlights, "There's a bitch in this theatre!" Greene, sitting in the dress circle, loudly fought her corner and one or two audience members joined in the argument on her side. Next to such a public haranguing, the Old Vic enterprise might seem a piece of cake. With star actors like Kevin Spacey and Dame Judi Dench onside and the company set to begin by 2002, Greene looks likely to emerge as a new and powerful force.

David Pugh

At the top of the bank balance, the standout success story of the younger generation – though he is also the oldest – is David Pugh. After serving his apprenticeship with Robert Fox, Pugh enjoyed respectable success with a stage version of the TV show *Bread*, followed it up with the long-running cult hit *A Tribute to the Blues Brothers* (which began its life as a one-off pub gig) and then he struck gold. Sean Connery had found a script which he loved and wanted to make

as a film, starring himself. Its French author, however, insisted that there be a major stage production first, and David Pugh was handed this play, called simply *Art*. Short (90 minutes), with three juicy roles, it has since been called, repeatedly, "the perfect West End play". One is reminded of the old saying that a good West End play confirms as many people as possible in as many prejudices as possible. Opinion is divided on *Art* – but anyone who thinks that contemporary art is a lot of tosh won't be disappointed. It opened at Wyndham's Theatre in 1996 with Albert Finney, Alan Bates and Tom Courtenay in the cast. An instant success, another cast was eventually called for, then another and another.

But where Pugh has been brilliantly clever is in his care over the recasting. Rather than let the bandwagon trundle merrily along on the strength of faded glories, Pugh keeps filling his stage with star names. Not only that but, as he explains, he meticulously constructs each trio so that they gel – and he gives them all nicknames. So there was the "American cast" with George Wendt, Stacey Keach and David Dukes, the "BBC period drama cast" led by Richard Griffiths, the "alternative comedy cast" featuring Jack Dee and Frank Skinner, and of course, what everyone fondly remembers as "the Nigel Havers cast". At the time of writing, Pugh has lured two of America's biggest old-time TV stars, Patrick Duffy and Richard Thomas. *Dallas* meets *Little House On The Prairie*. Not bad for a marketing ploy, and this cunning juggling act keeps the play in the papers and on TV chat shows as the big names do the obligatory rounds of publicity.

To date, *Art* has been replicated around the world and grossed over £40 million. Currently there are productions in London, New York, Los Angeles, and an American tour, and Pugh has sold the franchise to Australia, Chicago and Canada (though he retains the right to casting approval on every production). The young-looking 40 year-old producer is living proof of his favourite dictum (one which he announced in a full-page advert in *The Stage*) – "It can pay to write a play".

"However," he says, "although finding the right play is vital, 90 per cent of producing is the art of raising money. And if you have a success, you can probably raise double the amount of money for the next show. But then it only takes one flop to go belly-up again." Having found a success, he has seemed conspicuously reluctant to risk his reputation (surprisingly, Yasmina Reza's next two plays were given to other companies, the RSC and Islington's Almeida Theatre). Although he attests to having "several plays in development", the world is still waiting for his follow-up to *Art*. It will be interesting to see whether Pugh can bring his golden touch to bear elsewhere.

Sonia Friedman
Plucked from drama school by Laurence Olivier and Joan Plowright to stage manage a Sean Matthias double bill, Sonia Friedman was soon hired by the National Theatre where she worked on new plays with writers of the calibre of Harold Pinter, Tom Stoppard and Athol Fugard. That gave her a taste for new writing, although her first full producing job was a big AIDS benefit in Covent Garden (in which she replaced all of the shop assistants with celebrities). After leaving the National, Friedman joined forces with the director Max Stafford-Clark to create Out Of Joint, where she produced headline-winning plays including Mark Ravenhill's *Shopping and Fucking*. Most recently, she was headhunted by the Ambassador's Theatre Group. They were looking for an adventurous producer to continue the tradition of new writing at the New Ambassador's Theatre which had been kick-started by the Royal Court's temporary residence.

"The Ambassador's is my baby," Friedman tells me as we sit outside a pub opposite *Les Mis*, "Although it is a commercial West End theatre, I have an artistic policy of only producing new work or new interpretations of work there. The Royal Court's presence created an environment where a new play without stars could trust to word of mouth for good business. There is a hunger for that now. And my generation have to be the ones to do it. The precedents are there now that we *can* do this."

Thus far, her instincts have proved unerring. Almost every show at the Ambassador's sells out. The latest, a two-hander about film makers in Ireland called

Stones In His Pockets has, if the gossip columns are to be believed, had celebrities joining the audience unannounced almost nightly; Tom Hanks, Lauren Bacall, Andrew Lloyd Webber. The production has all the signs of becoming a cult success, and it exactly fits Friedman's philosophy of finding plays that are fresh and unusual: "I've always been told what a West End play is. I want to put on new works that I love, and see if I can make them work in a 400- or 500-seat theatre."

"Nevertheless, the real challenge lies ahead for Sonia Friedman. Within a few months of taking the job, her new employers acquired the Associated Capital Theatres empire and suddenly she was in charge of filling 16 theatres in the regions and the West End. Do the commercial pressures prove a strain on her artistic sensibilities? She is defiantly optimistic: "In the week that ATG took over ACT, four shows collapsed. How do you deal with that? With integrity, with passion. Can you do art and be commercially successful? That is the question that drives me every day."

Adam Kenwright

Friedman may have played the impresario to *Stones In His Pockets*, but it was actually produced by the long-established Paul Elliott and another young blood, the ebullient Adam Kenwright. Nephew to a famous uncle (Bill, if you haven't twigged), Adam is a fast-rising star, and as much a charmer as his uncle. As I sit, glass of wine in hand, in his Cambridge Circus office, I hear him earnestly reassuring a colleague

that her services will be required again soon – "I'm *desperate* for you to come in as much as you can."

The two Kenwrights (and Adam looks like a younger version of Bill) also share a love for football. In fact, Adam was by his own admission "an extremely good goalkeeper" who played for England schoolboys. In his early teens, he balanced the sport with working in his uncle's office, which he loved. At the age of 16, Arsenal Football Club offered him a contract. He thought about it, then phoned Bill and asked for a permanent job. And that was the end of the goalkeeping.

"Working for my uncle," he remembers, "was a bit of a double-edged sword. People tended to judge me by how they viewed him. And our relationship changed dramatically; it was no longer Uncle Bill. He is very kind, very generous, but wants to control everybody who works for him. Still, I adored it. I got in first in the morning and would be the last to leave." Having risen to be Bill Kenwright's number two, Adam eventually did leave after a quarrel.

Adam started a marketing company in Peggy Ramsay's old office in Barons Court. He was soon snapped up as a consultant by Andrew Lloyd Webber, then Cameron Mackintosh, then others, his reputation growing all the time. He has created eye-catching campaigns for *Jesus Christ Superstar*, *Art*, *Rent*, Adventures in Motion Pictures, the Reduced Shakespeare Company and plenty more.

Kenwright had always kept a hand in producing one or two shows, but he hit upon a winner in 1999, when he imported a highly energetic sort of dance show which employed bungee ropes to keep most of the action in the air. *De La Guardia* came to London's Roundhouse, and became a sell-out success. Moreover, it was the kind of unusual hit that set everyone talking.

"That," says Kenwright, "made me believe that there was something for my generation, that we could do. It also persuaded me that I could run my own company and we could produce from time to time. It certainly raised my position in the industry, especially internationally."

Next, he plucked a show from Edinburgh called *Cooking With Elvis*, a play by Lee Hall, brought it to London and put the popular comedian Frank Skinner in the cast. Kenwright had another success, although as he recalls, 'I had a horrible time trying to get a theatre. Nobody listens to kids."

"My mission," he says, "is to try and bring people who don't usually come to the theatre." He believes that this is "a marketing thing" as much as anything else. "There is so much competition for the theatre now, from computers, TV, cinema. We have got to constantly reinvent ourselves, in the same way that art does, that fashion does. You've got to accentuate the things you can only get from the live experience.

"And theatre needs to take notice of other art forms, like the pop world. We've got to work with artists who people can relate to. That's why I cast Frank Skinner in *Cooking With Elvis*, and I'm now working on a £3 million musical version of *Zorro* for which I'm hoping to get Robbie Williams, an old friend, to write the music. And the people now in power in the producing world are of a different generation, so how do they know what excites my generation?"

Kenwright believes that change must come: "At the moment theatre is insular, it's expensive, it's fucking uncomfortable – how much more difficult are we going to make it?"

One person in whom Kenwright places great faith (hailing him as "a genius") is the 22-year-old producer David Babani. Floppy-haired, hyperactive, Babani has a great deal to say for himself, but it is only a few minutes before the listener realises that there is substance in everything he says. Babani is one of the few young producers who came through without some sort of cushion – a mentor, or the comfort of a big subsidised theatre to ease any financial blow. That hasn't stopped him from becoming the youngest ever producer to mount a show in the West End (he presented the revue *Forbidden Broadway* at the Albery Theatre at the age of 21). "I beat Cameron Mackintosh!" he grins over lunch.

Babani's speciality is the production of small-scale musicals, and his preferred home is London's tiny Jermyn Street Theatre. "I like," he says, "to take American musicals which were perceived as not being suitable for Britain, and testing them, maybe jigging around with them and seeing if I can make them work here." This has led to productions including *Closer Than Ever*, a musical revue about thirty-somethings enduring mid-life crises. "It's by Richard Maltby and David Shire, who have won Oscars, Tonys, everything, but have nil name recognition over here." Babani reconceived the show for England, setting it in a New York subway train. "And it worked!" A similarly successful production of Stephen Sondheim's *Assassins*, also somewhat altered from the original, led to Babani being summoned to New York by an indignant Sondheim where, "Steve and I sat around a table and screamed at each other. He was furious that I had dared to change his work." But, reports Babani, he eventually won the composer's approval, and he and Sondheim are now friends.

I ask whether specialising in musicals, traditionally notoriously risky and money-gobbling enterprises, is a risky policy for a young producer. "Not if you're sensible," he replies. "Look, at Jermyn Street we use a typical cast of four, a band of two, the risks are acceptable. You can always expand a success, as we did with *Forbidden Broadway*."

Big long-runners, he believes, are far harder to come by. "I can't possibly compete on my own, nor do I want to, with scary multi-million pound conglomerates like SFX and Disney, who make a show just to break even, and then count on making their money by selling the franchises, by merchandise and by product awareness." But there are different kinds of long-runner. His latest success is a one-man Barbra Streisand tribute show that he picked up from New York. Called *Simply Barbra*, he has toured it to Edinburgh, Australia, Hong Kong and Singapore and its appeal shows no sign of abating.

"As a rule," he concludes, "you don't get long-runners in small theatres in London. In New York, performers are trained to perform in spaces other than big Broadway houses. Therefore there is this whole culture of smaller venues – 400- or 500-seaters – and the audiences go. London audiences take the view that if it is good it will transfer, and they will wait and see it then. However, the culture is slowly changing here, thanks in part to the success of places like the Donmar Warehouse. But I'd love to take a theatre like the Queen's on Shaftesbury Avenue – which almost never sells out its 1000 seats – and turn it into three smallish auditoriums all doing different kinds of things. A play in one, a musical in another, something like that would be exciting."

Julius Green
Julius Green, in his mid-thirties, also has grand designs on Theatreland. A former line producer for Bill Kenwright, he remembers being impressed by the sheer volume of shows that his former boss turned out. Since returning to independent

producing, in partnership with Ian Lenagan, he has applied the valuable lesson that "market share" is an important factor in successful commercial theatre production. "There's nothing wrong," says Green, "with trying to do as many different productions as you can, so long as you do them as *well* as you can." Furthermore, he believes that at a time when the "brand name theatres", principally the Almeida and the Donmar Warehouse, are threatening to dominate the straight drama scene in London, it is important for commercial producers such as himself to demonstrate that the old ways still work. Green is currently completing a doctorate on Binkie Beaumont, who created the blueprint for post-war commercial theatre production, and is the ultimate example of success based on market share.

Green and Lenagan's output so far (over 50 productions in the first three years of their partnership) certainly confirms their commitment to a wide variety of work. At the time of writing, Fanny Burney's Regency comedy *A Busy Day* (at the Lyric, Shaftesbury Avenue) rubs shoulders with *Saucy Jack and the Space Vixens* (an off-the-wall *Rocky Horror*-style piece which flopped on Shaftesbury Avenue but has since become a long-running cult hit in a specially converted London nightclub) and the latest Steven Berkoff work premiering at the Edinburgh Fringe. For the future, it looks as though Green and Lenagan are in the West End – and elsewhere – to stay.

Richard Jordan

One last young producer worth mentioning (though there are others) is the likeable Richard Jordan, who is described by his former employer and mentor Michael Codron as 'a young Michael Codron'. Twenty-five, he has just begun to make inroads into the West End with the production company he runs with his colleague Sally Vaughan. Though he has yet to set the arts alight, his first West End play *Anna Weiss* was respectably received, and a superbly atmospheric promenade production of Sondheim's *Sweeney Todd* (which Jordan directed under a pseudonym) at the Bridewell Theatre gave notice, perhaps, of great things to come. Whether he happens upon any runaway *Art*-like success has yet to be seen, but for now he is building solidly, and seems set to be the type of reliable producer on whom London will one day depend for quality staple fare. Jordan accepts that producing is incredibly financially risky, though he insists that a way will always be found to raise the money. "Nevertheless," he says, "producing is a struggle. Not many people want to be a producer because, unlike directing, you have to wear many caps. You'll never read a book on how to produce a show because every show needs a different approach. Essentially, good producers are optimists with both business acumen and, most important, a good eye. And there aren't a lot of those about."

It is true that it is more or less impossible to write a textbook on producing. However, since this book may be being read by emerging would-be producers, I asked some of those mentioned above – who are perhaps all near enough their beginnings to appreciate the particular problems to be faced today – to suggest a few tips for negotiating the minefield. "Producers' nuggets," as David Babani gleefully called them.

Producers' Tips

Sonia Friedman – "Never embark on a project unless you are financially stable for the downside as well as the upside. Make sure that you are protected. If you can't raise the money, start asking whether this is a project you *should* be sweating your guts out for – it could be a message."

Adam Kenwright – "You've got to treat it as a business. At the moment one in fourteen shows make their money back. I've started to tap the dotcom millionaires, also the City of London and Wall Street – in America there's an established tradition of big business investing in theatre. And it's cheaper for them to invest in a show in London than in New York. If you can get the one in fourteen statistic down to one in five, as I intend to, than we can begin to be seriously attractive to investors."

David Pugh – "You must be straight with investors. Tell them that it is like gambling on a horse, that they probably will lose it. And never take money from a friend."

Richard Jordan – "See as much theatre as you can. You learn much more from seeing

a flop than you do from a hit. And preferably you have to be able to do everyone else's job."

David Babani – "Someone once told me, 'You're in this business for the long run, act decently.' Work with one eye on the big picture – for instance, I could have brought my production *Assassins* into the West End, but it wasn't right for a bigger theatre. It killed me to walk away, but I did."

Sonia Friedman – "Very early on you become aware of that sense of control and power. But if you think of it that way, you're in trouble. Get preoccupied by that and you'll never get on and do the work. However, you must be ready to assert your views, while keeping everybody happy. It's a difficult balance to strike."

David Babani – "You've got to be a people person, much of the skill comes in putting the right people together. And you must be able to assimilate all the stress – make everyone feel that they have the freedom to fail, because that is when people do their best work."

Richard Jordan – "Believe in yourself; trust in your own tastes, and try and keep one step ahead of the public."

Sonia Friedman – "You need to be able to have emotional mechanisms to protect yourself. A failure can feel awful; when I had my first failure, Timberlake Wertenbaker's *The Break of Day*, I couldn't get myself out of bed in the morning. I felt sick, humiliated. You have to be able to deal with that – and keep believing in the show for the sake of the cast and crew."

David Pugh – "Always remember that whatever you put on will be for some people their first visit to a theatre. And if it is dreadful you will turn them off for life. That is a great responsibility."

Richard Jordan – "Avoid tunnel vision. When you're locked into a show, it is very easy to forget about the world outside. You lose your perspective, and then your judgment."

Adam Kenwright – "There are a lot of people out there who've lost hundreds of thousands of pounds, who've lost their houses. Unless someone has something really special – incredible business acumen, a great feel for what makes a successful show – I would not advise them to try. But once you do it, the difference between a good and a bad producer is that a good producer always fights his corner. We fight hardest when our backs are to the wall. When someone says 'You can't do this' you say 'Yes I can'. You find a way to do it. But anyone who chases it out of blind love ain't gonna make it. You have to *be the best*."

Sonia Friedman – "There are high stakes. We come across as nice and sweet, but you *must* be tough. However, as far as answering to investors goes, you've got to be able to do a good – your best – job every time. And if I know that I have, then I can put my head down and sleep."

And then, of course, some people simply thrive on danger.

APPENDIX

Major productions by the impresarios in this book

Listed below, major productions, selected to give a snapshot view of the range and quality of producers' achievements. Most have done more work than can be listed – in several cases well over 500 shows. Precedence has been given to London and Broadway productions. (When only the venue is given, then the location is London.) Brian McMaster is absent from this list, since the volume of work produced at the Edinburgh Festival each year is too enormous to do it justice.

Peter Hall

1988 *Orpheus Descending*, Williams (Haymarket, Broadway)

1989 *The Merchant of Venice*, Shakespeare (Phoenix, Broadway)

1990 *The Wild Duck,* Ibsen (Phoenix) *Born Again*, Ionesco (Chichester) *The Homecoming,* Pinter (Comedy)

1991 *Twelfth Night,* Shakespeare (Playhouse) *The Rose Tattoo*, Williams (Playhouse) *Tartuffe*, Molière (Playhouse)

1992 *Four Baboons Adoring the Sun,* Guare (New York) *Sienna Red*, Poliakoff (Liverpool) *An Ideal Husband*, Wilde (Globe, Haymarket and elsewhere)

1993 *Separate Tables*, Rattigan (Albery) *Lysistrata*, Aristophanes (Old Vic, Wyndham's, Greece) *She Stoops to Conquer*, Goldsmith (Queen's) *The Gift of the Gorgon*, Shaffer (Wyndham's) *Piaf*, Gems (Piccadilly)

1994 *An Absolute Turkey*, Feydeau (Globe) *On Approval*, Lonsdale (Playhouse) *Hamlet*, Shakespeare (Gielgud)

1995 *The Master Builder,* Ibsen (Haymarket)

1996 *Mind Millie for Me*, Feydeau (Haymarket)

1997 *A Streetcar Named Desire*, Williams (Haymarket) *Waste*, Granville-Barker (Old Vic) *The Seagull*, Chekhov (Old Vic) *Waiting for Godot*, Beckett (Old Vic, Piccadilly) *King Lear*, Shakespeare, (Old Vic)

1998 *The Misanthrope*, Molière (Piccadilly) *Major Barbara*, Shaw (Piccadilly) *Filumena*, De Filippo (Piccadilly) *Kafka's Dick*, Bennett (Piccadilly)

Bill Kenwright

1974 *West Side Story*, Bernstein, Sondheim and Laurents (Shaftesbury)

1979 *Joseph and the Amazing Technicolour Dreamcoat*, Lloyd Webber / Rice (UK Tour, Royalty)

1984 *Stepping Out - The Musical*, Harris (Albery)

1988 *Blood Brothers*, Russell (Phoenix, then Broadway in 1993)

1989 *Shirley Valentine*, Russell *A Streetcar Named Desire*, Williams (Peter Hall Company at the Haymarket)

1991 *Dancing At Lughnasa*, Friel (Garrick, Broadway 1992) *Travels With My Aunt*, Greene (Wyndham's, Broadway 1992)

An Ideal Husband, Wilde (Peter Hall Company, Globe, Haymarket and elsewhere)

1993 *She Stoops to Conquer,* Goldsmith (Wyndham's) *Separate Tables,* Rattigan (Albery) *Lysistrata,* Aristophanes (Peter Hall Company at the Old Vic, Wyndham's) *The Gift of the Gorgon,* Shaffer (Wyndham's) *Medea,* Euripides (Wyndham's, Broadway) *The Deep Blue Sea,* Rattigan (Apollo) *Moonlight,* Pinter (Comedy) *No Man's Land,* Pinter (Comedy)

1994 *An Absolute Turkey,* Feydeau (Peter Hall Company at the Globe) *Hamlet,* Shakespeare (Peter Hall Company at the Gielgud) *My Night with Reg,* Elliott (Criterion) *The Winslow Boy,* Rattigan (Globe) *The Miracle Worker,* Gibson (Comedy, Wyndham's)

1995 *The Master Builder,* Ibsen (Peter Hall Company at the Haymarket) *In Praise of Love,* Rattigan (Apollo) *Rupert Street Lonely Hearts Club,* Harvey (Criterion) *The Roy Orbison Story,* Kenwright (Piccadilly, Whitehall) *Design for Living,* Coward (Gielgud)

1996 *Mind Millie for Me,* Feydeau (Peter Hall Company at the Haymarket) *Chapter Two,* Simon (Gielgud) *Company,* Sondheim (Albery) *Passion,* Sondheim (Queen's) *Elvis – The Official Musical,* Good and Cooney (Prince of Wales) *The Odd Couple,* Simon (Haymarket) *The Aspern Papers,* James (Wyndham's) *Shakespeare for My Father,* Redgrave (Haymarket)

1997 *The School for Wives,* Molière (Piccadilly, Comedy) *Lady Windermere's Fan,* Wilde (Haymarket) *Pygmalion,* Shaw (Albery) *A Doll's House,* Ibsen (Belasco Theatre, Broadway) *Waiting for Godot,* Beckett (Peter Hall Company at the Old Vic, Piccadilly)

1998 *The Misanthrope,* Molière (Peter Hall Company at the Piccadilly) *Major Barbara,* Shaw (Peter Hall Company at the Piccadilly) *Filumena,* de Filippo (Peter Hall Company at the Piccadilly) *Kafka's Dick,* Bennett (Peter Hall Company at the Piccadilly)

1999 *The Chairs,* Ionesco (Golden Theatre, Broadway) *The Chiltern Hundreds,* Douglas-Home (Vaudeville) *Song At Twilight,* Coward (Gielgud)

Matthew Bourne

1987 *Overlap Lovers* (UK tour)

1988 *Does Your Crimplene Go All Crusty When You Rub?* (UK tour)

1989 *The Infernal Gallop* (UK tour)

1990 *Spitfire* (UK tour)

1992 *Town and Country* (UK tour)

1993 *Percy's Of Fitzrovia and The Infernal Gallop* (UK tour) *The Nutcracker* (double-bill with Opera North, UK Tour) *Deadly Serious* (UK tour, Hong Kong) *The Nutcracker* (Sadler's Wells)

1994 *Highland Fling* (UK tour, Donmar Warehouse production)

1995 *Swan Lake* (Sadler's Wells, West End, UK Tour, Broadway, Los Angeles)

1997 *Cinderella* (Piccadilly, Los Angeles)

Thelma Holt

1983 *Loot*, Orton (Ambassadors, Lyric Theatres Theatre of Comedy)

1985-87 *A Chorus of Disapproval*, Ayckbourn (NT transfer to Lyric Theatre) *The Petition*, Glanville (NT transfer to Wyndhams Theatre) *Brighton Beach Memoirs*, Simon (NT transfer to Aldwych Theatre) *Three Men on a Horse*, Abbott (NT transfer to Vaudeville Theatre) *A View from the Bridge*, Arthur Miller (NT transfer to Aldwych Theatre)

1987 *The Hairy Ape*, Eugene O'Neill (International '87 at the NT: Berlin's Schaubühne Theatre Company) *Miss Julie*, Strindberg (International '87 at the NT: Royal Dramatic Theatre of Stockholm) *Hamlet*, Shakespeare (International '87 at the NT: Royal Dramatic Theatre of Stockholm) *Macbeth*, Shakespeare (International '87 at the NT: Tokyo's Ninagawa Company) *Medea*, Euripides (International '87 at the NT: Tokyo's Ninagawa Company) *Tomorrow Was War*, Vassiliev (International '87 at the NT: Moscow's Mayakovsky Theatre Company)

1989 *The Fairy Queen* (co-production), Purcell (Aix-en Provence, Opera by Henry Purcell) *Tango Varsoviano*, Felix (International '89 at the NT: Buenos Aires' Teatro del Sur) *The Grapes of Wrath*, John Steinbeck (International '89 at the NT: Chicago's Steppenwolf Theatre Company) *Uncle Vanya*, Chekhov (International 89 at the NT: Moscow Art Theatre) *Suicide for Love*, Chikamatsu (International 89 at the NT: Tokyo's Ninagawa Company) *Orpheus Descending* (executive producer), Tennessee Williams (Haymarket and New York: Peter Hall Company) *The Merchant of Venice* (executive producer), Shakespeare (Phoenix: Peter Hall Company

1990 *The Wild Duck* (executive producer), Ibsen (Phoenix: Peter Hall Company) *Henry IV* (executive producer), Pirandello (Wyndham's: Triumph Theatre Production) *Hamlet*, Shakespeare (NT: Bucharest's Bulandra Theatre Company) *The Kingdom Of Desire (Macbeth)*, Shakespeare (NT: Taiwan's Contemporary Legend Theatre)

FOR THELMA HOLT LTD

1990 *Three Sisters*, Chekhov (Queen's, version by Nikolas Simmonds) *Tango at the End of Winter*, Kunio Shimizu (Piccadilly, adapted by Peter Barnes)

1991 *Electra*, Sophocles (Riverside Studios and tour: RSC)

1992 *Hamlet*, Shakespeare (Riverside Studios and tour) *Les Atrides*, Aeschylus (Robin Mills, Bradford: Le Theatre De Soleil) *Le Baruffe Chiozzotte*, Goldoni (NT: Piccolo Teatro) *Six Characters in Search of an Author*, Pirandello (NT: Bologna Teatro) *The Tempest*, Shakespeare (Barbican: Ninagawa Co in BITE season)

1993 *Medea,* Euripides (Zurich: Ninagawa Company) *Much Ado About Nothing,* Shakespeare (Queen's)

1994 *Peer Gynt,* Ibsen (International Tour: Ninagawa Co. version by Frank McGuinness) *The Clandestine Marriage,* Colman and Garrick (Queen's)

1995 *The Seagull,* Chekhov (UK regional tour, version by Nikolas Simmonds) *A Midsummer Night's Dream,* Shakespeare (Plymouth, Newcastle: Ninagawa Company) *Antony and Cleopatra,* Shakespeare (UK regional tour: Moving Theatre) *The Glass Menagerie,* Tennessee William's (Comedy: Donmar Warehouse)

1996 *Observe the Sons of Ulster Marching Towards the Somme,* Frank McGuinness (Barbican and regional tour: Abbey Theatre) *A Midsummer Night's Dream,* Shakespeare (Mermaid: Ninagawa Company) *A Doll's House,* Ibsen (Playhouse and Belasco, New York, in association with Bill Kenwright)

1997 *The Merchant of Venice,* Shakespeare (UK regional tour: Birmingham Rep) *The Maids,* Genet (UK regional tour: Donmar Warehouse) *Les Fausses Confidences,* Marivaux (Comédie Française, French Theatre Season at NT) *Shintoku-Maru* (Barbican: Ninagawa Co in BITE season) *Oh Les Beaux Jours,* Beckett (Riverside Studios, French Theatre Season)

1998 *The Relapse,* Vanbrugh (UK regional tour: Citizens Theatre Company) *Hamlet,* Shakespeare (Barbican: Ninagawa Co in BITE season)

1999 *Cleo, Camping,Emmanuelle and Dick,* Johnson (UK regional tour: RNT production) *Macbeth,* Shakespeare (Queen's) *King Lear,* Shakespeare (Saitama, Barbican and Stratford Ninagawa Co in association with RSC)

2000 *Miss Julie,* Strindberg (Haymarket, in association with Bill Kenwright Ltd)

Raymond Gubbay

1991 onwards: Twice-annual "Classical Spectacular" (Royal Albert Hall, many other UK arenas)

1996 Puccini's *La Bohème* (Royal Albert Hall)

1997 Bizet's *Carmen* (Royal Albert Hall)

1998, 2000 Puccini's *Madam Butterfly* (Royal Albert Hall, Birmingham's National Indoor Arena)

1999 Puccini's *Tosca* (Royal Albert Hall)

Annual Christmas season, consisting of various concerts at major UK venues including Royal Albert Hall, Barbican, Royal Festival Hall.

Cameron Mackintosh

1967 *Jane Eyre* (UK tour, Golders Green) *The Reluctant Debutante* (Henley) *The Chiltern Hundreds,* Douglas Home (Henley) *Little Women* (UK tour, Jeanetta Cochrane)

1969 *Murder at the Vicarage,* Christie (UK tour) *Anything Goes,* Porter (UK tour, Saville) *Rebecca,* du Maurier (UK tour)

1970 *At Home with the Dales,* Davis (UK tour)

1971 *Salad Days,* Slade (UK tour)

1972 *Trelawny of the Wells,* (Sadler's Wells, Prince of Wales)

1973 *The Card,* Waterhouse and Willis Hall (UK tour, Queen's)

1974 *Beyond the Fringe,* Revue (UK tour) *Winnie the Pooh* (UK tour, Phoenix) *Godspell,* Tebelak and Schwartz (UK tour, Phoenix, Her Majesty's, Prince of Wales, Shaftesbury)

1975 *John, Paul, George, Ringo...and Bert,* Russell (UK tour)

1976 *Side by Side by Sondheim,* Sondheim (revue arranged by Sherrin) (Mermaid, Wyndham's, Canada, Garrick, UK tour)

1977 *Oliver!,* Bart (UK tour, Albery)

1978 *My Fair Lady,* Lerner and Loewe (Leicester, UK tour, Aldelphi)

1979 *Oklahoma!,* Rodgers and Hammerstein II (Leicester, UK tour, Palace, Australia)

1981 *Cats,* Lloyd Webber (New London, Broadway, and various international prods)

1981 *Tom Foolery,* Lehrer (revue) (Brighton, Criterion, New York)

1982 *The Little Shop of Horrors,* Ashman and Menken (New York, Comedy, Australia, South Africa)

1983 *Song and Dance,* Lloyd Webber and Black (Palace, Australia, UK tour, Broadway) *Blondel,* Oliver and Rice (UK tour, Old Vic, Aldwych)

1984 *The Boy Friend,* Wilson (UK tour, Canada, Old Vic, Albery)

1985 *Les Miserables, (from RSC)* Schönberg and Boublil (Barbican, Palace, Broadway, and various international productions)

1986 *The Phantom of the Opera,* Lloyd Webber, Hart and Stilgoe (Her Majesty's, Broadway and various international productions)

1987 *Follies,* Sondheim and Goldman (Shaftesbury)

1989 *Just So,* Drewe and Stiles (Newbury, Trycicle) *Miss Saigon,* Schönberg and Boublil (Theatre Royal Drury Lane, Broadway, and various international productions)

1990 *Five Guys Named Moe,* Peters (Lyric, Broadway, USA and UK tours)

1991 *Moby Dick,* Longden and Kaye (Oxford, Piccadilly)

1992 *Putting It Together,* Sondheim (revue) (Oxford, New York inc Broadway, Los Angeles)

1993 *Carousel (*from RNT*)* Rodgers and Hammerstein II (Shaftesbury, New York, Tokyo (from NT)

1994 *Oliver!,* Bart (Palladium, UK tour, Canada

1996 *Martin Guerre* Schonberg and Boublil (Prince Edward, W Yorkshire Playhouse, UK tour, US tour)

1997 *Jack Tinker - A Life in Review,* Revue (Palladium) *The Fix* Dempsey and Rowe (Donmar Warehouse, Washington)

1998 *Swan Lake ,* Tchaikovsky (Broadway from AMP)

2000 *The Witches of Eastwick,* Dempsey and Rowe (Theatre Royal Drury Lane)

George Christie

1958 *Il Segreto Di Susanna*, Wolf-Ferrari
1959 *Fidelio*, Beethoven *Der Rosenkavalier*,
    R Strauss
1960 *I Puritani*, Bellini *Don Giovanni*,
    Mozart *La Voix humaine*, Poulenc
1961 *L'Elisir D'Amore*, Donizetti *Elegy for
    Young Lovers*, Henze
1962 *Pélleas et Mélisande*, Debussy
    L'incoronazione di Poppea, Monteverdi
1963 *Die Zauberflöte*, Mozart *Capriccio* R
    Strauss
1964 *La Pietra del Paragone*, Rossini
1965 *Il Matrimonio Segreto*, Cimarosa *Anna
    Bolena*, Donizetti
1966 *Jeptha*, Handel *Werther*, Massenet *Dido
    and Aeneas*, Purcell *L'heure Espagnole*,
    Ravel
1967 *L'Ormindo*, Cavalli *Don Giovanni*,
    Mozart *La Bohème*, Puccini
1968 *Die Entführung aus dem Serail*, Mozart
    Yevgeny Onegin, Tchaikovsky
1969 *Così Fan Tutte*, Mozart
1970 *The Rising of the Moon (world premiere)*,
    Il Turco in Italia, Rossini
1971 *Ariadne auf Naxos*, R Strauss *The Queen
    of Spades*, Tchaikovsky
1972 *Die Entführung aus dem Serail*, Mozart
    Il ritorno d'Ulisse in patria, Monteverdi
    Macbeth, Verdi
1973 *Le Nozze Di Figaro*, Mozart *Capriccio*,
    R Strauss *The Visit of the Old Lady*, Von
    Einem
1974 *Intermezzo*, R Strauss
1975 *The Cunning Little Vixen*, Janácek
    The Rake's Progress, Stravinsky

1976 *Pelléas et Mélisande*, Debussy
1977 *Don Giovanni*, Mozart *La Voix
    Humaine*, Poulenc *Die Schweigsame
    Frau*, R Strauss
1978 *Così Fan Tutte*, Mozart *Die Zauberflöte*,
    Mozart
1979 *Fidelio*, Beethoven
1980 *Die Entführung aus dem Serail*, Mozart
1981 *A Midsummer Night's Dream*, Britten
    Il Barbiere di Siviglia, Rossini
1982 *Orfeo ed Euridice*, Gluck *L'Amour des
    Trois Oranges*, Prokofiev
1983 *La Cenerentola*, Rossini
1984 *Where The Wild Things Are (world
    premiere)*, Knussen *L'incoronazione di
    Poppea*, Monteverdi *Arabella*, R Strauss
1985 *Carmen*, Bizet *Albert Herring*, Britten
    Higglety, Pigglety Pop! (world premiere),
    Knussen
1986 *Porgy and Bess*, Gershwin *Simon
    Boccanegra*, Verdi
1987 *L'heure Espagnole*, Ravel *L'enfant et les
    Sortileges*, Ravel *La Traviata*, Verdi
1988 *Katya Kabanova*, Janácek *The
    Electrification of the Soviet Union*,
    Osborne *Falstaff*, Verdi
1989 *Jenufa*, Janacek *Le Nozze Di Figaro*,
    Mozart
1990 *Die Zauberflöte*, Mozart *New Year*,
    Tippett
1991 *Così Fan Tutte*, Mozart *La Clemenza di
    Tito*, Mozart
1992 *Peter Grimes*, Britten *Death in Venice*,
    Britten *The Queen of Spades*,
    Tchaikovsky
1993 *Béatrice et Bénédict (concert
    performance)*, Berlioz

1994 *Le Nozze di Figaro*, Mozart *Don Giovanni*, Mozart *Yevgeny Onegin*, Tchaikovsky
1995 *The Second Mrs Kong*, Birtwhistle *The Makropoulos Case*, Janácek *Ermione*, Rossini
1996 *Lulu*, Berg *Theodora*, Handel
1997 *Manon Lescaut*, Puccini *Le Comte Ory*, Rossini
1998 *Rosalinda* Handel
1999 *Pélleas et Mélisande*, Debussy *Flight* Dove *The Bartered Bride*, Smetana

Duncan Weldon

1970 *When We Are Married*, Priestley (Strand)
1975 *The Case in Question*, Millar (Haymarket)
1976 *Three Sisters*, Chekhov (Cambridge) *The Seagull*, Chekhov (Duke Of York's) *The Circle*, Maugham (Haymarket)
1977 *Separate Tables*, Rattigan (Apollo) *Stevie*, Whitemore (Vaudeville) *The Good Woman of Setzuan*, Brecht (Royal Court)
1978 *Waters of the Moon*, Hunter (Haymarket) *A Family*, Harwood (Her Majesty's)
1979 *The Crucifer of Blood*, Giovanni (Haymarket)
1980 *Early Days*, Storey (RNT at the Comedy)
1981 *Virginia*, O'Brien (Haymarket) *Overheard*, Ustinov (Haymarket)
1982 *A Coat of Varnish*, Millar (Haymarket) *Hobson's Choice*, Brighouse

(Haymarket) *Uncle Vanya*, Chekhov (Haymarket) *Man And Superman*, Shaw (Haymarket, Cambridge)
1983 *The School for Scandal*, Sheridan (Haymarket) *Heartbreak House*, Shaw (Haymarket) Liza Minnelli, Revue (Apollo Victoria) *Beethoven's Tenth*, Peter Ustinov (Vaudeville) *Fiddler on the Roof*, Bock, Harnick, Stein (Apollo Victoria) *A Patriot for Me*, Osborne (Haymarket) *The Sleeping Prince*, Rattigan (Haymarket)
1984 *The Aspern Papers*, Redgrave, from the novel by Henry James (Haymarket) *Strange Interlude*, O'Neill (Duke Of York's) *Serjeant Musgrave's Dance*, Arden (Old Vic) *Aren't We All?*, Lonsdale (Haymarket) *American Buffalo*, Mamet (Duke Of York's) *The Way of the World*, Congreve (Haymarket)
1985 *The Lonely Road*, Schnitzler (Old Vic) *The Caine Mutiny*, Wouk (Queen's) *Waste*, Granville-Barker (Lyric) *Sweet Bird of Youth*, Williams (Haymarket)
1986 *Antony and Cleopatra*, Shakespeare (Haymarket) *Long Day's Journey into Night*, O'Neill (Haymarket) *Breaking the Code*, Whitemore (Haymarket) *Mr and Mrs Nobody*, Waterhouse (Garrick)
1987 *Kiss Me Kate*, Porter (Old Vic, Savoy) *You Never Can Tell*, Shaw (Haymarket)
1988 *A Touch Of The Poet*, O'Neill (Comedy) *The Admirable Crichton*, Barrie (Haymarket) *A Walk in the Woods*, Blessing (Comedy) *Richard II*, Shakespeare (Phoenix) *Orpheus*

Descending, Tennessee Williams (Haymarket)

1989 *Richard III*, Shakespeare (Phoenix) *Ivanov*, Chekhov (Strand) *The Merchant Of Venice*, Shakespeare (Peter Hall Company at the Phoenix) *Veterans Day*, Freed (Haymarket) *Another Time*, Harwood (Wyndham's)

1990 *An Evening with Peter Ustinov*, Ustinov (Haymarket) *Henry IV*, Pirandello (Wyndham's) *Kean*, Sartre (Old Vic)

1991 *Becket*, Anouilh (Haymarket)

1992 *Heartbreak House*, Shaw (Haymarket) *Lost in Yonkers*, Simon (Strand) *Cyrano De Bergerac*, Rostand (Haymarket)

1993 *Macbeth*, Shakespeare (RSC at the Barbican)

1994 *A Month in the Country*, Turgenev (Albery) *Home*, Storey (Wyndham's) *St Joan*, Shaw (Strand) *Lady Windermere's Fan*, Wilde (Albery) *The Rivals*, Sheridan (Albery)

1995 *The Duchess of Malfi*, Webster (Wyndham's) *Taking Sides*, Harwood (Criterion) *Old Times*, Pinter (Wyndham's) *The Hothouse*, Pinter (Comedy)

1996 *Uncle Vanya*, Chekhov (Albery) *Talking Heads*, Bennett (Comedy)

1997 *A Letter of Resignation*, Whitemore (Comedy, Savoy) *Electra*, Sophocles (Donmar Warehouse)

1998 *Rent*, Larson (Shaftesbury)

1999 *Richard III*, Shakespeare (RSC at the Savoy) *The Importance of Being Earnest*, Wilde (Haymarket)

Michael White

1961 *The Connection*, Gelber (Duke of York)

1963 *Cambridge Circus*, Idle, Oddie and Brooke-Taylor (Arts, Lyric) *Merce Cunningham*, Dance works (Sadler's Wells)

1964 *Son of Oblomov*, Arranyo (Comedy)

1966 *Loot*, Orton (Criterion) *Saturday Night and Sunday Morning*, Sillitoe (Prince of Wales) *The Blood Knot*, Fugard (Arts) *Yoko Ono*, Ono (Jeanette Cochrane)

1967 *American Hurrah*, van Itallie (Royal Court) *Philadelphia Here I Come*, Friel (Lyric)

1968 *Soldiers*, Hochhuth (New Theatre)

1969 *The Resistible Rise of Arturo Ui*, Brecht (Saville) *Oh, Calcutta!* Revue, devised by Tynan (New York, Roundhouse)

1970 *Annie*, Charnin and Meehan (Victoria Palace) *Sleuth*, Shaffer (St Martin's)

1971 *The Beard*, McClure (Royal Court)

1972 *Joseph and the Amazing Technicolour Dreamcoat*, Lloyd Webber and Rice (New Theatre) *The Threepenny Opera*, Brecht/Weill (Prince of Wales)

1973 *The Rocky Horror Show*, O'Brien (Royal Court)

1976 *A Chorus Line*, Bennett and Hamlisch (Drury Lane)

1978 *Deathtrap*, Levin (Garrick)

1982 *The Pirates of Penzance*, Gilbert and Sullivan (Drury Lane)

1984 *Pina Bausch*, Dance works (Sadler's Wells)

1985 *On Your Toes Rogers and Hart*, Abbot (Palace)

1989 *Metropolis*, Brooks and Hughes
(Piccadilly)

1993 *Crazy for You*, Gershwin and
Gershwin, adapted by Ludwig (Prince
Edward)

1994 *She Loves Me*, Bock, Harnick and
Masteroff (Savoy)

1995 *Fame, The Musical*, Fernandez
(Cambridge)

1996 *Voyeurz*, Lewis and Rafelson
(Whitehall)

2000 *Notre-Dame de Paris*, Plammondon
and Cocciante (Dominion)

Harvey Goldsmith

(No dates or venues are given because
Harvey Goldsmith has presented several
of these acts on many occasions:)

*Aida, Barbra Streisand, Barney the
Dinosaur, Bill Wyman, Billy Connolly, Billy
Joel, Bjorn Again, Black Sabbath, Bootleg
Beatles, Boyzone, Bros, Bruce Springsteen,
Carmen, Chris Rea, Cirque du Soleil, Club
Tropicana, Concert for G8 Heads of State,
Concerts for Kampuchea, Crystal Place Garden
Parties, Dancing on Dangerous Ground,
Depêche Mode, Disney Kids Awards, Elton
John, Eric Clapton, Explosive Dance in Aid of
The British Red Cross, Harry Connick Jnr,
Jools Holland and His Rhythm and Blues
Orchestra, Kenny Rogers, Led Zeppelin, Live
Aid, Lord of the Dance, Madonna, Music for
Montserrat, Neil Sedaka, Net Aid, New Kids
on the Block, Ozzfest, Paul Weller, Pavarotti,
Pet Shop Boys, Pete Townshend's LifeHouse,*
*Peter Gabriel, Pink Floyd, Prince, Prince's
Trust Gala, Queen, Rod Stewart, Shania
Twain, Sheryl Crow, Sting, The Bee Gees, The
Eagles, The Kinks, The Prague Heritage Fund
Classical Concert, The Rolling Stones, The
Three Tenors, The Total Eclipse Festival, The
Wall in Berlin, Tosca, Tribute to Freddie
Mercury, Van Morrison, Woody Allen and His
New Orleans Jazz Band*

Michael Codron

1956 *Ring for Catty*, Cargill and Beale
(Lyric)

1957 *A Month of Sundays*, Savory
(Cambridge) *The Wit To Woo*, Peake
(Arts) *Share My Lettuce*, Revue (Lyric
Hammersmith, Comedy, Garrick,
Cambridge, Duke of York's)

1958 *The Dock Brief and What Shall We Tell
Caroline?*, Mortimer (Lyric
Hammersmith, Garrick) *The Birthday
Party*, Pinter (Lyric Hammersmith)

1959 *Fool's Paradise*, Coke (Apollo)

1960 *The Wrong Side Of The Park*, Mortimer
(Cambridge, St Martin's) *The
Caretaker*, Pinter (Arts, Duchess)

1961 *Three*, Pinter, Mortimer and Simpson
(Arts, Criterion) *Stop It Whoever You
Are*, Livings (Arts) *Under Milk Wood*,
Thomas (Lyric Hammersmith) *Big Soft
Nellie*, Livings (Theatre Royal
Stratford East)

1962 *Two Stars for Comfort*, Mortimer
(Garrick) *Doctors Of Philosophy*, Spark
(Arts) *End Of Day*, Beckett (Arts)

1963 *The Lover and The Dwarfs*, Pinter (Arts)
Cockade, Wood (Arts) *Cider With Rosie*,
Lee (Garrick) *Out of the Crocodiles*,
Cooper (Phoenix)

1964 *Poor Bitos*, Anouilh (Arts,Duke of
York's) 1964 *Entertaining Mr Sloane*,
Orton (Arts,Wyndham's,Queen's)

1965 *Loot*, Orton (tour) *The Killing Of Sister
George*, Marcus (Duke Of York's)

1966 *Little Malcolm And His Struggle
Against The Eunuchs*, Halliwell
(Garrick) *There's A Girl in My Soup*,
Frisby (Globe,Comedy, Broadway)
When Did You Last See My Mother?,
Hampton (Comedy)

1967 *The Judge*, Mortimer (Cambridge) *Fill
The Stage With Happy Hours*, Wood
(Vaudeville) *Wise Child*, Gray
(Wyndham's) *The Boy Friend*, Wilson
(Comedy)

1968 *Not Now Darling*, Cooney and
Chapman (Strand) *The Real Inspector
Hound*, Stoppard (Criterion)

1970 *The Contractor*, Storey (Royal
Court,Fortune) *The Two Of Us*, Frayn
(Garrick) *The Philanthropist*, Hampton
(Royal Court, Mayfair, Broadway)

1971 *A Voyage Round My Father*, Mortimer
(Haymarket) *Butley*, Gray (Criterion)
Slag, Hare (Hampstead, Royal Court)
The Changing Room, Storey (Royal
Court, Globe)

1972 *Veterans*, Wood (Royal Court) *Me
Times Me*, Ayckbourn (tour) *Time And
Time Again*, Ayckbourn (Comedy)

1973 *Collaborators*, Mortimer (Duchess)
Savages, Hampton (Royal Court)

Habeas Corpus, Bennett (Comedy,
USA) *The Sea*, Bond (Royal Court)
Absurd Person Singular, Ayckbourn
(Criterion, Broadway)

1974 *Knuckle*, Hare (Comedy) *The Norman
Conquests*, Ayckbourn (Globe,USA)
John, Paul, George, Ringo...and Bert,
Russell (Lyric)

1975 *Alphabetical Order*, Frayn (Mayfair)
Absent Friends, Ayckbourn (Garrick)
Otherwise Engaged, Gray (Queens,
Comedy, USA) *Stripwell*, Barker
(Royal Court)

1976 *Treats*, Hampton (Royal Court,
Mayfair) *Teeth 'N' Smiles*, Hare (Royal
Court, Wyndham's)

1977 *Dusa, Stas, Fish and Vi*, Gems
(Hampstead, Mayfair) *The Old
Country*, Bennett (Queens)

1978 *The Rear Column*, Gray (Globe) *Ten
Times Table*, Ayckbourn (Globe) *The
Homecoming*, Pinter (Garrick) *Night
And Day*, Stoppard (Phoenix,
Broadway)

1979 *Joking Apart*, Ackbourn (Globe)

1980 *Make And Break*, Frayn (Lyric
Hammersmith, Haymarket) *The
Dresser*, Harwood (Queens,
Broadway) *Hinge and Bracket*, Revue
(Globe)

1981 *Quartermaine's Terms*, Gray (Queens)

1982 *Noises Off*, Frayn (Lyric
Hammersmith, Savoy, Broadway)
The Real Thing, Stoppard (Strand,
Broadway)

1984 *Benefactors*, Frayn (Vaudeville,
Broadway)

1985 *Jumpers*, Stoppard (Aldwych)

1986 *Woman in Mind*, Ayckbourn (Vaudeville,Broadway)

1988 *Hapgood*, Stoppard (Aldwych, Los Angeles) *Henceforward...*, Ayckbourn (Vaudeville)

1990 *Man Of The Moment*, Ayckbourn (Globe) *Hidden Laughter*, Gray (Vaudeville)

1991 *The Revengers Comedies I and II*, Ackbourn (Strand)

1992 *The Rise And Fall Of Little Voice*, Cartwright (RNT at the Aldwych, Chicago, Broadway)

1993 *Time Of My Life*, Ayckbourn (Vaudeville) *Jamais Vu*, Campbell (Cottesloe, Vaudeville)

1994 *Dead Funny*, Johnson (Vaudeville) *Arcadia*, Stoppard (RNT at the Theatre Royal, Haymarket)

1995 *Indian Ink*, Stoppard (Aldwych) *Dealer's Choice*, Marber (Cottesloe, Vaudeville)

1997 *Tom and Clem*, Churchett (Aldwych)

1998 *Things We Do for Love*, Ayckbourn (Gielgud, Duchess) *The Invention Of Love*, Stoppard (Haymarket)

1999 *Copenhagen*, Frayn (Cottesloe, Duchess) *Comic Potential*, Ayckbourn (Lyric)

2000 *Peggy for You*, Plater (Comedy)

Alan Sievewright

1968 *Les Huguenots*, Meyerbeer (Royal Albert Hall) *Marilyn Horne Concert Debut*, Various (Royal Albert Hall)

Lucrezia Borgia, Donizetti (Royal Festival Hall) *Nabucco*, Verdi (Theatre Royal Drury Lane)

1969 *Semiramide*, Rossini (Theatre Royal Drury Lane) *Il Pirata*, Bellini (Theatre Royal Drury Lane) *La Gioconda*, Ponchielli (Theatre Royal Drury Lane)

1970 *Andrea Chenier*, Giordano (Theatre Royal Drury Lane) *Roberto Devereux*, Donizetti (Theatre Royal Drury Lane) *Montserrat Caballe London Recital Debut*, Various (Theatre Royal Drury Lane)

1971 *Norma*, Bellini (Royal Festival Hall) *Maria Stuarda*, Donizetti (Royal Festival Hall)

1972 *Mefistofele*, Boito (Royal Festival Hall)

1973 *La Juive*, Halévy (Royal Festival Hall) *Samson et Dalila*, Saint-Saëns (Royal Festival Hall) *Caterina Cornaro*, Donizetti (Royal Festival Hall) *An Evening of Musical Lollipops* (Royal Albert Hall)

1974 *I Puritani*, Donizetti (Royal Festival Hall) *Renata Tebaldi and Franco Corelli London Farewell Concert*, Various (Royal Albert Hall) *Attila*, Verdi (Royal Festival Hall) *Ernani*, Verdi (Royal Festival Hall)

1975 *Adriana Lecouvreur*, Cilea (Royal Festival Hall) *Macbeth*, Bloch (Royal Festival Hall)

1977 *The Soldier's Tale*, Stravinsky (Argo/ Decca) *An Evening with Placido Domingo* (Wyndham's) *An Evening with Dame Joan Sutherland* (Albery)

1980 *Encore! An Evening with Victoria de los Angeles* (Duke of York's) *Encore! An*

Evening with Jose Carreras and Katia Ricciarelli (Duke of York's) *Encore! An Evening with Dame Elizabeth Scwarzkopf* (Duke of York's)

1982 *Turandot* (world premiere of authentic Puccini / Alfano ending), Puccini (Barbican Hall)

1983 *La Gioconda,* Ponchielli (Barbican Hall) *Medée,* Cherubini (Barbican Hall) *An Evening of Gershwin* (Barbican Hall)

1987 *Maria Callas Exhibition* (Royal Festival Hall) *Callas Sings Again* (Purcell Room)

1989 *Festival of Sydney*

1990 *International Gala of Opera and Ballet* (Los Angeles)

1991 *Jose Carreras and Friends* (Theatre Royal Drury Lane) *Serenade for a Princess* (Banqueting House)

1992 *Fanfare for a New World* (Liverpool)

1992 *Fanfare for Europe* (Brussels) *International Opera Gala* (The Royal Opera House)

1993 *An International Gala of Italian Opera* (Megaron, Athens)

1994 *International Gala Concert* (Savoy)

1997 *Gala in Tokyo*

1998 *Catarina Cornaro* (staged), Donizetti (Queen Elizabeth Hall)

1999 *Il Re Pastore*, Mozart (St John's Concert Hall, Smith Square, fully staged)

Andrew Lloyd Webber

1983 *Daisy Pulls It Off,* Deegan

1984 *Starlight Express,* Lloyd Webber and Stilgoe (Apollo Victoria) *On Your Toes,* Rodgers and Hart (Palace)

1989 *Aspects of Love,* Lloyd Webber, Black and Hart (Prince of Wales, Broadway)

1993 *Sunset Boulevard,* Lloyd Webber, Black and Hampton (Adelphi, Broadway)

1996 *By Jeeves,* Lloyd Webber and Ayckbourn (Albery) *Jesus Christ Superstar,* Lloyd Webber and Rice (Lyceum, Germany) *Whistle Down the Wind,* Lloyd Webber and Sherman (Washington, Aldwych)

2000 *The Beautiful Game,* Lloyd Webber and Elton (Cambridge)

Victor and Lilian Hochhauser

1960 Brought the Leningrad Philharmonic Orchestra to UK

1961, 1966 Brought the Kirov Ballet to the Royal Opera House

1963, 1969 Brought the Bolshoi Ballet to the Royal Opera House

1972 Brought the Peking Opera and other Chinese companies to London

1973 Brought the Bolshoi Ballet to the London Coliseum

1973–83 Ten years of Rudolf Nureyev Festival, with 36 international ballet companies

1988 Presented Verdi's *Aida* at Earl's Court

1991 Presented Verdi's *Aida* at Birmingham's National Indoor Arena

1993, 95, 97 Brought the Kirov Ballet to the London Coliseum

1994 Promoted Birmingham Royal Ballet

1998 Brought the Royal Ballet to the London Coliseum

1999 Brought the Bolshoi Opera and the Bolshoi Ballet to the London Coliseum

2000 Brought Kirov Ballet to the new Royal
Opera House.
Promoted Royal Ballet at the new
Royal Opera House

Notable artistes Hochhauser has
promoted include:

Yehudi Menuhin, Igor Oistrakh,
David Oistrakh, Sviatoslav Richter,
Eugeny Mavrinsky, Mstislav
Rostropovich, Emil Gilels, Leonid
Kogan, Margot Fonteyn, Natalia
Makarova, Rudolf Nureyev, Mikhail
Baryshnikov